Artifacts of Thinking

Artifacts of Thinking

READING HANNAH ARENDT'S
DENKTAGEBUCH

ROGER BERKOWITZ AND IAN STOREY

Editors

FORDHAM UNIVERSITY PRESS

New York   2017

Fordham University Press has no responsibility for the persistence or accuracy of URLs for external or third-party Internet websites referred to in this publication and does not guarantee that any content on such websites is, or will remain, accurate or appropriate.

Fordham University Press also publishes its books in a variety of electronic formats. Some content that appears in print may not be available in electronic books.

Visit us online at www.fordhampress.com.

Library of Congress Cataloging-in-Publication Data

Names: Berkowitz, Roger, 1968– editor. | Storey, Ian (Ian N.), editor.
Title: Artifacts of thinking : reading Hannah Arendt's Denktagebuch / Roger Berkowitz and Ian Storey, editors.
Description: First edition. | New York, NY : Fordham University Press, 2017. | Includes bibliographical references and index.
Identifiers: LCCN 2016014313 | ISBN 9780823272174 (cloth : alk. paper) | ISBN 9780823272181 (pbk. : alk. paper)
Subjects: LCSH: Arendt, Hannah, 1906–1975 Denktagebuch. | Political science—History—20th century.
Classification: LCC JC251.A74 A825 2017 | DDC 320.01—dc23
LC record available at https://lccn.loc.gov/2016014313

Printed and bound in Great Britain by
Marston Book Services Ltd, Oxfordshire

19 18 17   5 4 3 2 1

First edition

For Jerome Kohn and Elisabeth Young-Bruehl
for their long dedication

Das Interpretieren, das Zitieren—doch nur,
um Zeugen zu haben, auch Freunde.
—Hannah Arendt, Denktagebuch *XXVII.*7

CONTENTS

vii

ARTIFACTS OF THINKING

Introduction

Ian Storey

Hannah Arendt's intellectual diary, her *Denktagebuch*,[1] is a unique record of an intellectual life and one of the most fascinating and compelling archives of twentieth-century literature, political thought, and philosophy. Comprising twenty-eight handwritten notebooks—primarily in German but partly in English and Greek—the *Denktagebuch* begins in 1950 and trails into sporadic notes in the early 1970s. By far the majority of entries, ranging from personal reflections to dense, argumentative engagements with other thinkers, are from the 1950s and 1960s. In these two decades, during which Arendt published *The Human Condition*, *Between Past and Future*, *Men in Dark Times*, *On Revolution*, and *Eichmann in Jerusalem*, as well as a number of essays, the *Denktagebuch* makes evident how closely Arendt read the works of her interlocutors, records previously hidden sources, and displays the dynamic, evolving nature of Arendt's thinking.

Neither an Augustinian confessional nor an autobiography like those of Virginia Wolff, still less a narrative journal like the diaries of Samuel Pepys or Andy Warhol, the *Denktagebuch* is an uneasy fit in familiar literary categories. It is far more structured than the collection of musings and quotations that comprise Thomas Jefferson's commonplace book, but less formal than a collection of drafts and unfinished essays. The majority of entries are thematic, and some of the most common themes (often announced in Arendt's own subheadings) include "Thinking and Acting," "Plato," "Plurality," "Means—Ends Categories in Politics," "Metaphor and Truth," "The Path of Wrong," "Love," "Marx," "Hegel," "On Labor," "On Loneliness," "On Heidegger," and "On Philosophy and Politics." Arendt's utterly unconstrained intellectual range, combined with the unusual form of the record, makes it nearly impossible to align the *Denktagebuch* with any familiar genre or subject heading, as the humorously strained classification of the work by the Library of Congress under "Political Theory. Theories of the State: The Modern State" attests.

Even the usual English translation of the title, *Thought Diary*, can be misleading, insofar as Arendt herself as a figure appears only rarely in her *Denktagebuch* and the first-person voice is almost never used. There are pieces of poetry and aphorisms by herself and others, as well as favored quotations and musings that stretch for pages. Some entries are polished short essays. Many are intense textual readings with etymological and philosophical commentary. Others are the rough working out of new ideas, which will later appear in her published writing. The notebooks manifest Arendt's thinking and writing process and betray the intensity of her reading and thinking in a community of thinkers, but Arendt herself as a thinking subject occupying the privileged seat of *I*, remains elusive.

The absence of the authorial voice adds to the peculiar intimacy of reading the *Denktagebuch*, precisely because the text bears none of the signs and disturbances of having any potential audience other than herself in mind. The first notebook, written on Arendt's return from a still war-shattered Europe and her first postwar encounter with Martin Heidegger, opens with a long, troubled reflection on responsibility for the past and reconciliation among its survivors. Belying the clearly personal nature of her reflections, Arendt's tone is often a conceptually rigorous distillation of thoughts. She may be responding to conversations with Heidegger, as detailed in her letters, and readings of Nietzsche, but neither thinker is mentioned in entries. The opening metaphor of the weight of the past that is born on one's shoulders is taken from Friedrich Hölderlin, who again is not named and disappears behind Arendt's analytical accounts of forgiveness, revenge, and reconciliation. The first reconciliation narrative is a personal working out of her thoughts, a seemingly finished product that Arendt nevertheless returns to in the *Denktagebuch* and amends many times over the next twenty years. Never do Arendt's conceptually detailed and seemingly considered reflections on reconciliation appear in her published writings.

There is another voice in the notebooks, one evident in the opening entry of the last notebook, dated 1971. Arendt begins poetically as she struggles to come to terms with a life without her longtime partner and husband, Heinrich Blücher. The one-sentence entry bears the title "*Ohne Heinrich*" (Without Heinrich) and reads: "*Frei—wie ein Blatt im Wind.*" Blücher's death, Arendt's entry suggests, leaves her "free, like a leaf in the wind," a suggestive line that Arendt then includes in a letter to her friend Mary McCarthy. In that letter, Arendt goes on to cite explicitly from "Reif Sind," the same poetic fragment of Hölderlin about the burden of the past that she takes as her inspiration for the inaugural entry of the *Denktagebuch* in 1950. Not only does this opening of the final notebook hearken to the book's origin, but it also sets a once playful expression of freedom into a context of both grief and respect for the past. Arendt is profoundly aware of the mixed blessings of unconstrained freedom; the unbounded freedom of a leaf in the wind is without the tether to a past that gives life meaning.

If the *Denktagebuch* has a consistent voice, it is Arendt's unique and unceasing interrogation of her world, a world that, as she once wrote to Gershom Scholem, is the world of German philosophy—"If I 'come out of' anywhere," Arendt writes in denying Scholem's claim that she is part of the "German left" or the "German intellectuals," "it is out of German philosophy."[2] But even as Arendt engages in the tradition of German philosophy—with numerous entries on Kant, Nietzsche, Hegel, Marx, and Heidegger—the notebooks widen our sense of the scope of her intellectual homeland. In the *Denktagebuch*, we see her in close and careful conversation with her spiritual family: Plato, Aristotle, Montesquieu, Alfred Portmann, William Faulkner, Wallace Stevens, and Friedrich Hölderlin. We might think of the *Denktagebuch* as a kind of antithesis to Rousseau's *Confessions*: if, as Cicero said, "the face is a picture of the mind as the eyes are its interpreter,"[3] then Rousseau has put on his best (and worst) face for us, but in her twenty-eight fragmentary and eloquent notebooks, we have something as close to Arendt's literary eyes as we could ever hope to see.

The singular nature of the *Denktagebuch* as a glimpse through Arendt's own way of reading and thinking raises important questions for how to think about its contribution to our understanding of Arendt's monumental life spent in thought, and how it can be used for scholarship when it is read other than for sheer pleasure. There will be a temptation to read the *Denktagebuch* as any other of Arendt's books, but this is a seduction that must be resisted: The *Denktagebuch* is not a finished product, and its conceptual categories are rarely finalized. We may never know why Arendt chose not to publish certain of her insights recorded in the *Denktagebuch*, but that choice cannot be ignored.

Early forays such as those of David Marshall and Sigrid Weigel have shown the considerable promise of looking to the *Denktagebuch* to help illuminate Arendt's published writings, and in the process they have shed light an equal danger: that, presented with a treasure trove of hints and gestures, one might treat the *Denktagebuch* as a kind of definitive guide, a historical trump card when confronted with difficult, unavoidable trials of hermeneutics that come with interpreting a writer as dense and original as Arendt.[4] An honest perusal of the *Denktagebuch* itself—an unsteady terrain of shifting arguments, investments, architectures, and conjectures—should trouble this impulse. For those of us without the mental grammar of the sole mind by and for whom it was written, the *Denktagebuch* can constitute neither more nor less than Whitman's "backward glance o'er travel'd roads": entrancing, instructive, illuminative, but no more final than the thoughts each entry brings us.

Finally, there will be a competing tendency by skeptics to diminish the importance of the *Denktagebuch*, arguing that its motley collection of notes, aphorisms, and tentative formulations may have been useful to Arendt herself but is unreliable as a window into her thought. Just as we must resist the temptations to rely too fully on the *Denktagebuch*, we must also resist the urge to write it off as a private fancy. The *Denktagebuch* offers insights into both formative and advanced stages of Arendt's thinking, a halting and often incomplete yet ultimately invaluable guide through her intellectual and philosophical development.

This question of how to read, interpret, and employ the immense wealth of the *Denktagebuch* guides all of the essays in this volume, and each author has tried to approach these questions explicitly and to do so in a way that uses a substantive concern or theme in the book to model their approach. Taken together, the essays, most of which began their life during a weeklong workshop in the summer of 2012 sponsored by the Hannah Arendt Center for Politics and Humanities at Bard College, attempt to present a conversation on how to begin what will be a long, slow, but infinitely fruitful process of integrating the *Denktagebuch* into our understanding of Hannah Arendt and her world.

The opening essay, Roger Berkowitz's "Reconciling Oneself to the Impossibility of Reconciliation," explores themes of responsibility and reconciliation in the long first entry and beyond of the *Denktagebuch*, and how those themes are repeatedly reflected (and altered) in Arendt's later works. Looking solely at Arendt's published writings, Berkowitz argues, one could be forgiven for seeing reconciliation as "meaningful, but not central to her larger effort to rethink the practice of politics in the modern age." "All this changes" though, "when one opens Arendt's *Denktagebuch*," within which reconciliation is a constant, fluid trope to which she returns often in the face of an enormous variety of intellectual problems. In order to emphasize the extraordinary flexibility and incisive influence of the idea of reconciliation for Arendt's thought, Berkowitz eschews putting forward a unitary account of Arendt's theory of reconciliation in favor of nine interrelated but distinct (and sometimes in tension) understandings of reconciliation to be found in the *Denktagebuch*. The formal architecture of Berkowitz's essay presents a way of thinking about the content of the *Denktagebuch* that emphasizes Arendt's own resistance to systematicity in favor of conceptual flexibility and responsiveness to the world around her.

Ursula Ludz, one of the two editors who took on the monumental task of compiling and annotating it, explores the unique perspective the *Denktagebuch* provides into perhaps the most publically tumultuous period of Arendt's life and work: her report on the trial of Adolf Eichmann and the ensuing furor. In "On the Truth-and-Politics Section in the *Denktagebuch*," Ludz uses a detailed account of three entries as a platform to contemplate not only the background and motivations of Arendt's singular decision only to respond to her critics collectively and at arms length, but also what the *Denktagebuch* reveals philosophically about the claim, sometimes made, that she understood Eichmann's banality to be a simple factual truth. The question of what is a factual truth becomes central Ludz's reading of Arendt's own thinking about the Eichmann controversy.

Picking up from Berkowitz the strands in the opening notebook that would become Arendt's central political concerns of the 1950s, Thomas Wild provides a meditation on what he views as Arendt's extraordinary translation of her specific political diagnosis of an "unprecedented break in history and tradition" into new modes of writing and expression that confront the political structure of thinking itself. Entwining Arendt's frequent meditations in this period on poetics with the signs the notebook provides of her developing account of totalitarianism and judgment, "'By Relating It': On Modes of Writing and Judgment in the *Denktagebuch*" suggests that we can read the *Denktagebuch* as an alternative practice of writing and judgment, one that recrafts historical understanding as a response to her early question, "Is there a way of thinking which is not tyrannical?"

Like Wild, Wout Cornelissen focuses his "Thinking in Metaphors" on the particular, deliberate practices of thinking recorded in *Denktagebuch*. Cornelissen constructs a dialogue between the *Denktagebuch* and *The Human*

Condition on thinking and the dangers of *herstellen* (making) as a mode of approaching the world. In a striking series of interconnections between Arendt's texts, Cornelissen provides a reading of three different metaphors or literary motifs that he suggests all point to modes of thought Arendt embraces to resist the anticommunicative (and ultimately antipolitical) nature of a *herstellen* and its tendency to "mute violence." Rather than read *Denktagebuch* through Arendt's more canonical texts, the essay suggests that we need to learn to read those published texts more in the mode of the *Denktagebuch* and take more seriously Arendt's commitment not just to perspectival plurality but also to its implications for the very thinking of theory itself.

In "The Task of Knowledgeable Love: Arendt and Portmann in Search of Meaning," Anne O'Byrne explores Arendt's long fascination and engagement with the natural scientist and thinker Adolf Portmann, who emerges as a central figure in Arendt's discussion of appearance in *The Life of the Mind*. In dialogue with Portmann, O'Byrne writes, Arendt found an account of the natural world that resonated with her own approach to the political one, a "hermeneutic phenomenology, a way of looking at the world that engages and transforms the viewer." Portmann's antifunctionalism and focus on "intensified life" shared and fed Arendt's anti-instrumental revaluation of appearance in which "appearances are *sensed*, and that sensing is the province of all sentient beings." The unreliability of sensed appearance as well as its diversity supports Arendt's turn from knowledge to meaning and from singularity to plurality. For both Arendt and Portmann, this attunement to meaning-making through knowledge was what made it possible to love the world as it is, thus leading Arendt to imagine education as the decision to "love the world enough to take responsibility for it."

Expanding beyond the particular form of love of the world, Tatjana Noemi Tömmel argues that the *Denktagebuch* is a source for understanding love as the deepest and most systematic of Arendt's investments which never the less rarely entered her published work. In "*Vita Passiva*: Love in Arendt's *Denktagebuch*," Tömmel observes that we might "distinguish three or even four different concepts of love in the *Denktagebuch*" that allow for "a systematic reconstruction of her . . . ambivalent, partly paradoxical theories of love." The key, according to the Tömmel, is to accept provisionally Arendt's impulse to conceptual formalism and explore the ways in which she both deliberately contrasts passion, recognition, and *amor mundi*, while also cultivating their intersections. The result is a way of understanding the enormously important role of love in Arendt's thinking that both and allows us to pick up and interweave "loose ends . . . waiting to be tied up" while still keeping "the diversity of her concepts and the liveliness of her thinking." Tömmel's essay provides an elegant defense and demonstration that resisting the impulse to logical systematicity in interpreting Arendt need not entail abandoning systematic interrelation altogether.

Tracy Strong's "America as Exemplar: The *Denktagebuch* of 1951" takes as its departure a starting point of Arendt's own, her turn after the publication of *The Origins of Totalitarianism* toward "making sense" of her new adoptive country and searching in the "American revolutionary experience" for "what a human society would be that was truly political." Tracing the genealogy of European thinkers to whom Arendt turns to begin to make sense of what might be distinctive about the American experiment as "an example of what an understanding of politics that did not rest upon any kind of absolute would look like," Strong builds a conversation between Nietzsche and Arendt on contracting and promising, and the specifically political relation entailed in Arendt's admonishment to Nietzsche that when we promise, we can only ever promise "to each other." This concept of the political space founded in the creation of the revolutionary contract, for Strong, allowed Arendt to begin to explore what models of judgment were still open to the world after totalitarianism had left the thinking world with an inescapable and "legitimate distrust of all moralizing." In this early section of the *Denktagebuch*, we discover just how important "America was, in Arendt's reading" as "an exemplar of what the political could be."

Although the concept of "natality" has become one of the central concerns of recent Arendt scholarship, she used the term itself only quite rarely in her published corpus, and as Jeff Champlin points out in his "'Poetry or Body Politic': Natality and the Space of Birth in Hannah Arendt's *Thought Diary*," still less in the *Denktagebuch*, where the word appears only once. Nevertheless, Champlin argues, it comes at a crucial moment, and examining the section in which natality appears not only helps us understand the specific, novel alteration she is trying to introduce to the concept of politics but also highlights the ways in which "Arendt uses the narrative and poetic dimensions of the idea to expand the philosophical concepts of novelty and change." For Champlin, the way in which the *Denktagebuch* interweaves traditionally "poetic" and "philosophical" voices is a technique that puts into literary practice the conceptual demand of her new vision for a "poetry of the body politic," a way of understanding the necessarily embodied character of all political beginnings for Arendt, which belies Habermas's reduction of her thoughts on revolution to just another "contract theory of natural law."

Finally, Ian Storey's "Facing the End: The Work of Thinking in the Late *Denktagebuch*" inverts the traditional gaze of reading archival material forward into the work that resulted from it. It asks what can be learned by looking on the *Denktagebuch* as a rearview mirror on Arendt's thought as well. Arendt's intertwined late meditations on the nature of "thinking, death, and purpose" can be read, Storey suggests, as the preparatory notes for *Thinking* that they are, but they should also trouble our established sense of Arendt's concerns in her early works as well, particularly her consistent concern with what she saw as the increasing instrumentalization of the shared human world. The twenty-seventh notebook of the *Denktagebuch*, the last substantive *Heft*, provides a language for teasing apart the multiple senses in which ends and end-orientation are an integral piece of Arendt's view of the human condition, and for resuscitating some of the essential ambiguity in Arendt's relationship to instrumentality. It also provides, in the end, some important gestures toward a way of thinking about political ethics that Arendt never finished exploring, some fascinating glimpses at what might have been and, in the afterlife of the *Denktagebuch*, what might yet be.

NOTES

1. Hannah Arendt, *Denktagebuch. Bd. 1: 1950–1973. Bd 2: 1973–1975.* ed. Ursula Ludz and Ingrid Nordmann (München Zürich, 2002).

2. Arendt to Scholem, July 20, 1963, *Der Briefwechsel Hannah Arendt and Gershom Scholem*, ed. Marie Luise Knott, #133, 438.

3. Cicero: "*Ut imago est animi voltus sic indices oculi,*" *Orator* 60.

4. David Marshall, "The Origin and Character of Hannah Arendt's Theory of Judgment," *Political Theory* 38, no. 3 (2010): 367–393, and "The Polis and Its Analogues in the Thought of Hannah Arendt," *Modern Intellectual History* 7, no. 1 (2010): 123–149; Sigrid Weigel, "Poetics as a Presupposition of Philosophy: Hannah Arendt's *Denktagebuch*," *TELOS* 146 (2009): 97–110.

CHAPTER I

Reconciling Oneself to the Impossibility of Reconciliation: Judgment and Worldliness in Hannah Arendt's Politics

Roger Berkowitz

Hannah Arendt's *Denktagebuch* begins with a reflection on how to respond to wrongs: "The Wrong that one has done is the burden on the shoulders, what one bears, because one has laden it upon himself"[1] (*D* I.1.3). The strange phrase of a "burden upon the shoulders" refers to the poetic fragment "Reif Sind" by Friedrich Hölderlin. Arendt and Martin Heidegger had discussed Hölderlin's poem months earlier while walking in the Black Forest on Arendt's first trip to Germany since fleeing the Nazis. Upon returning to New York, she wrote Heidegger and requested the citation. Heidegger provided the citation in a letter of May 6, when he writes: "I am happy for you that you are surrounded by your books again. The line with 'the burden of the logs' is in 'Ripe and dipped in Fire'—around the same time you probably wrote it [presumably a lost letter], I had been thinking about the burden of logs."[2] Just weeks later, Arendt inaugurated her *Denktagebuch* with a reflection on the proper response to past wrongs.[3]

In calling upon Hölderlin's poem, Arendt raises the problem of memory and of how to respond to past wrongdoings. The stanza Arendt cites announces her theme:

*Und vieles
Wie auf den Schultern eine Last von Scheitern ist
Zu behalten.*

And as
A load of logs upon
The shoulders, there is much
To bear in mind.[4]

We must remember our past wrongs and sufferings and bear them as
our burden. At the same time, Hölderlin insists, we need to let go of the
past and to taste the ripeness of the present. Ripe hanging fruit may have
deep roots, but we cannot live looking backward. We need to forgo the
temptation of nostalgia as well as the security of knowing what was. Instead,
Hölderlin writes, we should "Let ourselves rock, as on a boat, lapped by
the waves." Without disavowing the past, "Reif Sind" is a clarion call to
grasp the fruit now while it is ripe.

In Arendt's opening entry of her *Denktagebuch* in 1950, she names the
embrace of the now over and against the past "reconciliation" (*Versöhnung*).
Reconciliation, she writes, "has its origin in a self-coming to terms with
what has been given to one" (*D*, I.1, 4). To reconcile with the given is a
willful act—a judgment—to love the world as it is. Reconciliation with a
wrongful act or an evil world is "only possible on the foundation of grati-
tude for what has been given" (*D* I.1.4). It is a judgment that amidst pain,
injustice, and heartbreak, we must love the world as it is. As an act of loving the world—what Arendt later in the *Denktagebuch* calls *amor mundi*—
reconciliation is at the very core of political judgment.

Arendt's *Denktagebuch* begins and ends with reflections on reconciliation. For those unfamiliar with Arendt's *Denktagebuch*, her decision to
begin with a discussion of reconciliation may seem circumstantial, a mere
accident. Reconciliation appears sporadically in Arendt's published writing. It does not appear in *On Revolution* (although the problem of revolution—the imperative of a new beginning to meet the challenge of living
together in a world without authority—is to be understood within the
guiding framework of reconciliation). In *The Origins of Totalitarianism*,
the idea is present, but is spoken under the name "comprehension." In *The
Human Condition*, reconciliation is mentioned only once, although the
discussion of forgiveness in the section on Action is heavily influenced by
Arendt's approach to reconciliation. Arendt's book most indebted to the
thinking of reconciliation is *The Life of the Mind*, her unfinished final book,
which contains important passages on reconciliation, many of which origi-

nate in the *Denktagebuch*. Most important, however, reconciliation figures prominently in numerous published essays such as "Understanding and Politics," "The Gap Between Past and Future," "The Crisis in Education," "Truth and Politics," "On Humanity in Dark Times: Thoughts About Lessing," and "Isak Dinesen 1885–1963."[5] To look simply at Arendt's published texts reveals Arendt's account of reconciliation to be meaningful, but not central to her larger effort to rethink the practice of politics in the modern age.

All this changes when one opens Arendt's *Denktagebuch*. Beyond the opening entry, Arendt energetically returns to the theme of reconciliation over the two decades that she actively engages with her *Denktagebuch*. Reconciliation is one of the recurrent ideas in the *Denktagebuch*, showing deep resonances with Arendt's development of action, thinking, understanding, comprehension, forgiveness, politics, and the love of the world. In conversation with her readings of Hegel, Marx, Nietzsche, and Heidegger, Arendt reworks the question of reconciliation into one of the fundamental if hidden questions of her work. To follow the thread of reconciliation through the *Denktagebuch*, as I do in this essay, is to see that Arendt both begins and ends her inquiry into reconciliation in relation to her engagement with Heidegger.

I argue in this essay that reconciliation is a central and guiding idea that deepens our understanding of Arendt's fundamental conception of politics, plurality, and judgment. I also show that the judgment to reconcile with world is inspired by Arendt's engagement with Heidegger on the questions of thinking, forgiveness, and reconciliation, as well as by her own efforts to think through her personal and intellectual reconciliation with Heidegger. Arendt characterizes Heidegger's fundamental "error" to be his refusal of reconciliation with the world. His wakeful standing-in-the-clearing of being leads him to attend to being as that which withdraws. By focusing on the presence of what is absent, Heidegger's thinking retreats from the world of appearances in its concern with the unseeable and the unsayable. It is against Heidegger's unworldly escapism—his refusal of reconciliation with the world as it is in a standing-in the clearing of being—that Arendt embraces reconciliation as one way to name politics, the worldly standing-in amidst the battle that is man's struggle to make a home on earth.

I present nine theses that Arendt advances around the theme of reconciliation found in her *Denktagebuch*. Theses 1–4 address reconciliation—as distinct from forgiveness, guilt, and revenge—as a political act of judgment, one that affirms solidarity in response to the potentially disintegrating experience of evil. Thesis 5 situates Arendt's discussion of reconciliation in her critiques of Hegel and Marx. Thesis 6 considers the central role of reconciliation in Arendt's book *Between Past and Future* and argues that the "gap between past and future" is Arendt's metaphorical space for a politics of reconciliation understood as the practice of thinking and judging without banisters, as she put it, in a world without political truths. Theses 7 and 8 turn to Arendt's engagement with Heidegger on the question of reconciliation, arguing that her embrace of reconciliation within an evil world is a response to the errors of Heidegger's worldless thinking. Finally, Thesis 9 turns to Arendt's final judgment of Adolf Eichmann, arguing that her refusal to reconcile herself with Eichmann exemplifies the limits of reconciliation; Arendt's decision not to reconcile with Eichmann and to demand his death is Arendt's paramount example of political judgment. Judgments for reconciliation and nonreconciliation are judgments that can reenliven and reimagine political solidarity in the wake of great acts of evil.

Not one of these theses encompasses all the others. Reconciliation is not a single or controlling concept in Arendt's work; it is, however, a multifaceted idea that touches nearly every aspect of Arendt's work. Attention to the depth of Arendt's engagement with reconciliation in the *Denktagebuch* offers new insights into her fundamental ideas of politics, solidarity, and judgment. Read in this way, the *Denktagebuch* shows that Arendt places the question of reconciliation—and at times nonreconciliation—at the very center of her inquiry into the activities of thinking and judging in politics.

Thesis 1: Reconciliation is an act of political judgment affirming solidarity in response to a wrong.

Arendt develops her understanding of reconciliation by setting reconciliation against forgiveness and revenge as one of the three possible responses to wrongdoing. When confronted with a wrongdoer who has done a wrong, she writes, forgiveness and revenge both are incapable of political judgment. Forgiveness—at least human forgiveness as opposed to divine forgiveness—proceeds on the Christian assumption that what the wrongdoer has done is something that anyone could have done. "Forgiveness is perhaps possible insofar as it is only the express recognition that we-are-all-sinners, thus it claims that everyone could have done anything, and in this way it produces an equality—not of rights, but of nature" (*D* I.1.4). In order to forgive, we assume that "but for the grace of God" we could have committed similar wrongs. Forgiveness therefore erases the difference between the one who forgives and the wrongdoer; thus, forgiveness erases the distance necessary to judge and makes judgment impossible.

Revenge similarly follows the Christian precept of a natural equality of all, but in the reverse direction. If forgiveness assumes we are all equally sinful and fallen and thus might have committed a wrong, revenge presumes we all have the right to do wrong. Revenge proceeds from out of a concept that "we are all born poisoned" by our vengeful lusts (*D* I.1.5). The avenger asserts his equal right as a human animal to take the law into his hands instinctively and without reflection, just as the wrongdoer has done. To avenge a wrong is to claim the same passionate right as the wrongdoer. Acting on unthinking passions, revenge also negates judgment.

Both revenge and forgiveness, Arendt writes, "spring from the Christian solidarity between mankind, that all are equally sinners and all are capable of everything just as their fellow man, even the greatest evil" (*D* I.1.6). For Arendt, this Christian solidarity with all men is "grounded on the fundamental mistrust in the human substance" (*D* I.1.6). Since revenge and forgiveness imagine all people to be the same in their sinfulness, both erase human plurality and difference. Christian solidarity is a "negative solidarity, which springs out of the idea of original sin" (*D* I.1.6). In such a Christian solidarity, we are all the same by nature. If everyone is the same, no one can judge another. Neither forgiveness nor revenge allow for political judgment that could articulate a positive ideal of a common world that might gather a plurality of persons into a political world.

Reconciliation is different from forgiveness and revenge in two ways that are crucial for politics. First, the political power of reconciliation proceeds from its ability to create and affirm solidarity in the face of a wrong that threatens to dissolve that common sense of belonging to a common world. By affirming one's acceptance of the world with the wrong in it, reconciliation accepts the wrong in its difference—for example, for Arendt to reconcile with Heidegger means to accept that what he did was wrong and yet still affirm that the world is better with him and his wrongdoing in it than without them. Politically, reconciliation means to accept and affirm the reality of people whose acts we consider to be fundamentally wrong; thus, while Arendt disagrees with anti-Semites and racists as well as communists and laissez-faire capitalists, she believes that they and their opinions are part of the common world. Reconciliation is thus open to radical plurality in a way that forgiveness and revenge are not.

Second, reconciliation has a specifically political judgment at its core. Reconciliation is an act of solidarity; unlike the presumptive solidarity of Christian forgiveness and vengeance, however, reconciliation is a political judgment that first brings solidarity to be. The "solidarity of reconciliation is firstly not the foundation of reconciliation (as the solidarity of being sinful is the foundation of forgiveness), but rather the product [of recon-ciliation]" (*D* I.1.6). When I decide to reconcile with the world as it is, I affirm my love for the world and thus my solidarity with the world and those who live in it. In this sense, reconciliation is the precondition for the being of a *polis*: It is the judgment that in spite of our plurality and differ-ences, we share a common world. To reconcile with a wrong is to affirm one's solidarity with the world as it is and is, therefore, to help bring into being a common world. Arendt thus turns to reconciliation as a more properly political response to wrongdoing, one that might help to build "a new concept of solidarity" (*D* I.1.6).

The fact that solidarity is connected to political judgment means that it includes a judgment about the constitution of a people, a "we."[6] The "we" appealed to in solidarity is not a pregiven essence but is the result of a judg-ment that finds something common among a plurality. Solidarity, for Arendt, offers a unity that emerges not out of sympathy or pity, both of which develop togetherness based upon a feeling for depersonalized others, the poor. In the judgment to reconcile with others out of solidarity, people "establish deliberately, and, as it were, dispassionately a community of interest with the oppressed and exploited."[7] Solidarity moves beyond pity and embraces "the strong and the rich no less than the weak and the poor."[8] Solidarity, therefore, is a conceptual judgment of reconciliation that is open to uniqueness and meaningful differences (of opinion, status, religion, and race), a judgment that appeals to a "common interest" not in majority opin-ion but in "the grandeur of man," or "the honor of the human race," or the dignity of man. Political solidarity is the outcome of reconciliation insofar as we reconcile ourselves to faction, disagreement, and plurality.

Thesis 2: Reconciliation replaces guilt with mutual release.

In order to reconcile and find solidarity with the human world inclusive of wrongdoing, reconciliation must not confront all wrong as proceeding from guilt. Reconciliation focuses less on the wrongdoer subjectively and instead confronts the wrongful act itself—as an act, rather than as the doing of a guilty person. "*Reconciliation* has its origin in the coming to terms with [*Sich-abfinden*] what has been sent one as given [*dem Geschick-ten*]"[9] (*D* I.1.4). Reconciliation addresses not the sin of the wrongdoer but the fact of the wrong itself—that factual act or doing that has happened, that has been given.

Arendt expands upon her point that reconciliation avoids the assignment of guilt in a later *Denktagebuch* entry from April 1951. The wrong, she writes, is different from guilt. She distinguishes "the mere wrong-doing" from "the reality of being-guilty" (*D* III.22.69). Guilt gives the wrongful act permanence and continuity in the world. She writes: "What is so difficult to understand is that wrong can have permanence and even continuity. We call this guilt—wrong as continuity of the that-which-cannot-once-again-be-undone"[10] (*D* III.22.69). Where guilt is something that attaches to a person and lasts in the world, the permanence of wrong in the sense of guilt cannot be overcome. Lasting guilt rends the body politic and disrupts the solidarity amid a plurality that is the essential achievement of politics. This is because the "actually guilty—and not those who have done a wrong—are expelled by society and must be thrown out of society, because with such guilty people history is no longer possible"[11] (*D* III.22.69). Guilt poisons politics. With guilty people, one cannot share a common world unless one punishes them or forgives them. While guilt is important for punishment and is the common foundation of Christian forgiveness, it is destructive of politics, which requires that we discover that common thing around which we affirm our solidarity.

Arendt finds a way out of the problem guilt poses for politics by turning to reconciliation, which she develops from the example of Jesus Christ. Against the Christian conception of a guilty and a "perverted nature," "Jesus seeks to dissolve being-guilty into a merely having-done-of-a-wrong [*blosses Unrecht-getan-Haben*]" (*D* III.22.69). The result is that the wrong does not stick to the wrongdoer himself, and the wrongdoer can be freed from the permanence of guilt.[12] By separating guilt from wrong, it is possible for the wrong to be politically overcome and thus not allowed to persist as a rip in the body politic. The removal of wrong from the person to the world, while not sufficient for reconciliation, is a condition of its possibility.

Arendt argues two further activities are required for reconciliation to reestablish solidarity in the wake of a wrong. First, the wrongdoer must show himself ready to immediately correct his wrongdoing. Second, the wronged person must be ready to no longer insist that a wrong has occurred—that is, must no longer comport himself as if a wrong has occurred. "This," she writes, "is the sense of reconciliation, in which, in distinction from forgiveness, always both parties are engaged" (*D* III.22.69). There is in reconciliation a "mutual release," the sense that both the wrongdoer and the wronged affirm their willingness to accept the wrong, albeit in different ways. The wrongdoer accepts the wrong and changes his action, and the wronged accepts the wrong as something that has happened, as simply a part of the world. They thus both make the judgment that continued coexistence in a shared political world is preferable to persisting in the doing or naming of a wrong.

To explicate what she means by the mutual release of reconciliation, Arendt enlists two sayings of Jesus. Jesus, she writes, had reconciliation— and not forgiveness—in mind when he wrote, in the Lord's Prayer, "And forgive us from our sins, as we forgive our sinners," and second, from the book of John, that the sinners must "go forth and sin no more" (*D* III.22.69). The very "sense of reconciliation" is this two-sided approach in which both wrongdoer and wronged are engaged. The wronged person must release the wrongdoer, but only if and when the wrongdoer admits and repents his wrong.

Even though the English translation of the Lord's Prayer speaks of forgiveness, Arendt argues that Jesus's teaching is better understood as counseling reconciliation. We do not make peace with the wrongdoer who does not repay; that wrongdoer has done a wrong, and we neither erase that guilt nor affirm that we might have acted in the same way. What Jesus calls for, in Arendt's interpretation, is that we focus not on the wrongdoing of the debtor but on the fact of his wrong. To reconcile, she writes, means to judge that the wrongful act is something the wronged person can live with. Reconciliation means that one make a judgment not to hold the very-real-and-not-forgiven wrongs of the wrongdoers against them. But reconciliation is just only when the wrongdoer also admits and repudiates his act.

When both parties reconcile themselves—the one by admitting error and ceasing further wrongdoing and the other by accepting the wrongdoing as something he can live with—they can and *do* affirm their willingness to live together in a world of common understanding amidst their plurality and disagreements. It is in this way that reconciliation offers to rebuild political a common world together, a world that is threatened by wrongful acts. Reconciliation as the mutual release leading to an affirmation of solidarity is what Arendt means when she says that reconciliation is at the very core of political judgment.

Thesis 3: Reconciliation is the political side of forgiveness that rebuilds a broken common world.

Arendt picks up this sense of reconciliation as a mutual release when she writes about forgiveness in *The Human Condition*. Once again, Arendt turns to Jesus: "The discoverer of the role of forgiveness in the realm of human affairs was Jesus of Nazareth."[13] Arendt cites numerous sources from the New Testament where Jesus preaches that the power to forgive is foremost a human power and not a prerogative of God. Thus in Matthew, Jesus says: "The Son of man hath power upon earth to forgive sins," and Arendt adds that "the emphasis being 'upon earth.'"[14] She cites Matthew, again, where

Jesus says, "For if ye forgive men their trespasses, your heavenly Father will also forgive you: But if ye forgive not men their trespasses, neither will your Father forgive your trespasses."[15] Her point is that "the power to forgive is primarily a human power."[16] It is humans, not God, for whom forgiveness is a fundamental capacity.

Arendt traces the reason for Jesus's insistence on human forgiveness to the insight that men "know not what they do." Since human action is irreversible and unpredictable, forgiveness is necessary to enable action. The human capacity to forgive becomes an ontological ground for action and politics. Since no man can know the distant and unpredictable consequences of his action, he is "'guilty' of consequences he never intended or even foresaw."[17] Without the capacity to forgive and thus free man from the burden of the irreversibility and unpredictability of his actions, man would cease all action: "The possible redemption from the predicament of irreversibility—of being unable to undo what one has done though one did not, and could not, have known what he was doing—is the faculty of forgiving."[18] Forgiveness, in Arendt's telling, offers the solution to the predicament of action.

Arendt's use of the word "forgiveness" in *The Human Condition* is deceptive. Even as she insists on the need for forgiveness in politics, she limits the province of forgiveness. Human forgiveness, she writes, "does not apply to the extremity of crime and willed evil, for then it would not have been necessary to teach in the Gospel of Luke: 'And if he trespass against thee seven times a day, and seven times in a day turn again to thee, saying, I repent; thou shalt forgive him.'"[19] If we usually think of forgiveness as a response to willful wrongs, Arendt here uses it otherwise. She is not talking about forgiving sins or crimes, but mere "trespasses."

The emphasis on trespasses rather than on wrongs is important. If wrongs are rare, "trespassing is an everyday occurrence."[20] Trespass is simply part of action, the fact that every human act will create "new relationships within a web of relationships" that will inevitably lead to some wrongs. It is in this sense that forgiveness is necessary for action, and forgiveness is addressed not to intentional or willful wrongs but simply to the trespasses that inhere in human actions in the public realm.

Arendt's attention to Luke's limitation of forgiveness to everyday trespasses allows her to clarify her idiosyncratic understanding of forgiveness. The original Greek word in the Gospel that is traditionally translated as "forgiveness" is *aphienai*, which Arendt suggests means to "'dismiss' and 'release' rather than 'forgive.'"[21] By forgiveness, then, Arendt does not mean the act of forgiving one his sins—the Christian act of finding solidarity in a human sinfulness—but rather the "constant mutual release" that allows men to continue to act in the world. As Arendt argues: "Only through this constant mutual release from what they do can men remain free agents, only by constant willingness to change their minds and start again can they be trusted with so great a power that to begin something new."[22]

In turning to the language of "mutual release" in her redefinition of forgiveness, Arendt surreptitiously points back to her understanding of reconciliation developed in the *Denktagebuch* and discussed earlier here. Her discussion of forgiveness in *The Human Condition*—often mistakenly thought to address questions of criminal and moral wrongs—is actually an argument about the possibility of political action; political action is possible only insofar as those whose acts lead to wrongs ask to be released from their past decisions and those who have been wronged agree to release them. This mutual release is what Arendt understands to be reconciliation as opposed to forgiveness, a distinction Arendt once made in a letter to W. H. Auden.[23]

Why, in defining forgiveness as a "mutual release," does Arendt collapse the distinction between forgiveness and reconciliation that occupied much of her earlier work? One possible answer is that Arendt actually integrates forgiveness into her political idea of reconciliation. This is possible because reconciliation and the act of forgiveness are, as Arendt wrote already in a 1953 note in the *Denktagebuch*, two sides of a single coin: "Therefore no action is possible without mutual forgiveness (what is called reconciliation in politics)" (*D* VIII.17.303). Mutual forgiveness, or mutual release, is actually called reconciliation in politics, even if in *The Human Condition* she leaves out the word "reconciliation" itself. "Forgiveness" is the name for the ontological possibility of action based in mutual release, while "reconciliation" names the political impact of the possibility of mutual release.

Both forgiveness and reconciliation are human capacities that make action possible, albeit in response to different kinds of wrongs. Forgiveness is what makes human action possible in light of the unavoidable fact that all human action carries with it the uncertain risk of transgression, of intentionally or not, causing harm and doing wrong. Forgiveness is geared to trespasses. Reconciliation, as opposed to forgiveness, is what makes human action possible when the offending action is elevated from a mere transgression to a sin or a crime. Once the transgression becomes crime and inserts itself in the public realm to demand a political response, forgiveness remains politically impotent.

In criminal law, the question is neither forgiveness nor reconciliation, but punishment—although punishment is itself a version of reconciliation in which the criminal's accepting of his punishment allows for him eventually to be reintegrated into political society. But in response to certain crimes—such as the Nazi genocide and the trial of Adolf Eichmann—even punishment becomes impossible because Eichmann's wrongs are of such an enormity as to explode the possibility of political solidarity with a world in which actions such as bureaucratic genocide can exist. In extreme cases, legal judgment must cede to political judgments of reconciliation or non-reconciliation.[24]

It is in this sense that reconciliation offers an understanding politics based upon a conceptual solidarity that attends to "'the grandeur of man,' or the 'honour of the human race', or the dignity of man,'" as opposed to a politics based upon pity that aspires to unity only of the unfortunate and poor.[25] Reconciliation is what makes possible the political reconstitution of a common world that includes a meaningful plurality. Thus, Arendt can say that no political action is possible without reconciliation.

Thesis 4: Reconciliation is an act of understanding and imagination that enables politics amidst plurality.

One essential difference between forgiveness and reconciliation concerns the question of understanding. Forgiveness, Arendt writes, "has so little to do with understanding that it is neither its condition nor its consequence."[26] Take the example of totalitarianism: "To understand totalitarianism is not to condone anything, but to reconcile ourselves to a world in which such things are possible at all."[27] Instead of forgiveness, understanding is connected to both reconciliation and action.

As Arendt elaborates in the *Denktagebuch*: "In understanding happens the reconciliation with the world that first makes possible all acting" (*D* XIV.16.331). Writing in 1953, one year before "Understanding and Politics" was published, Arendt emphasizes that understanding is an "a priori condition for acting." In reconciliation and understanding, we "come to terms with" what is in the world and thus "come to terms with my belonging to that reality as an acting person" (*D* XIV.16.331). In other words, in understanding, one reconciles with what is even when it is not what it ought to be; understanding commits oneself to acting in the world as one tries to make it anew. This is why "Understanding is the specifically political way of thinking ('the other fellow's point of view!')" (*D* XIV.16.332). Only someone who is reconciled with the world even when it is not as he or she would have it—someone who accepts the world as it is and comes to terms with the world with others in it—can politically act in that world among people who are unique and thus have divergent opinions. It is in understanding that we experience the political virtues of friendship and respect for others with whom we differ. Thus do understanding and reconciliation open the door to politics amidst a world of plurality.

When Arendt publishes her account of reconciliation and understanding in "Understanding and Politics (The Difficulties of Understanding)," in *Partisan Review* in 1954,[28] she raises the core question of reconciliation with regard to evil: How can one reconcile with a totalitarian world and with individuals who bring it about? Understanding means reconciling and facing up to totalitarianism, and making knowledge of totalitarianism meaningful. Understanding is a "strange enterprise," and an "unending activity" by which we "come to terms with and reconcile ourselves to reality, that is, try to be at home in the world."[29] But why should we make totalitarianism meaningful? Why reconcile with evil? Arendt argues that by making what it understands "meaningful," and reconciling with what we hate, understanding "prepare[s] a new resourcefulness of the human mind and heart."[30] Reconciliation does not mean embracing evil, but understanding it and accepting it as real. Pursuing further the example of totalitarianism, understanding means seeing that totalitarianism is a new governmental form that has ruined "our categories of thought and our standards of judgment."[31] It is only such a reconciling understanding—a facing up to the new and unprecedented in totalitarianism—that makes a space for "a being whose essence is beginning" to respond to totalitarianism by judging "without the customary rules" of morality; only understanding and reconciliation can rebuild a new home amidst others with whom one disagrees in a political way.[32]

Both understanding and reconciliation, as political judgments, depend upon imagination. Arendt explains the importance of imagination to reconciliation through a discussion of King Solomon's prayer asking God for the gift of an understanding heart. Solomon prayed for this gift "because he was a king and knew that only an 'understanding heart,' and not mere reflection or mere feeling, makes it bearable for us to live with other people, strangers forever, in the same world, and makes it possible for them to bear with us."[33] Imagination, "which actually is understanding," is what "allows us to take our bearings in the world."[34] It is through imagination that we take the world we are given, even a world of totalitarianism and evil, and make ourselves at home in this world. That is what it means to reconcile oneself to the world.

Thesis 5: Reconciliation travels "the Path of Wrong."

One frequent heading under which Arendt explores reconciliation is "the Path of Wrong" (*Der Pfad des Unrechts*)"[35]—a title that Ursula Ludz and Ingeborg Nordmann, editors of the *Denktagebuch*, tell us Arendt at one point considered for the German edition of *The Origins of Totalitarianism* (*D* III.22 n. 1.937). In one passage on "The Path of Wrong," Arendt says that "the cardinal question" is to understand and reconcile ourselves to the importance of wrongs.

> "The Path of Wrong"—anti-Semitism—imperialism—world histori-
> cally—totalitarianism—. How is it that only the paths of wrong have
> been accessible (*gangbar*), have been relevant, above all still had a rela-
> tion to the actual questions, difficulties and catastrophes and that there
> are never paths of right and cannot be? This is the cardinal question.
> (*D* III.27.72)

Arendt makes the same point about the privilege of wrongs in history at the end of her preface to *The Origins of Totalitarianism*.[36] The path of this evil is no doubt harrowing and inhuman, but "it is also true that without it we might never have known the truly radical nature of Evil."[37] This is not to defend totalitarianism or deny its wrongness—and just to be clear, she is speaking of totalitarianism, which is different from the Final Solution. Arendt does say that wrongs like totalitarianism are important events in human history. They are tragedies. But tragedies, for Arendt, are part of human history, even the main parts.

Tragic wrongs are the only meaningful events of human history. Arendt quotes Hegel's maxim that "a ripped stocking is better than a darned stocking," which she glosses to mean, "being ripped first makes noticeable the original unity. . . . The stocking thus appears as a 'living unity' in the ripped stocking precisely then when it proves its uselessness for life" (*D* XXVI.28.726). As Arendt writes, "Hegel's original personal experience is of being ripped, his first worldly-experience is the French Revolution. Both lead 1) to negation as the beginning and the power that brings forth think-ing, and 2) to the ideal living within thinking—reconciliation, and recon-ciliation with thought itself and with the world" (*D* XXVI.27.725). The root of Hegelian reconciliation is the profound need to make whole in thought a world that is broken in reality. In thinking and reconciling with the wrongs of the world, we can reaffirm the unity and goodness of a common world.

There are obvious limitations to Hegel's account of reconciling with what is. Hegel's refusal of politics and his reconciliation with the present—

his claim that what *is* is what is rational—can justify inaction in the face of even the worst injustice. As Arendt writes, "Hegel's satisfaction with the present may be risible (*empörend*)" (*D* III.28.72). But Arendt rightly insists that Hegel's "purely contemplative" political method is actually born from utterly correct "political instincts" to heal the real world in thought and to remove philosophical concepts from the political will to improve the future. That is why Hegel has better political instincts than does Marx, as she explains in a later entry on the "Path of Wrong." Arendt repeats the thought-chain of wrongs linking anti-Semitism, imperialism, and totalitarianism, while also adding to the list "Marxist world history" (*D* III.22.68). A few entries later, Arendt explains what she means by the addition of Marxist world history. There is, she writes, "only one essential difference between Hegel and Marx, one that has in any case a catastrophic and decisive significance." The difference is that Hegel's world-historical view is only backward-glancing, ending in the present, while Marx's history is "'prophetic,' projected to the future and understands the present only as a springboard" (*D* III.28.72). It is Marx's forward-looking world history, his effort to mobilize philosophy for politics, which "introduced the truly deadly anti-political principle into politics" (*D* III.28.72).

The antipolitical principle that Marx introduces to politics is scientific materialism, the "tyrannical" principle of logic. Plato, in Arendt's telling, was the first to corrupt politics with the antipolitical principle of logic. Leibniz and Descartes brought politics into the scientific age with their declaration "*adequatio rei et intellectus*," insisting that the world conform to laws of reason and science.[38] Hegel's political logic followed, holding the world to logic and reason. For Plato, Leibniz, and Hegel, the rationality of world was a perpetual limitation on human freedom and thus on politics: "Against the unalterable laws of logic there is no freedom" (*D* II.20.45). All human action is, when seen under the rationalist perspective, simply a working out of rational laws. Scientific politics thus cannot allow for either freedom or plurality.

Marx goes further, however. Under Marx's world history, it is the singular laborer (the sovereign individual) who in the service of his own freedom sets out to master and remake the world of plurality that both confronts and frustrates his own plans. It is this "plurality, which since Plato (and through until Heidegger) is in the way of the [individual] man— in the sense that it does not allow him his sovereignty" (*D* IV.1.79–80). In the name of the sovereignty of the individual laborer or politician, "everything is permitted that serves the end." For Marx, "The statesman produces the ideal society, for which he uses and abuses all others only as a helper"

(*D* IV.1.80). Marx's unwillingness to reconcile with the wrongs of the world leads him, Arendt argues, to justify the ultimate wrong of tyranny and totalitarianism.

What all these wrongs from totalitarianism to Marxism show us—if we are willing to truly face up to them—is the antipolitical face of evil in our world today. Modern evil is the ideological, thoughtless, and superficial denial of human action and human judgment encapsulated in all theories and ideologies that offer a single and all-inclusive explanation of human events. What evil requires is not escapism, but that we face up to the seductiveness of modern evil in an age of scientific explanation. Wrongs call for comprehension, "the unpremeditated, attentive facing up to, and resisting of, reality—whatever it may be."[39] The path of wrong requires thinking and understanding and, in Arendt's words, reconciliation.

Thesis 6: Reconciliation beyond Hegel requires settling down in the gap between thinking and the world.

In *Between Past and Future*, Arendt writes: "The task of the mind is to understand what happened, and this understanding, according to Hegel, is man's way of reconciling himself with reality; its actual end is to be at peace with the world."[40] In *Truth and Politics*, Arendt again raises the problem of a thoughtful reconciliation to reality alongside a reference to Hegel: "Who says what is always tells a story. To the extent that the teller of factual truth is also a storyteller, he brings about that 'reconciliation with reality' which Hegel, the philosopher of history *par excellence*, understood as the ultimate goal of all philosophical thought."[41] And in *The Life of the Mind*, Arendt addresses the Hegelian foundation of reconciliation in two places. Reconciliation, she writes in the section on "Willing," "is at the center of the whole Hegelian system." It is a "*reconciliation* . . . between the 'Divine,' with which man spends his time while thinking, and the 'secular,' the affairs of men." The importance of reconciliation is that it gives meaning to human life that has been severed from the meaning of truth and tradition. Reconciliation, for Hegel, affirms that "the course of history would no longer be haphazard and the realm of human affairs no longer devoid of meaning."[42]

The touchstone for Arendt's own thinking about reconciliation is Hegel. Hegelian thinking, as a kind of reconciliation with the world, is the activity in which human beings work to understand and comprehend the world around them. This understanding-reconciliation is necessary because without it we would not live in a world that we could understand or make our way in. Objects for which we have no understanding and no language to describe them are nonexistent. There is a basic truth to Hegel's idealism: that the real world only is for humans insofar as we humans think that world and reconcile ourselves to it.

Even as she founds her approach to reconciliation on Hegel's thinking, it is also clear that Arendt finds Hegel's view of reconciliation incomplete and in need of revision. There is a hint of her critique in one sentence from "The Gap Between Past and Future;" after the lines quoted earlier grounding her thinking on Hegel's view of reconciliation, Arendt adds a caveat: While reconciliation is necessary to be at peace with the world, we thinkers of politics may no longer be in position to seek peace in the world: "The task of the mind is to understand what happened, and this understanding, according to Hegel, is man's way of reconciling himself with reality; its actual end is to be at peace with the world. *The trouble is that if the mind is unable to bring peace and to induce reconciliation, it finds itself immediately engaged in its own kind of warfare.*"[43]

Arendt explicitly questions whether reconciliation and the peace it would bring are possible. Against Hegel, Arendt asks: What happens when reconciliation fails?

The problem Arendt grasps hold of under the title of reconciliation is that the "break in tradition" and the "death of God" disrupt the traditional philosophical effort to rationalize politics. The Marxian response—to force reality into a new progressive reason guided by science—is part and parcel of totalitarianism. Instead, Arendt councils a new idea of reconciliation: reconciliation to a world without political truths, one in which politics is closer to a kind of warfare—one specifically suited to the human mind.

Arendt reiterates her worries about Hegelian reconciliation in a passage from *The Human Condition*:

> The idea that only what I am going to make will be real . . . is forever defeated by the actual course of events, where nothing happens more frequently than the totally unexpected. . . . The political philosophy of the modern age, whose great representative is still Hobbes, founders on the perplexity that modern rationalism is unreal and modern realism is irrational—which is only another way of saying that reality and human reason have parted company. Hegel's gigantic enterprise to reconcile spirit with reality (*den Geist mit der Wirklichkeit zu versöhnen*), a reconciliation that is the deepest concern of all modern theories of history, rested on the insight that modern reason foundered on the rock of reality.[44]

The political philosophy of the modern age "founders on the perplexity" that reconciliation—the effort to prove and sustain the rationality of the world—has finally been shown to be impossible. Hegel's "gigantic enterprise," Hobbes's scientific reconceptualization of reason as interest, and Marx's scientific materialism are all heroic yet futile efforts to submit reality to rationality and thought. They represent a striving to have the political world make sense. To institute peace.

In questioning Hegelian reconciliation, however, Arendt does not abandon reconciliation. Rather, she reimagines reconciliation as a facing up to the basic fact of the modern world: That Hegelian reconciliation fails to institute peace and that politics in the age of the death of God is necessarily a battle. Arendt insists we reconcile ourselves to the fact that there is no truth in politics, and all politics is a struggle among opposing opinions, or *doxai*. This does not mean there are no political facts or that truth is politically irrelevant, but there are fewer political facts than most people think. Further, such facts as there may be are themselves cemented only by persuasion and opinion. They are settled political facts that come, by weight of overwhelming persuasiveness, to be part of the shared common world. Political truth, in Arendt's poetic formulation, is "the ground on which we stand and the sky that stretches above us."[45] We must reconcile ourselves, she argues, to a world of plurality absent authority and absent all but the most foundational truths.

The *Denktagebuch* offers a path toward deepening our understanding of the scattered comments about reconciliation in Arendt's published writings. This is especially true with regard to Arendt's understanding of and her critique of Hegel's theory of reconciliation. In an entry from 1953 titled "Concerning Hegel's Historical Philosophy," Arendt writes:

> This rests on the concept of reconciliation. The central sentence stands at the end of the Philosophy of World History and reads: "That the History of the World, with all the changing scenes which its annals present, is the process of development and the realization of Spirit—this is the true *Theodicea*, the justification of God in History. Only *this* insight can reconcile Spirit with the History of the World— viz., that what has happened, and is happening every day, is not only not 'without God,' but is essentially His Work."[46] Hegel's philosophy says ultimately: Only if "the infinite is the truth of the finite" (Philosophy of Religion), can I bear that I am finite; only if "world history and actuality" is the "work of God himself," can I bear to live in them. That is reconciliation." (*D* XIV.23.337)

In a later passage from 1970, Arendt points toward certain passages from Hegel's *Encyclopedia* that are central to her reading of reconciliation. Hegel clarifies the specific importance of reconciliation in his philosophical system with these words from his *Encyclopedia*:

"The highest and final aim of philosophic science is to bring about . . .
a reconciliation of the self-conscious reason with the reason which *is* in
the world—in other words, with actuality."[47] What this means, Hegel
writes in his *Lectures on the History of Philosophy*, is that "the ultimate
aim and business of philosophy is to reconcile thought or the Notion
with reality."[48]

For Hegel, reconciliation means all that *is* only insofar as it is thought.
This is "completely correct," Arendt adds, this is true at least subjectively
(*D* XXVII.50.776–777).

Arendt's response to Hegel appears in another entry from the same
year. She asks: "What makes us think? Hegel's answer: Reconciliation.
Reconciliation with what? With things as they are. But this we do constantly anyhow by establishing ourselves in the world. Why repeat it in
thought?" (*D* XXVII. 58.782). For Hegel, reconciliation is experienced as
a response to his fundamental experience of the world ripped asunder. In
other words, the world appears to man as that which is foreign, wrong, and
in need of rationalization. Man stands against the objects and things of the
world, which are separate from him. And man's dream and drive is to
reunite himself with the world. But if reconciliation is almost unconscious
and natural, why then, Arendt asks, do we have to repeat this reconciliation
in thought?

Arendt's rethinking of reconciliation follows her conviction that sometime in the early part of the twentieth century, philosophy and thinking
ceased to be able "to perform the task assigned to it by Hegel and the
philosophy of history, that is, to understand and grasp conceptually historical reality and the events that made the modern world what it is."[49] For
Arendt, somehow, the "human mind had ceased, for some mysterious
reasons, to function properly."[50] In other words, what happens in the
twentieth century is that a gap emerges between reality and thinking. This
gap between thinking and reality itself, Arendt writes, is not new. It may
be, she supposes, "coeval with the existence of man on earth." But for centuries and millennia, the gap was "bridged over by tradition." At a time
when our efforts to understand the real world forever fall short, reconciliation assumes a different and distinctly non-Hegelian sense. Reconciliation
demands that we forgo the will to absolute knowledge or scientific mastery
of the world. We must instead reconcile ourselves to the reality of the gap
between thinking and acting. We must, in other words, reconcile ourselves
to our irreconcilability to the world.

Thinking today requires accepting the irreconcilability of the world that Arendt names "settling down in the gap between past and future." It demands that we continually recommit ourselves to the loss of a knowable and hospitable world and instead commit ourselves to the struggle of thinking and acting in a world without banisters. Only if we think and reconcile ourselves to the reality of our irreconcilable world can we hope to resist the ever-present possibility of totalitarianism.

Thesis 7: Arendt's reconciliation is a response to Heidegger's worldless thinking.

Unlike Hegel, Heidegger is not known as a thinker of reconciliation. And in Arendt's published writings, there is no discussion of Heidegger in connection to reconciliation. In the *Denktagebuch*, however, the connection between Heidegger and reconciliation is powerful and explicit. The *Denktagebuch* reveals that Heidegger is the silent partner in Arendt's lifelong reflection on reconciliation.

As discussed earlier, Arendt begins the *Denktagebuch* with an essay on reconciliation that was inspired at least in part by her visit with Heidegger in the winter of 1949. In the same letter in which Heidegger answers Arendt's query about the Hölderlin poem "Reif Sind," he adds: "Hannah, reconciliation is rich, but apparently we must wait for a turning point, when the world changes and overcomes the spirit of revenge."[51] In another letter one week later, Heidegger continues: "But you remember: on a walk in a valley, we talked about language. You are right about reconciliation and revenge. I have been thinking about that a great deal. In all this thinking, you are so near."[52] Invoking Nietzsche's reflections on revenge and reconciliation[53] in *Also Sprach Zarathustra*, Heidegger offers wariness about reconciliation, suggesting that redemption from revenge would be very nearly superhuman or, as Nietzsche expressed it, "the bridge to the highest hope, and a rainbow after long storms."[54] What is clear, however, is that Arendt's earliest thinking about reconciliation emerges out of a conversation with Heidegger.

Twenty years after her original conversation with Heidegger, Arendt resumes her meditation, this time thinking through the place of reconciliation in Heidegger's own thought. The occasion is her preparation for her speech honoring Heidegger on his eightieth birthday. In her longest entry on Heidegger in the *Denktagebuch* that concludes with a discussion of reconciliation, Arendt takes her bearings from Heidegger's book *Zur Sache des Denkens*.

The question she takes up is: "What is it that most properly goes on in thinking?" For Heidegger, thinking means to hearken to Being ("*Sein vernimmt= Denken*"). Such a "pure thinking, thus thinking as thinking" is timeless. It is, as Heidegger writes, standing-in (*einstehen*) in the time in which Being is most properly heard. What is decisive, Arendt writes, is the experience of thinking as standing-in; as an experience, thinking is not a process or a method but simply that which brings a person to himself. To be human is to have the experience of thinking, that is, of standing-in in the nearness of Being. It is the Heideggerian claim that "I become a self qua self first and most properly insofar as I think" that Arendt argues is the "error of *Being and Time*" (*D* XXVI.27.723).

Heidegger's "error," Arendt writes, is the error of all professional philosophers. It is to imagine that "insofar as I think I cease to be a being. I am ageless, without qualities, etc. It is as if I am not a man, but man" (*D* XXVI.27.723). Thinking thus becomes a kind of Kantian "thing in itself," a non-thing: It is "worldless." Thinking is something we cannot talk about. It has the character of a retreat or an evacuation from the world.

Once she has established Heidegger's error with regard to thinking, Arendt contrasts Heidegger and Hegel on the question of thinking. For Hegel, thinking is reconciliation. From out of Hegel's "original personal experience" of being-ripped and separated from the world, he develops the ideal of thinking as the reunification of the self with the world. Arendt then returns to Heidegger and writes: "For Heidegger instead of reconciliation: to erect oneself in the finite as what is most properly given to one: the *Ereignis* as the manifestation of this finitude (being limited) qua property" (*D* XXVI.27.725). Unlike Hegel, whose original experience is negation, from which follows the need for thinking as a reunifying reconciliation, Heidegger's "fundamental experience" is the "seeing and hearing of what is absent" (*D* XXVI.27.725–726). Thinking for Heidegger is a standing in the presence of what withdraws: "The Matter of Thinking: To transform the absent into the present" (*D* XXVI.27.726). In all thinking there is an act of transcending, of stepping beyond oneself into the clearing of being.

In a much earlier entry from 1950 — one of the many in the *Denktagebuch* titled "Acting and Thinking" — Arendt argues that Heidegger's idea of thinking is a "fulfilled concentration" or "absolute wakefulness." It is a waking to the experience of the world; thus, thinking is understood as a way of being for men that is also active: "Thinking would then be the being-freed-for action in man" (*D* I.11.12). Understood in this way Heidegger's activity of thinking can be seen as one precursor for Arendt's reconciliation with thinking as the settling down in the gap between past and future.

By the 1970s, however, Arendt is clear that Heidegger's approach to thinking goes wrong insofar as the thinker withdraws from the world. "In thinking," she writes in 1970, there is a partial "pulling of oneself back out of the world of appearances" (*D* XXVII.76.792). Thinking, in other words, can be apolitical and unworldly. Thinking is trapped within itself: "The activity of thinking is as relentless and repetitive as life itself, and the question whether thought has any meaning at all constitutes the same unanswerable riddle as the question for the meaning of life."[55] As a seeing into the unseeable and the unsayable, thinking is even analogous to death in its rejection of the world.

Thesis 8: Reconciliation is thinking as the battleground between past and future.

If Heidegger chooses a worldless thinking instead of Hegelian reconciliation of world and thought, Arendt comes by the late 1960s and 1970s to see reconciliation as a facing up to the fact that politics is a battle. Arendt repeatedly invokes Kafka's parable of "He" who is pushed forward by the past and who is pushed backward by the future. The parable illustrates, metaphorically, "the activity of thought."[56] Elsewhere, Arendt writes that the metaphor names "the location of thought."[57] The place of thinking, Arendt writes, is "a battleground."[58] "This battleground for Kafka is the metaphor for man's home on earth."[59] The dream of the "He" in Kafka's parable is the ability to jump outside of the "Now" where the forces meet, to become an umpire, spectator, or judge, to be able to judge the battle from "outside the game of life."[60] That is the "old dream Western metaphysics has dreamt from Parmenides to Hegel, of a timeless region," the dream of Hegelian reconciliation. But man, Arendt insists, "Man lives in this in-between."[61]

The battleground of the past and future as well as the place and time of thinking between them is not something true. There is no one true and eternal space of thinking. It proceeds from what Arendt calls her "basic assumption of this investigation": that metaphysics and philosophy must be dismantled because "the thread of tradition is broken and that we shall not be able to renew it."[62] Reconciliation is no longer possible. Or, in other words, the act of reconciliation—of thinking the unity of thought and action—requires today a reconciliation to the irreconcilability of the world with thought, which is another way of saying that reconciliation becomes a question amidst the break of the tradition and the failure of the metaphysical effort to subordinate the world to truth. This may be why Arendt embraces for reconciliation Kafka's metaphor of a battleground and abandons Hölderlin's image from "Reif Sind" of a boat rocking on the waves of the hear and now, having let go of the past and the future.[63]

We have, in the end, only one judgment and decision before us. Here is Arendt: "Finally, we shall be left with the only alternative there is in these matters—we either can say with Hegel: *Die Weltgeschichte ist das Welt-gericht*, leaving the ultimate judgment to Success, or we can maintain with Kant the autonomy of the minds of men and their possible independence of things as they are or as they have come into being" (LOM, 216). This is the judgment we have before, us, our burden. To reconcile ourselves with the break in our tradition and with the loss of the guarantee of dignity and of truth. To follow what Arendt calls the "path of wrong" to its conclusion means that we must love the world with wrong in it and without the now shattered promise of truth and solidarity.

The challenge of reconciliation is to love the world as it is, that is, as potentially irreconcilable and inclusive of evil. It is well known that Arendt considered calling the book that would become *The Human Condition* by the title *Amor Mundi*—For the Love of the World. In 1955, there are at least three entries in the *Denktagebuch* dedicated to *Amor Mundi*. The first asks simply: "Amor Mundi—Why is it so difficult to love the world?" (*D* XXI.21.522). The answer is clear enough: anti-Semitism, racism, totalitarianism, poverty, corruption, and a feeling of utter powerlessness to make change. What reconciliation and understanding require is a commitment to politics and plurality that can come about only through a dedication to the world as it is.

Thesis 9: Arendt's final judgment of Adolf Eichmann is a judgment of nonreconciliation and a paramount example of political judgment.

Arendt began thinking about reconciliation in the aftermath of World War II during her first return to Germany and her reunion with Heidegger. In distinguishing reconciliation from forgiveness, she was clearly grappling with her own response to the wrongs of her friends and acquaintances. Arendt determined that she could reconcile with even those people she could not forgive. If they would admit their error, she could make the effort to live with them in a common world. Reconciliation names this power to face up to wrongs of the world and still commit oneself to living with them in a political community.

The case that tested Arendt's limits of the power of reconciliation was that of Adolf Eichmann. In Eichmann she confronted someone who did not admit his error in participating in the machinery of genocide—or, to the extent he did repent of his errors, so fully misunderstood his error to be that he simply followed the wrong side. Eichmann could be neither reconciled with nor forgiven. Faced with a wrong and a wrongdoer who refuses to repent, reconciliation would preserve the existence of the wrong and persistence of the wrongdoer. Reconciliation, therefore, would be powerless to remake the shattered human community.

In cases such as Eichmann's, there is another choice beyond reconciliation, forgiveness, or punishment. In the face of that which is irreconcilable, one can choose to deny reconciliation. This is the choice that Arendt makes in her own judgment of Eichmann: to act beyond the boundary of reconciliation's power to inaugurate a common world. "Reconciliation has a merciless boundary," Arendt writes, a boundary that "forgiveness and revenge don't recognize—namely, at that about which one must say: This ought not to have happened" (*D* I.1.7). Arendt explains what she means by reference to Kant's discussion of the rules of war, where Kant says that actions in war that might make a subsequent peace impossible are not permitted. Such acts, like pogroms and genocides, whether in war or peace, are examples of "radical evil"; they are "what ought not to have come to pass." Such acts are also those that cannot be reconciled, "what cannot be accepted under any circumstances as our fate" (*D* I.1.7). Nor can one simply silently pass by in the face of radical evil.

Arendt cannot forgive Eichmann. But neither can she reconcile either with him or with what he has done. That is the meaning of her final judgment offered in the epilogue, the one she says the judges in Jerusalem should have "dared" to offer. Arendt's judgment reads:

> You admitted that the crime committed against the Jewish people during the war was the greatest crime in recorded history, and you admitted your role in it. . . . We are concerned here only with what you did, and not with the possible noncriminal nature of your inner life and of your motives. . . . Let us assume, for the sake of argument, that it was nothing more than misfortune that made you a willing instrument in the organization of mass murder; there still remains the fact that you have carried out, and therefore actively supported, a policy of mass murder. For politics is not like the nursery; in politics obedience and support are the same. And just as you supported and carried out a policy of not wanting to share the earth with the Jewish people and the people of a number of other nations . . . we find that no one, that is, no member of the human race, can be expected to want to share the earth with you. This is the reason, and the only reason, you must hang.[64]

The reason Eichmann must hang is that no human being must be expected to share the earth with him. He must hang, in other words, because what he did was so horrific that it must simply be rejected, eradicated, and said no to. This does not mean it should be forgotten, not at all. Rather, the world in which Eichmann's crimes could and did happen must simply be said no to. In short, Eichmann must hang because his crimes are irreconcilable with a civilized world.

In an interview with Günter Gaus, Arendt says that Eichmann's role in the Final Solution exceed the bounds of what is reconcilable.[65] She describes how she and her husband, Heinrich Blücher, originally could not believe the reports emerging from Auschwitz, reports based on the testimony of two escapees Rudolf Vrba and Alfred Wetzler. Once the facts were confirmed and irrefutable, her response was: "Well, one has enemies. That is entirely natural. Why shouldn't a people have enemies? But this was different. It was really as if an abyss had opened."[66] The abyss that opened separates the Nazis involved in Auschwitz from humanity.

Most wrongs can be reconciled. Before she knew of the mass killings in administrative massacres, Arendt tells Gaus, she "had the idea that amends could somehow be made for everything else, as amends can be made for just about everything at some point in politics." But the administrative terror and genocide in Auschwitz was something new and different, something that, in her words, "*ought not to have happened.*" What ought never to have been is not the number of victims, but the "method, the fabrication of corpses and so on." These horrors, these abominations, meant that "something happened there to which we cannot reconcile ourselves. None of us ever can."[67] It is the irreconcilable nature of simply inhuman and unbelievable crimes that, for Arendt, is the lesson she takes from the Holocaust. And it is this irreconcilability to the crimes that underlies Arendt's judgment of Adolf Eichmann.

Arendt's embrace of reconciliation as a response to the wrongs of the world is not absolute. Not every wrong and not every wrongdoer can or should be reconciled. And some wrongs, while not irreconcilable, are bad enough that they do not merit active reconciliation. This indeed is the framework through which she approaches her judgment of Eichmann. While Eichmann himself and thousands like him "were, and still are, terribly and terrifyingly normal," while his subjective will was banal rather than consumed by willful evil, it is nevertheless the case that his deeds—his willing participation in the machinery of genocide—are horrific and radically evil. Arendt condemns Eichmann to be banished from the Earth. Even if the memory of Eichmann's deeds is inextinguishable, the judgment to banish Eichmann and refuse reconciliation to a world with him and his actions in it is a political judgment that affirms one's solidarity with a world in which Eichmann's actions are not simply criminal, but unimaginable.

Eichmann and his crimes are incapable of reconciliation. Such an act of nonreconciliation is—as is forgiveness in the private sphere—a spontaneous and unexpected act. Unlike a legal judgment grounded in precedent, an act of reconciliation or nonreconciliation has the revolutionary quality of a break, a crisis, a new beginning, one that makes a claim either to reaffirm a common world (reconciliation) or to reimagine and reform our common world (nonreconciliation). Just as politics might depend on reconciliation as a way of binding oneself to a common world, so too may politics at times demand that actions and persons be excluded from that world so that it might remain a world we can share.

Reconciliation and nonreconciliation both are judgments made on the battlegrounds of past and future and thought and action. Both affirm a political solidarity inclusive of plurality, but with limits. The great decision facing all of us is whether we can and will reconcile ourselves to the world as it is. In this sense, judgments of reconciliation and nonreconciliation are exemplary actions of political judgment in a world without banisters.

NOTES

1. "*Das Unrechte, das man getan hat, ist die Last auf den Schultern, etwas, was man trägt, weil man es sich aufgeladen hat.*" All internal references are to Hannah Arendt, *Denktagebuch*, ed. Ursula Ludz and Ingeborg Nordmann (Munich: Piper Verlag, 2003).

2. Hannah Arendt and Martin Heidegger, *Letters: 1925–1975*, ed. Ursula Ludz, trans. Andrew Shields (New York: Harcourt, 2004), 85.

3. See Roger Berkowitz, "Bearing Logs on Our Shoulders: Reconciliation, Non-Reconciliation, and Building of a Common World," *Theory & Event* 14 (2011).

4. Friedrich Hölderlin, *Hyperion and Selected Poems*, ed. Eric L. Santner (New York: Bloomsbury Academic, 1990), 274–275.

5. See Hannah Arendt, "Understanding and Politics (The Difficulties of Understanding)," in *Essays in Understanding, 1930–1954*, ed. Jerome Kohn (New York: Harcourt, 1994); Hannah Arendt, "The Gap Between Past and Future," "The Crisis in Education," and "Truth and Politics," in *Between Past and Future* (New York: Viking Press, 1968); Hannah Arendt, "On Humanity in Dark Times: Thoughts About Lessing" and "Isak Dinesen 1885–1963," in *Men in Dark Times* (New York: Harcourt, 1968).

6. I am indebted to Michal Eldred for this formulation in a comment he made on a draft version of this essay posted on academia.edu.

7. Hannah Arendt, *On Revolution* (Penguin Books: New York, 1965), 89.

8. Ibid.

9. *"Versöhnung dagegen hat ihren Ursprung im Sich-abfinden mit dem Geschickten."*

10. *"Was so schwer zu verstehen ist, ist, dass Unrecht Permanenz und sogar Kontinuität haben kann. Dies nennt man Schuld—Unrecht als Kontinuität des Nicht-wieder-ungeschehen-machen-Könnens."*

11. *"Den wirklich Schuldigen, nicht den, der Unrecht getan hat, stösst die Gesellschaft aus ihrer Mitte und muss es tun, weil mit ihm Geschichte nicht mehr möglich ist."*

12. In this way, reconciliation potentially speaks to a Jewish as opposed to a Christian conception of forgiveness, one tied to judgment as opposed to the unilateral forgiveness. I am indebted to Julia Lupton for this insight.

13. Hannah Arendt, *The Human Condition*, 2nd ed. (Chicago: University of Chicago Press, 1998), 238.

14. Ibid., 239 n. 76. Note that Arendt is citing Matthew 9:4–6: "But that ye may know that the Son of man hath power on earth to forgive sins, (then saith he to the sick of the palsy,) Arise, take up thy bed, and go unto thine house."

15. Matthew 6:14–15 (KJV, Cambridge Edition).

16. Arendt, *The Human Condition*, 239 n. 77.

17. Ibid., 233.

18. Ibid., 237.

19. Ibid., 239–240.

20. Ibid., 240.

21. Ibid.

22. Ibid.

23. On Arendt's refusal of Christian forgiveness, see Julia Lupton, "Judging Forgiveness: Hannah Arendt, W. H. Auden, and The Winter's Tale," *New Literary History* 45, no. 4 (2014): 641–663. Lupton writes: "Auden communicated his concerns directly to Arendt, who followed up with a formal typed letter dated February 14, 1960 (St. Valentine's Day). There, she takes issue with several points raised in 'The Fallen City.' First, she uses the Gospels against Auden to argue that even in Christianity, forgiveness is not unconditional: 'Jesus said, "If thy brother trespass against thee, rebuke him; and if he repents, forgive him."' Whereas Auden wants forgiveness to flow freely regardless of the attitude of the one being forgiven, Arendt insists on the transactional character of the gesture, which demands consideration of the comportment of the transgressor as well as the moral judgment, not just the moral attitude of the absolver." As Lupton sees it, for Arendt, forgiveness is not the Christian forgiveness of sins but the conditional mutual release of reconciliation.

24. See the following section.

25. Arendt, *On Revolution*, 88–89.

26. Hannah Arendt, "Understanding and Politics (The Difficulties of Understanding)," in *Essays in Understanding*, 308.

27. Ibid.

28. Ibid., 307 ff. Originally published in *Partisan Review* 20, no. 4 (1954). The essay, as Kohn notes, is based on a long manuscript called "On the Nature of Totalitarianism: An Essay in Understanding."

29. Ibid., 308.

30. Ibid., 310.

31. Ibid., 318, 321.

32. Ibid. 321.

33. Ibid., 322.

34. Ibid.

35. See, e.g., Arendt, *Denktagebuch*, XXVI.27.725; III.27.72; III.22.68; III.28.72.

36. Listing the same series of grievous wrongs—"Antisemitism (not merely the hatred of Jews), imperialism (not merely conquest), totalitarianism (not merely dictatorship) . . ."—Arendt again concludes that political thought must focus on wrongs, not the good. "We can no longer afford to take that which was good in the past and simply call it our heritage, to discard the bad and simply think of it as a dead load which by itself time will bury in oblivion." See Hannah Arendt, *The Origins of Totalitarianism* (San Diego: Harcourt Brace, 1973), ix.

37. Ibid.

38. See Roger Berkowitz, *The Gift of Science: Leibniz and the Modern Legal Tradition* (Cambridge, Mass.: Harvard University Press, 2005).

39. Ibid., viii.

40. Hannah Arendt, *Between Past and Future* (New York: Viking Press, 1968), 7.

41. Ibid.

42. Hannah Arendt, *Life of the Mind* (New York: Harcourt Brace Jovanovich, 1978), 2:46. See also an unsourced remark reported by Melvyn A. Hill in which she says, "I can very well live without doing anything. But I cannot live without trying at least to understand whatever happens. And this is somehow the same sense in which you know it from Hegel, namely where I think the central role is reconciliation—reconciliation of man as a thinking and reasonable being. This is what actually happens in the world." See *Hannah Arendt, The Recovery of the Public World*, ed. Melvyn A. Hill (New York: St. Martin's Press, 1979).

43. Arendt, *Between Past and Future*, 7 (italics added).

44. Arendt, *The Human Condition*, 300–301.

45. Arendt, "Truth and Politics" in *Between Past and Future*, 259.

46. George Wilhelm Friedrich Hegel, *The Philosophy of History*, trans. John Sibree (Mineola, N.Y.: Dover, 1956), 457.

47. George Wilhelm Friedrich Hegel, *The Science of Logic*, trans. William Wallace (Oxford: Clarendon Press, 1975), §6, 107–108.

48. George Wilhelm Friedrich Hegel, *Vorlesungen über die Geschichte der Philosophie* (Frankfurt: Suhrkamp, 1993), 3:455.

49. Arendt, *Between Past and Future*, 8.

50. Ibid.

51. Arendt and Heidegger, *Letters*, 85. This letter is from Heidegger to Arendt, 5/5/1950. The reference is here to Nietzsche's *Also Sprach Zarathustra*. See Roger Berkowitz, "Bearing Logs on Our Shoulders: Reconciliation, Non-Reconciliation, and the Building of a Common World," *Theory & Event* 14, no. 1 (2011).

52. Arendt and Heidegger, *Letters*, 88.

53. For a discussion of Arendt's account of Nietzsche as it relates to reconciliation, see Berkowitz, "Bearing Logs on Our Shoulders."

54. Friedrich Nietzsche, *Also Sprach Zarathustra: Ein Buch für Alle und Keinen*, ed. Giorgio Colli and Mazzino Montinari (New York: De Gruyter, 1993) 128.

55. Arendt, *The Human Condition*, 171.

56. Arendt, *Between Past and Future*, 12.

57. Hannah Arendt, *Life of the Mind* (New York: Harcourt Brace Jovanovich, 1978), 1:210.

58. Ibid., 203.

59. Ibid., 205.

60. Ibid., 207.

61. Ibid., 205.

62. Ibid., 212.

63. I thank Samantha Hill for inspiring this insight.

64. Hannah Arendt, *Eichmann in Jerusalem: A Report on the Banality of Evil* (New York: Penguin Books, 1977), 279.

65. Hannah Arendt, "What Remains? The Language Remains: A Conversation with Günter Gaus," in *Essays in Understanding*, 14.

66. Ibid.

67. Ibid. (both quotations).

CHAPTER 2

On the Truth-and-Politics Section in the *Denktagebuch*

Ursula Ludz

"Wahrheit und Politik" (Truth and Politics) is entered in the *Denktagebuch* like a title on page 1 of Notebook XXIV, introducing a section that actually consists of forty-three individual entries. Unlike the other notebooks constituting Arendt's thought diary, which usually record a month and a year, Notebook XXIV does not give a date at the beginning. Here the title replaces the date, while the first date appears on handwritten page 28 as "Weihnachten [Christmas] 1964." Notebook XXIII covers the period from August 1958 through January 1961. Only thirty pages of this notebook were used, the rest left empty. The empty pages indicate a remarkable gap in the *Denktagebuch*, a gap that parallels a highly dramatic period in Hannah Arendt's life and intellectual biography.

In April 1961, Arendt traveled to Jerusalem to attend the Eichmann trial. As a reporter for *The New Yorker*, she stayed in the courtroom between April 11 and May 7 and a second time from June 20 through June 23, during the first sessions when Eichmann was on the witness stand. Between these two visits in Israel and afterward, she traveled and worked in Europe, returning to the United States at the end of July. In 1962, she began to write her report. The manuscript she delivered to *The New Yorker* in October

1962 was first published between February 16 and March 16, 1963, in a series of five installments. Apparently Arendt did not take her *Denktagebuch* with her when she was visiting Israel and various places in Europe in 1961, and she did not use it when she was writing her report in 1962. For the evaluation of the diary character of the *Denktagebuch*, this is highly significant, since, as we know, encountering Eichmann in the courtroom and reporting about the trial was a highly emotional undertaking for Arendt.

It seems likely that Arendt started Notebook XXIV with the section on "Wahrheit und Politik" in 1963, either shortly before or after she had made a decision concerning the attacks launched against her after the publication of *Eichmann in Jerusalem*. On October 3, 1963, she wrote to Mary McCarthy from Chicago: "I am convinced that I should not answer individual critics. I probably shall finally make, not an answer, but a kind of evaluation of the whole strange business. This, I think, should be done after the furor has run its course and I think that next spring will be a good time. I also intend to write an essay about 'Truth and Politics,' which would be an implicit answer."[1]

Interestingly enough, most of the entries introduced by the title "Wahrheit und Politik" in the *Denktagebuch* are written in German, although the bulk of the public attacks on Arendt, her articles and her book were published in English. In addition, another striking observation should be mentioned: "Truth and Politics," she wrote to McCarthy, was meant as an "implicit answer" to her critics. Indeed, the answer is so "implicit" that there is hardly any mention of a critic's name or of a special argument, neither in the *Denktagebuch* nor in any version of her later articles on "Truth and Politics." In the *Denktagebuch* Arendt simply jots down notes of thought with regard to "Truth and Politics" she wanted to keep, to save from getting lost. As she said to Günter Gaus in the 1964 interview: "If I had a good enough memory to really retain everything that I think, I doubt very much that I would have written anything—I know my own laziness."[2] In other words, in the section "Wahrheit und Politik" in the *Denktagebuch*, Arendt was collecting material that she might or might not ultimately use when composing on "Truth and Politics" itself. There is nothing refined about most of these notes in the sense that Arendt put much thinking into them, as she did in many previous *Denktagebuch* entries. They are hasty notes, certainly not meant to be published as such. Compared to other *Denktagebuch* entries, they lack the quality of free-floating thought found by so many of the other authors in this volume. Neither can something like a thinking process be detected in them: indeed, Arendt hardly engages in "exercises in political thought." Only in entry no. 21 do we see beginnings of a reflection that shows signs of that exercise.

Understanding this solitary section "Wahrheit und Politik" requires first a report of its forty-three entries in a kind of systematic overview. I will then single out two entries (nos. 10 and 21) for more specific presentation. They are the ones in which Arendt refers directly to her personal case and condition at the time, being complemented by the first entry following the truth-and-politics section, entry no. 44: "Weihnachten 1964." Finally, I return to the question that haunted the seminar discussion and indeed many of the essays in this volume: What is "truth on a factual level"?

An Overview

Arendt begins the truth-and-politics section in the *Denktagebuch* by noting distinctions[3] important to her treatment of the issue: truth vs. opinion (no. 1); truth vs. lie (no. 2). Actually, most of the entries can be systematized under the Arendtian effort of making distinctions. Truth vs. opinion is the topic of entry no. 30 too, while truth vs. lie can also be found under nos. 34 and 41 as well as entry no. 46. In addition, Arendt concerns herself with a constellation of related distinctions: truth vs. ideology (nos. 8 and 12); philosophical truth vs. scientific validity (no. 9); truth and thinking (no. 14); truth by agreement (no. 15); general vs. particular truth (no. 20); absolute or philosophical truth vs. factual truth (no. 32); facts or political facts (nos. 27 and 35). However, the *Denktagebuch* provides no elaborate formulations for any of these distinctions. One has to turn to the published essays in order to find out what her respective thoughts are, which requires rather extensive work of textual criticism, since Arendt published several pieces under the heading of "Wahrheit und Politik" or "Truth and Politics."[4] But even if one consults the published essays, one may not find definitive answers.

In addition to making distinctions, in the *Denktagebuch* Arendt refers to examples[5] for lies by noting the following keywords or phrases: "France," "Resistance Movement," "Jewish martyrs," "greatest pogrom" (all in no. 3); "Silesians" (in no. 5); "Diaspora vs. Jewish home" (in nos. 8 and 11); "class struggle" (in no. 12); "Elders of Zion" (in no. 17); "man at the watchtower" (in no. 19); the "stab-in-the-back legends" (in no. 29). Again, she is hardly specific about these examples; why they are indications for lies needs explanation, which would require an extensive interpretation in each case and thus go beyond this essay's scope. For the purposes at hand, it may suffice to mention those examples she uses in her final essay "Truth and Politics:" (1) the lie held and presented by Adenauer, who claimed "that the barbarism of National Socialism had affected only a relatively small percentage of the country;" (2) De Gaulle's lie that, as she puts it, "France belongs among the victors of the last war and hence is one of the great powers." Lies of this kind, she continues, "whether their authors know it or not, harbor an element of violence; organized lying always tends to destroy whatever it has decided to negate."[6] Furthermore, she notes some examples more pertinent to the Eichmann case, which appear under the keywords "Jewish martyrs" and "greatest pogrom" in no. 3; they are treated more elaborately in entries nos. 8 and 11; in no. 17 she mentions the "Elders of Zion."

Arendt concerns herself, then, with the mechanisms of distorting truth, e.g., by interests and interest groups (nos. 24, 25, and 28), or just by creating and communicating factual errors (no. 38). In two entries, she points out that lies and factual errors, for whatever reasons they may have been invented or accepted in public, become dangerous not only to the liar but also endanger the world in which they are communicated (nos. 26 and 29). "A 'world,'" she notes, "can also be erected on the basis of a lie: An organization based on a lie is no less powerful than that erected on the basis of the truth" (no. 29), it may even be more powerful, but in the end "the strength of truth" outlasts "the power of the lie" (no. 34). "Images," she writes in "Truth and Politics,"[7] "have a relatively short life expectancy."

There are two entries, however, that merit special attention. As mentioned before, nos. 10 and 21 are related directly to Arendt's personal case, that is, to the controversy that arose after the publication of *Eichmann in Jerusalem*. These as well as note no. 44 ("Weihnachten 1964"), examined in detail, provide us with something more of the flesh of "Truth and Politics."

"Die Rolle der Big Lie"

Entry 10 in Notebook XXIV is entitled "Die Rolle der Big Lie" (The Role of the Big Lie), but there is no indication to what Arendt means by Big Lie, both capitalized. Not knowing a specific answer to this question, Ingeborg Nordmann and I, when editing the *Denktagebuch*, gave a rather general hint to Arendt's essay "Lying in Politics" (1095). Now, however, we know a bit more. It was Patchen Markell who, by browsing through the *New York Times* index, found an article titled "German Posters Done from '19 to '61 Demonstrate Effect of Propaganda." The article, which hints at the "big

lie" in Germany's history of the twentieth century, reports about the exhibition "Weimar–Nürnberg–Bonn: Art as a Political Weapon" organized
by the Art Center of the New School for Social Research.[8] Arendt may
have read this article, but she could not have seen the exhibition, since it
was shown (May 8 through June 15, 1963) when she was traveling in
Europe. The *Times* reported that the example of posters displayed at the
exhibition "vividly" illustrated "how the 'big lie' was put over in Germany,"
from the Weimar Republic through the Nazi era to the Cold War period.
In any case, this would have reminded Arendt of the "Big Lie" as it became
known by an anticommunist propaganda film produced by the US Army in
1951, which became a centerpiece of American political rhetoric against
the USSR. The film begins with a quote from Hitler's *Mein Kampf*: "The
great masses will more easily fall victim to a big lie than to a small one." In
terms of content, Hitler's "big lie" seems intuitively related to what Arendt
in Entry 17 of Notebook XXIV refers to as the "Elders of Zion," that is,
the forged "Protocols of the Elders of Zion" which she had addressed in an
article in 1945.[9]

Entry no. 10 deserves to be considered more carefully because of the
way it reflects on the reasoning it contains with regard to Arendt's personal
case. She states: "I am reproached for saying certain things because I am a
'self-hating Jew.'"[10] This, she reflects, is an accusation against which she
could defend herself if she wished, while against other accusations, such as
that she is a defender of Eichmann or a "behaviorist" thinker, there is no
possibility of defense since these accusations have no relation to reality and
are thus absurd. Nevertheless, she asks herself: "If these statements are
absurd, why then are they uttered"? Without giving a direct answer, she
adds that reality is limited, but that absurd statements presented as facts
belong to a sphere of unlimited possibilities, thus pointing to her argument
that lies, like images, create a reality which "can always be explained and
made plausible," while factual truth is characterized by "this stubborn there-
ness, whose inherent contingency ultimately defies all attempts at conclusive explanation."[11]

Framing the problem in the terms of jurisprudence, Arendt continues, "I
would have to file a libel suit, and this would mean that I would have to
defend myself. It would force me to present[12] everything I have ever written.
If one is completely innocent, then one cannot argue. This is why in court it
is always the prosecutor who must prove the defendant's guilt. 'Proof of
innocence' cannot be given." In the same vein and later in the *Denktagebuch*
as well as in "Truth and Politics," Arendt notes a quote from Montaigne: "If
falsehood, like truth, had but one face, we should know better where we are,

for we should then take for certain the opposite of what the liar tells us. But the reverse of truth has a thousand shapes and a boundless field."[13]

"Fang an mit"

Entry no. 21, the longest in the "Wahrheit und Politik" section, is the only one that includes questions and answers Arendt posed to herself when engaging in an inner dialogue on truth and politics. She asks herself questions, for instance, about Socrates. Was he cautious? No, she answers. Was he moderate? Yes, insofar as he admitted that no man is wise. She discusses possible interpretations with regard to Lessing's quote that seems so meaningful to her thoughts: "Let each man say what he deems truth, and let truth itself be commended unto God."[14] She then concerns herself with the question "Who am I to judge?" and notes, just as a reminder, the old saying "*Fiat justitia, et pereat mundus*" (Let there be justice, though the world perish). This is followed by a quote from Bacon and reflections on the "obligation of the scholar to 'the truth as he finds it.'"

Entry 21 starts as an admonition of the author to herself: "*Fang an mit*" (begin with), which is a rather rare feature in the *Denktagebuch*. Presumably, she wrote this when planning her essay "Truth and Politics." However, what she writes thereafter hardly can qualify as an outline for that essay, but it is highly telling with regard to her self-perception in this "whole strange business." Arendt conceives of herself as having sought and found "some truth."[15]

She elaborates on this thought in "Truth and Politics" when she writes about the standpoint of the truthteller. "This standpoint . . . is clearly characterized as one of the various modes of being alone. Outstanding among the existential modes of truthtelling are the solitude of the philosopher, the isolation of the scientist and the artist, the impartiality of the historian and the judge, and the independence of the fact-finder, the witness, and the reporter."[16] From Entry 21, it is quite obvious that she considers herself to be the truthteller regarding Eichmann: "None of the things I spoke of were secret, all were in the Trial. It speaks for the power of the press or rather the magazines that they appeared in the open only after I had published them" (626). Even more clearly, in a letter to Mary McCarthy: "My point would be that what the whole furor is about are facts, and neither theories nor ideas. The hostility against me is a hostility against someone who tells the truth on a factual level."[17]

Arendt ends Entry 21 with the statement "Truth . . . because it can be discovered and told by the One only, has no power; it lacks the capacity to organize. Only if Many consent to one truth, then truth develops power. However, what creates power in this case is the fact of consenting, not truth as such" (627). It is this generally skeptical view regarding truth that informs Arendt's essay on "Truth and Politics," and that she specifies with regard to "truth on a factual level," as will be shown later.

"Weihnachten 1964"

Like Entry 21, Entry 44 is unique, but this time because it reveals some of Arendt's inner life, which in principle she keeps hidden almost all through her thought diary. This entry, following the "Wahrheit und Politik" section, is dated Christmas 1964.[18] It was written at a time when *"die Welt lächelt,"* that is, when the world was smiling on the author of the *Denktagebuch,* a surprising notation. In Arendt's life, 1964, like the second half of 1963, was a time in which she had to cope with the many private and public, mostly unfair criticisms after the publication of *Eichmann in Jerusalem* in the spring of 1963—a year, one would think, that rather would have made her doubt whether the world will ever smile on her again.

The good mood, however, may not have been due only to what Arendt mentions in Entry 44, namely, as she puts it, the fact that the world complies with her vanity and rewards her ambition in such a way that she is willing to settle her posthumous affairs, among them the preservation of her papers in the Manuscript Division of the Library of Congress. But it also may have been owing to an occurrence in 1964, which is known from the "Kant-Heft,"[19] included in the published *Denktagebuch.* There we find a telling entry under the heading "Nacht vom 28. zum 29. April 1964" (Night of April 28–29, 1964), which she presumably noted in Chicago when she was struck by an inspiration concerning Kant's *Critique of Judgment*: "In the *Critique of Judgment* . . . the political man has his say."[20] This discovery at night, probably an allusion to the well-known anecdote from the life of the young Descartes,[21] seems to have overwhelmed her, although there had been signals for it in former times.[22] It points to the path ahead for Arendt's work—the path that leads her, via "Thinking and Moral Considerations," to the Judgment part of *The Life of the Mind.*

The Haunting Question: What Is "Truth on a Factual Level"?

Among the many distinction, examples, and thoughts Arendt notes in her *Denktagebuch* truth-and-politics section, one item can be singled out as fundamental. It may be phrased in the question, What is truth on a factual level? This question receives a specific twist when debated within the realm of Arendt's now notorious concept of the "banality of evil," which, by the way, is never mentioned in the *Denktagebuch*. Roger Berkowitz, in his introductory remarks to the Conference on "Truthtelling: Democracy in an Age Without Facts," held at Bard College in 2011, proposed that in Arendt's terms "Eichmann is banal" and that Arendt had meant this to be a statement of factual truth.[23] But did she really? The question has lingered ever since.

Before entering into the discussion, a short reminder may be appropriate. At the end of *Eichmann in Jerusalem*, Arendt reports the last words uttered by Eichmann on the gallows, concerning which she comments: "It was as though in those last minutes he was summing up the lesson that this long course in human wickedness had taught us—the lesson of the fearsome, word-and-thought-defying banality of evil."[24] This is the only place in the book where Arendt uses the formula she had put in the subtitle. Only later, in her 1964 preface to the German edition (and accordingly in 1965 in the postscript to the second English edition), does "banality of evil" come up again. She writes (in the second English edition): "When I speak of the banality of evil, I do so only on the strictly factual level, pointing to a phenomenon which stared one in the face at the trial."[25] The "banality of evil," a phenomenon staring the reporter in the face, which is "fearsome" in such a way that it is "word-and-speech-defying"—these component parts of Arendt's interpretation cannot be overemphasized. Many critics, however, have overlooked both the adjectives "fearsome" and "word-and-speech defying," a point made by Ernst Vollrath in his speech of acceptance of the Bremen Hannah Arendt Prize for Political Thinking in 2001.[26] Vollrath also highlighted that for Arendt the phenomenologist, the "banality of evil" is a "phenomenon" and in so doing implied that a statement like "Eichmann is banal" remains off the mark. Arendt may have confirmed "banalities" (in Jerome Kohn's phrasing) of Eichmann, but she never made a statement to the effect that Eichmann was banal. The fearsome "phenomenon" was word-and-thought-defying, but Arendt was able to describe what she had experienced in confronting herself with the reality of Eichmann. She could write a report; however, as she later confessed in a letter written to Rabbi Arthur Hertzberg in 1966: "The whole truth is that I did not know the answers myself when I wrote the book."[27]

In Arendt's understanding, then, may we consider "Eichmann is banal" a statement of factual truth? Since Arendt writes explicitly in "Truth and Politics" that she wants to understand truth in the sense in which men commonly understand the word,[28] we cannot simply look up philosophical dictionaries for definitions and then decide how to answer the question. However, it does make sense to look at Arendt's concept of factual truth by examining the concept in the works of thinkers to whom she is indebted: Martin Heidegger, Karl Jaspers, and, as Peg Birmingham points out,[29] Walter Benjamin.

Arendt's hint to the distinction (known since Leibniz) between rational truth and factual truth does not help much, since she writes: "I shall use this distinction for the sake of convenience without discussing its intrinsic legitimacy."[30] Rather, we are left with the examples she provides and with those statements she formulates in the course of her reflections on "Truth and Politics." Concerning the examples, Arendt is very clear about what Eichmann is not. He "was not Iago and not Macbeth, and nothing would have been farther from his mind than to determine with Richard III 'to prove a villain.'"[31] He was not a monster, as has often been pointed out. But are these negative examples sufficient to empirically feed the statement "Eichmann is banal" in a way that it can be claimed to be a statement of factual truth?

With regard to Arendt's reflections on truth and politics, things become even more complicated. "Factual truth," she writes, is "political by nature,"[32] it "informs political thought," and, as she has it in the final German version, "*hält Spekulation in Grenzen*"[33] (provides limits to speculative thinking). There exist "brutally elementary data" like that to which the French politician Georges Clemenceau is said to have referred during a talk on the question of guilt for the outbreak of the First World War: "I know for certain that they [i.e., future historians] will not say Belgium invaded Germany."[34] Certainly, the statement "Eichmann is banal," does not belong to these "brutally elementary data," but there is a striking parallel between the two. Arendt's guess holds for both: "It is as if people commonly are incapable of coming to terms with things of which cannot be said any other way than that they are as they are—things in their naked facticity."[35] However, when she continues to say that factual truth is "beyond agreement, dispute, opinion, or consent,"[36]—or put even more directly, when it comes to factual truth, persuasion is useless, so is discussion—one can no longer follow the argument on factual truth with regard to her view on Eichmann.

Furthermore, Arendt differentiates her description of Eichmann from the concept "banality of evil" by declaring that with the latter she is drawing one conclusion, or rather "the most general" conclusion from what she had seen and described: "My 'basic notion' of the ordinariness of Eichmann is much less a notion than a faithful description of a phenomenon. I am sure there can be drawn many conclusions from this phenomenon and the most general I drew is indicated: 'banality of evil.' I may sometime want to write about this, and then I would write about the nature of evil."[37] Unfortunately, this is a work she never wrote.

Arendt's views on Eichmann as well as her way of introducing the "banality of evil," are basically tentative and open to debate. The portrait she painted of Eichmann was multifaceted, which Jerome Kohn brings to attention. Arendt's Eichmann, Kohn argues, is a "murderer," an "idealist," and a "clown."[38] To claim as a statement of factual truth that Arendt's Eichmann is banal would reduce this multifacetedness. One would miss part of the story Arendt wanted to tell and did tell, even though she did not claim to have told a story, but rather to have learned a lesson[39]. She had sought to initiate a "real" or "authentic" controversy, as she wrote to Rabbi Hertzberg: "I had hoped for a real controversy."[40] It was a debate that she did not get.

Such deficiency, if it is really one, hardly comes as a surprise to those, myself included, who believe that Arendt's *Eichmann in Jerusalem* and particularly the concept "banality of evil" left not only truths on a factual level but also a Socratic sting to posterity.

Two Concluding Observations

Returning to the "Wahrheit und Politik" section in the *Denktagebuch*, I want to put on record two more general observations. One is directly related to the *Denktagebuch* entries discussed here, the other one places the section in the broader context of the *Denktagebuch* as a literary genre.

The "Wahrheit und Politik" entries are a collection of eclectic observations, thoughts or "trains of thought" (to use Margaret Canovan's phrase), and quotations; they obtain some structure only if seen in the light of the later publications on "Wahrheit und Politik" and "Truth and Politics." When reviewing "Truth and Politics" for the second edition of *Between Past and Future*, Arendt gave a decisive hint by adding an asterisked footnote: "This essay was caused by the so-called controversy after the publication of *Eichmann in Jerusalem*. Its aim is to clarify two different, though interconnected, issues of which I had not been aware before and whose importance seemed to transcend the occasion. The first concerns the question of whether it is always legitimate to tell the truth—did I believe without qualification in '*Fiat veritas, et pereat mundus*'—Be there truth, even if the world may perish? The second arose through the amazing amount of lies used in the 'controversy'—lies about what I had written, on one hand, and about the facts I had reported, on the other."[41] It is with both these issues that Arendt tried to come to grips in her essay "Truth and Politics," and it is for both these issues that she collected materials in the *Denktagebuch*. But there are also thoughts and materials in the *Denktagebuch* section that did not enter the "Truth and Politics" publications, and vice versa.

Considered in the context of the *Denktagebuch* as a whole, the "Wahrheit und Politik" section is proof of the "Arbeitsjournal" (logbook) or "Werkstatt" (workshop) character of the *Denktagebuch*, namely, Arendt's practice of using her thought diary during a period when she was preparing a special publication. Only marginally does this section show the real quality of the *Denktagebuch*: the kind of Socratic inner dialogue, the two-in-one dialogue, and the free flow of thinking that our working group has enjoyed and has been concerned with in other sessions. One may even argue that after the break or gap in 1961–62, a general change in the *Denktagebuch* can be detected. The prolific time of the 1950s is over, more and more the diary becomes instrumental up to the end in the 1970s, when it serves the purposes of only a traveling calendar.[42]

With Gary Ulmen as "Englisher"

NOTES

1. Hannah Arendt to Mary McCarthy, October 3, 1963; *Between Friends: The Correspondence of Hannah Arendt and Mary McCarthy, 1945–1975*, ed. Carol Brightman (New York: Harcourt Brace, 1995), 151. In fact, Arendt acted in accordance with this announcement: She wrote "a kind of evaluation" in the spring of 1964, which was first published as her "Vorrede" to the German translation of *Eichmann in Jerusalem*, and she worked on "Truth and Politics." For more details, see Ursula Ludz, "Nur ein Bericht? Hannah Arendt und ihr Eichmannbuch," in *Interessen um Eichmann: Israelische Justiz, deutsche Strafverfolgung und alte Kameradschaften*, ed. Werner Renz (Frankfurt: Campus Verlag, 2012), 259–288.

On October 3, 1963, Hannah Arendt wrote another letter. It was addressed to Emory University, to which she was invited to give two Walter Turner Candler Lectures in 1962. Because of the Eichmann trial, this commitment was postponed to 1964. Originally, she was scheduled to talk about Revolution and Freedom and, in a second lecture, on Bertolt Brecht. Now she announced that she wanted to change the topic of her first lecture to "Truth and Politics," and in fact the official announcement of her lectures, preserved among her papers in the Library of Congress, lists "Truth and Politics" as the topic of her first lecture on April 30, 1964. I owe this information to Patchen Markell.

2. Hannah Arendt, "'What Remains? The Language Remains': A Conversation with Günter Gaus," in *Essays in Understanding, 1930–1954*, ed. Jerome Kohn (New York: Harcourt Brace, 1994), 1–23, at 3.

3. For the significance to Arendt of the methodological approach of making distinctions, see her remarks at the 1972 Toronto Conference: Hannah

Arendt, "On Hannah Arendt," in *Hannah Arendt: The Recovery of the Public World*, ed. Melvin A. Hill (New York: St. Martin's Press, 1979), 301–339, at 337f. See also Susanne Lüdemann, "Vom Unterscheiden: Zur Kritik der politischen Urteilskraft bei Hannah Arendt und Giorgio Agamben," *HannahArendt.net* 6, nos. 1–2 (2011).

4. The earliest public comments by Arendt on "Truth and Politics" or "Wahrheit und Politik" came as a lecture read for Sueddeutscher Rundfunk (taped in New York on December 15, 1963, and published in Germany in 1964); it was entitled "Die Wahrheit in der Politik." Arendt worked on the topic till 1967, when the first English version appeared in *The New Yorker*, which she revised several times and finally published in the second edition of *Between Past and Future* in 1968. Still, she did not give up the topic. She rewrote the essay in German after a translation failed. Put otherwise, for Arendt's final word on "Truth and Politics" the German publication of 1969 must be consulted. In this essay I will refer to both the last English and the last German version: "Truth and Politics," in Hannah Arendt, *Between Past and Future: Eight Exercises in Political Thought* (Harmondsworth: Penguin Books, 1983), 227–264; "Wahrheit und Politik," in Hannah Arendt, *Zwischen Vergangenheit und Zukunft: Übungen im politischen Denken I*, ed. Ursula Ludz (Munich: Piper Verlag, 1994), 327–370.

5. Methodologically speaking, examples may be looked at as being as significant to Arendt's thinking as the noting of distinctions. In her *Lectures on Kant's Political Philosophy*, she points to and explains Kant's "exemplary validity" and his quote "examples are the go-cart of judgments" in particular, Hannah Arendt, *Lectures on Kant's Political Philosophy*, ed. Ronald Beiner (Chicago: University of Chicago Press, 1982), 76f.

6. For references, see "Truth and Politics," 252.

7. Ibid., 256.

8. *New York Times*, May 10, 1963. Materials about the exhibition, including the catalog, are preserved at the Archives of New School University.

9. Hannah Arendt, "The Seeds of a Fascist International" (1945), reprinted in Arendt, *Essays in Understanding*, 140–150.

10. This reproach occurs in Eva Michaelis-Stern, "Tragt ihn mit Stolz, den gelben Fleck!" in *Die Kontroverse: Hannah Arendt, Eichmann und die Juden*, ed. F. A. Krummacher (Munich: Nymphenburger Verlagshandlung, 1964), 152–160, at 154; see also Norman Fruchter, "Arendt's Eichmann and Jewish Identity" (1965), reprinted in *For a New America: Essays in History and Politics from Studies on the Left, 1959–1967*, ed. James Weinstein and David W. Eakins (New York: Random House, 1970), 423–454, esp. 444ff.

11. "Truth and Politics," 327f.

12. She writes "*vorlesen*" (read aloud), which, in my understanding, should be read as "*vorlegen*" (present).

13. *Denktagebuch* XXV.20.665; "Truth and Politics," 258.

14. *"Jeder sage, was ihm Wahrheit dünkt, und die Wahrheit selbst sei Gott empfohlen!"* See Arendt at the end of her speech "On Humanity in Dark Times: Thoughts about Lessing," in *Men in Dark Times* (New York: Harcourt, Brace & World, 1968), 3–31, at 31.

15. I made the respective passage in Entry 21 the subject of my "Quote of the Week," published under the title "One Against All" on the Hannah Arendt Center website on September 3, 2012.

16. "Truth and Politics," 259f; see also, on "loneliness" as a topic that is present throughout the *Denktagebuch*, Ursula Ludz and Ingeborg Nordmann in their "Nachwort" to the *Denktagebuch*, 825–862, at 854f.

17. Arendt to McCarthy, September 20, 1963, *Between Friends*, 148.

18. The reference to Christmas as such should be stressed. See Arendt in her letter of December 25, 1950, to Karl Jaspers, Hannah Arendt and Karl Jaspers, *Correspondence, 1926–1969*, ed. Lotte Kohler and Hans Saner, trans. Robert Kimber and Rita Kimber (New York: Harcourt Brace Jovanovich, 1992), 159: "To Monsieur's amusement, I've bought a little tree for the first time since my childhood."

19. *Denktagebuch*, 807–824. See Ian Storey's essay later in this volume, as well as Ludz and Nordmann, "Nachwort," 844–847.

20. *Denktagebuch*, 818.

21. Arendt refers to Descartes's "famous night" in *Denktagebuch* (XXVII.16.759), i.e. the night in 1619 when Descartes was struck by the idea that there is *"un accord fondamental entre les lois de la nature et les lois des mathématiques"* (a fundamental agreement between the laws of nature and the laws of mathematics).

22. See, for example, Hannah Arendt in her letter to Karl Jaspers (August 29, 1957): "At the moment I'm reading the *Kritik der Urteilskraft* with increasing fascination. There, and not in the *Kritik der praktischen Vernunft*, is where Kant's real political philosophy is hidden." Arendt and Jaspers, *Correspondence*, 318. See also *Denktagebuch* (XXII.571ff).

23. Roger Berkowitz, introductory lecture to the Arendt Center 2011 Fall Conference, on the Center's website on October 28, 2011.

24. Hannah Arendt, *Eichmann in Jerusalem: A Report on the Banality of Evil*, introduction by Amos Elon (New York: Penguin Books, 2006), 252.

25. Ibid., 287; see also Arendt to Joachim Fest: "banality was a phenomenon that really couldn't be overlooked." Hannah Arendt, "Interview by Joachim Fest" (1964), translated by Andrew Brown, in *The Last Interview and Other Conversations* (Brooklyn: Melville House, 2013), 39–85, at 47.

26. Ernst Vollrath, "Vom radikal Bösen zur Banalität des Bösen: Überlegungen zu einem Gedankengang von Hannah Arendt," in *Hannah Arendt: Ihr Denken veränderte die Welt: Das Buch zum Film von Margarethe von Trotta*, ed. Martin Wiebel (Munich: Piper Verlag, 2012), 129–139.

27. Hannah Arendt to Rabbi Arthur Hertzberg, April 8, 1966, reprinted as facsimile from the Papers of Hannah Arendt at the Library of Congress, in *Mittelweg 36: Zeitschrift des Hamburger Instituts fuer Sozialforschung* 3, no. 1 (1994): 73.

28. "Truth and Politics," 231.

29. Peg Birmingham, "Why Are We So Matter of Fact About the Facts?" *HA: The Journal of the Hannah Arendt Center for Politics and the Humanities* 1 (2012): 65–80.

30. "Truth and Politics," 231.

31. *Eichmann in Jerusalem*, 287.

32. "Truth and Politics," 238.

33. "Wahrheit und Politik," 339.

34. "Truth and Politics," 239.

35. "Wahrheit und Politik," 337f.

36. "Truth and Politics," 239, and further pages about the "tyrannical tendency" of truth.

37. Arendt to McCarthy, October 3, 1963, *Between Friends*, 152.

38. Jerome Kohn, "Arendt's Eichmann: Murderer, Idealist, Clown," *HA: The Journal of the Hannah Arendt Center for Politics and the Humanities* 1 (2012): 96–108. One may argue with Kohn whether "murderer" is the proper term. Shouldn't it better be "criminal," or, referring to Arendt (*Eichmann in Jerusalem*, 288), "one of the greatest criminals of that period"?

39. Arendt, *Eichmann in Jerusalem*, 252, 288.

40. Arendt to Hertzberg.

41. "Truth and Politics," 227. No such reference is given in any of the German publications of "Truth and Politics."

42. Ludz and Nordmann, "Nachwort," 834f., 858.

CHAPTER 3

"By Relating It": On Modes of Writing and Judgment in the *Denktagebuch*

Thomas Wild

"The question is: Is there a way of thinking which is not tyrannical?" (*Die Frage ist: Gibt es ein Denken, das nicht tyrannisch ist?*), wrote Hannah Arendt in December 1950, a few months after she began writing the *Denktagebuch* (*D* II. 20.45). It is a thought in the form of a question, which begins and forms the center of Arendt's work of the next several years as she rethinks the political, rereads dominant and hidden traditions of philosophy, and develops unprecedented modes of writing in the face of an unprecedented break in history and tradition (dealing with the legacy of totalitarianism, the Nazi past, and the Shoah). At the time of this entry, *The Origins of Totalitarianism* was already in manuscript form. In the winter of 1949–50, Arendt had returned to Germany for the first time since her flight in 1933. In her "Report from Germany," published in October 1950 in *Commentary*, she formulated the challenge of the present era: "to face and to come to terms with what really happened."[1] It is a challenge of understanding, of judgment, and not least of writing itself regarding the literal process of "coming to terms with."

What is the context of Arendt's question about the possibility of non-tyrannical thought in the *Denktagebuch*? What do the surroundings of this passage look like? The entry itself deals with "the affinity of the philosopher and the tyrant since Plato" (*D* II. 20.45). The tradition of Western thought that identifies thinking and reason with logic begins with Plato. The irrevocable laws of logic, according to Arendt, are "by definition" connected not to freedom, but rather to tyranny. If one understands this tradition where the political is the concern of man and of a rational constitution, then only tyranny can produce good politics. The political, however, is not intrinsic to humans, it is not part of the human essence: The human being is apolitical, Arendt states in a neighboring entry. As Arendt conceptualizes it and explains in *The Human Condition*, the birthplace of freedom and the political lies "between people" (*Zwischen-den-Menschen*): "Politics arises in the space between people and establishes itself *as the relationship*" (*Politik entsteht im Zwischen und etabliert sich* als der Bezug; 17, my emphasis).

The question of the relationship between tyranny and thought is a political and theoretical one. How can the connection between the occurrences of the world and the capacity of humans to understand and think through them be effectively conceived? In an immediately preceding entry from December 1950, Arendt recalls a powerful guiding principle of the philosophical tradition: *adaequatio rei et intellectus*, the correspondence theory of truth which claims the adequacy of knowledge, or intellect and subject. According to Hegel, Arendt notes, the movements of the mind and the movements of events match insofar as the intellectual "swimming" (*Schwimmbewegungen*) of man continues to match the "tide" (*Strombewegungen*) of world events. Marx, according to Arendt, concludes from this that the swimmer is in fact stronger than the tide, and even able to channel the river of world events into specific channels. "Naturally, this is possible only within the laws of the tide" (*innerhalb der Stromgesetze*), since the laws of the tide "are also the laws of swimming" (*zugleich auch die Schwimmgesetze sind*), she comments. In anaphoric unison with her question about nontyrannical thought, Arendt responds: "The question is how one can avoid swimming in the tide at all" (*Die Frage ist gerade, wie man das Schwimmen im Strom überhaupt vermeiden kann*; *D* II.19.45).

Arendt calls into question the *et*/and between *rei* and *intellectus* in a twofold manner, as well as the conjunction in "the conception of truth and world security" (*Wahrheitsbegriff und Weltsicherheit*), as the entry is titled in the *Denktagebuch*. In questioning the binding power of these conjunctions, she breaks up the assumptions of traditional connectors.

The cited notes, including Arendt's emphatic questions, precede an entry that is literally broken up. "The path of life" (*Der Lebensweg*), as it is titled, runs metaphorically on land, instead of swimming in the tide of history. The "deserts and wildernesses of life" (*Wüsten und Wildnisse des Lebens*), with which the entry begins, however, lay no solid ground for the paths of thought to follow. As protection from the worst perils of the "human jungles" (*Menschendschungel*), society has built "a few tracks" (*ein paar Wege*), which provide orientation, at least in "bright times" (*in ruhigen Zeiten*). And what happens to men in dark times? After a dash she begins the contrary argument: "Whoever does not these tracks . . ." (*Wer diese Wege nicht . . .*) and the note breaks off. But just two entries later (*D* II.21.45), a voice seems to continue this reflection on the "path of life":

> Up life's hill with my little bundle,
> If I prove it steep,
> If a discouragement withhold me,
> If my newest step
> Older feel than the hope that prompted,
> Spotless be from blame
> Heart that proposed as heart that accepted,
> Homelessness for home.

The voice that speaks here in Arendt's *Denktagebuch* belongs to Emily Dickinson. Like Arendt, she vexed her contemporaries and left no one untouched but many uncomprehending. The theorist answers her own question about the unsettled relationship between reality and the contemplation of reality with a poem. Is there a conjunction that connects these disparate pieces that Arendt places next to one another in her *Thinking Notebook*?

To accept "homelessness for home" was a new kind of experience for Arendt upon her reencounter with Germany. Her "Report from Germany" uses the word twice in the first paragraph. The "peculiarly modern touches of physical homelessness," Arendt says, had been added to the general picture of catastrophe in the devastated land of postwar Europe; she describes "homelessness on an unprecedented scale" in her preface to the *Origins*, written at the same time in summer 1950. "Heartlessness," which rhymes with "homelessness" and echoes Dickinson's poem, is the remarkable word with which Arendt brings the core observation of her report to light.[2]

The heartless and stubborn refusal of many Germans to accept the blatant and shocking realities revealed a difficult legacy of the Nazi regime. Arendt saw the inability of many of those she spoke with to distinguish facts from opinions as a variation on this problem. "The reality of the death factories" had often been "transformed into a mere potentiality," Arendt reports from numerous conversations.[3] This was the burdensome inheritance of totalitarian rule, which fostered an understanding of reality in which "what is true today may already be false tomorrow."[4] The refusal of countless Germans to confront and understand what actually happened comes to Arendt as an image: "Amid the ruins, Germans mail each other picture postcards still showing the cathedrals and marketplaces, the public buildings and bridges that no longer exist."[5] Arendt does not look "behind the facades," but rather describes what she perceives in front of her eyes. She does not refer to a preexisting system of conception, nor does she deduce a theory to present her thoughtful observations. Her way of writing describes a process: "to face and to come to terms with what really happened."[6]

Arendt does not arrange the two activities "to face" and "to come to terms with" in a chronological, intentional, or causal order. Instead, the sentence expresses a mode: to look reality in the face, to confront what happened and to find words for what one thus discovers, to bring it into language. An oscillating "and" that joins, and creates distance. A break and a space between. "Stop and think." "Between" is a political word for Arendt: It is a place for interactions that are unpredictable and not fully controllable; it is a birthplace for freedom. Totalitarianism tried to radically destroy this space of freedom with an "iron band" of ideology and terror, Arendt writes in *The Origins of Totalitarianism*. In the *Denktagebuch* she takes up the word "band" and links it in a new and different way. It is not the coercive logic of reason but rather the imagination that forms a "band between people" (*Nicht die Vernunft, sondern die Einbildungskraft bildet das Band zwischen den Menschen*), she says, in regard to the political aptitude of different intellectual capacities: "Against the self-sense, reason, which grows from the thought of the "I"/ego, stand the world-sense, public spirit (passive) and imagination (active) which grow from others" (*Gegen den Selbst-Sinn, die Vernunft, die aus dem Ich-denke lebt, steht der Welt-Sinn, der als Gemeinsinn (passiv) und als Einbildungskraft (aktiv) von den Anderen lebt*; D XXII.19.570).

In the immediately following paragraph of the same entry (from August 1957), Arendt considers the relationship between art and politics and comes to the conclusion that "both have to do with the world" (*beide haben es mit der Welt zu tun*). A year later, the thought resurfaces in *The Human Condition* (as well as in the German version *Vita activa* of 1960). In the section on "The Permanence of the World and the Work of Art" (*Die Beständigkeit der Welt und das Kunstwerk*) Arendt speaks of the human faculty to be "open and related to the world" (*weltoffene und weltbezogene Fähigkeit*) from which art is produced. This is the human capacity "to think and to sense" (*zu denken und zu sinnen*) as she refers to it later in the same paragraph.[7] It is a surprising "and"-connection of two traditionally separate capacities again reminiscent of the mode "to face and to come to terms with."

This wording exists only in the German edition of *Vita Activa*, while in the American *Human Condition* merely "the human capacity for thought" is discussed. Whereas the connection "to face and to come to terms with" is only in Arendt's publications in English (see "Report from Germany" and *Origins*), compared with simply "*verstehen*" (understand) or "*begreifen*" (grasp, conceive) in the German (*Elemente und Ursprünge totaler Herrschaft*). In one of two entries in the *Denktagebuch* on "Metaphor(s) and Truth" that directly follow the Dickinson poem "Up life's hill with my little bundle," Arendt creates another counterpart for "come to terms" which carries significant and remarkable echoes of the English, down to the very syllable: First the "coming-to-words" (*Zum-Wort-Werden*) makes the "shock of reality" (*Schock der Wirklichkeit*) bearable; "this may indeed underlie the '*adaequatio rei et intellectus*'" (*dies liege vielleicht doch der 'adaequatio rei et intellectus' zugrunde*; D II.25.48). As fragile as the already difficult relationship between reality and the reflection on reality becomes in the face of the modern breaks in tradition, Arendt persistently considers the particles of that divide, while "shock of reality" and "coming to words" act as if they were transcriptions of *rei* and *intellectus*, the focus remains on *et*/and. The question then becomes how these conjunctions can be conceived and presented today.

In Arendt's writing, the word "and" continually appears not as a simple connector to be taken for granted, but rather as a word for making distinctions and as a particle noting engagement (*Verbindlichkeit*). "And" can make seemingly incompatible concepts confront each other. Such arrangements can be surprising and confusing. "And" can hold abutting concepts in limbo and leaves space for further thought, regroupings, and new beginnings. "And" cannot be resolved into one concept; it needs two to come to life. "And" brooks no negation. Metaphorically, "and" is a word of poetry— and of poetic thinking.

In her speech accepting the Lessing Prize, "On Humanity in Dark Times," Arendt pursues the question of "how much reality must be retained even in a world become inhuman if humanity is not to be reduced to an empty phrase or phantom" (*wieviel Wirklichkeit auch in einer unmenschlich gewordenen Welt festgehalten werden muss, um Menschlichkeit nicht zu einer Phrase oder einem Phantom werden zu lassen*).[8] Arendt imagines a friendship between a German and a Jew under the conditions of the Third Reich.

Under such circumstances, would it not have been a sign of humanness, if these friends had said, "Are we not both human beings" (*Sind wir nicht beide Menschen*)? No, according to Arendt: "in keeping with a humanness that had not lost the solid ground of reality, a humanness in the midst of the reality of persecution, they would have had to say to each other: 'A German and a Jew, and friends' ('*Ein Deutscher und ein Jude, und Freunde*')." It is a double "and" that enables an "unpremeditated facing up to, and resisting of, reality" in thought and writing,[9] a doubled "and" whose two sides cannot be united, but that rather live from and in the distinction.

This thought of Hannah Arendt's on distinctions that are binding without being tyrannical is related to her reflections on "plurality." The beginnings of these thoughts are noted in her early entries in the *Denktagebuch*. We know from later writings, such as *The Human Condition* (1958) or *On Violence* (1968) that plurality—the existence of the many and the various—was a prerequisite for politics for Arendt. Politics, whose raison d'etre is freedom, arises from the spontaneous thinking and acting together of the many and the various. At the beginning of the *Denktagebuch*, she makes a connection between her reflection on plurality (as a political concept) and a "plurality of languages" (*Pluralität der Sprachen*), and in fact renews and contextualizes her original question of nontyrannical thought.

"If there were only one language, perhaps we would be sure of the nature of things," Arendt writes (*Gäbe es nur eine Sprache, so wären wir vielleicht des Wesens der Dinge sicher*; D II.15.42). "*Gäbe*," "*wäre*," "*vielleicht*"/"If," "were," "perhaps"—the distance between this uncertainty and the certainty of "one language" or "the nature of things" has the potential for humor, or at least polemical possibility. This is intentional, as Arendt sees concepts like one "world language" (*Weltsprache*) not only as "nonsense" (*Unsinn*) but also as "artificially enforced disambiguation of the ambiguous" (*künstlich gewaltsame Vereindeutigung des Vieldeutigen*), a totalizing abolition of plurality. The decisive case for a plurality of languages is made in her opinion by the fact that a multiplicity of languages exists. These languages differ in vocabulary and grammar, and therefore in their "mode of thinking" (*Denkweise*), and all are learnable. It is primarily the learnability of foreign languages, according to Arendt—who knew Greek, Latin, French, and English—which enables the discovery that there are other "'counterparts' to the physically identical world that we have in common" (*dass es noch andere 'Entsprechungen' zur gemeinsam-identischen Welt gibt als die unsere*). We, who are many and various, and more than simply descendants of one "animal rationale" or "*zoon logikon*," we are beings gifted not with reason or language, but with languages and with the faculty of speaking to one another.

But why does Hannah Arendt put the "other 'counterparts' of our collectively shared world" in quotes? If one now reconsiders this entry on the "fluctuating ambiguity of the world and the insecurity of humans in it" (*schwankenden Vieldeutigkeit der Welt und [der] Unsicherheit des Menschen darin*) as a reflection of the fluctuating relationship of *rei* and *intellectus*, one notices that Arendt speaks of the *adaequatio*, with echoes of the original Latin (*'adäquierende'. . . adjustierende Erkenntnis*), as "adjusting knowledge" (*D* II.15.43). So why "Entsprechungen/counterparts"? This German entry on the "plurality of languages" is bordered by a quote in French (Blaise Pascal), and an entry by Arendt in English. In this echo chamber, what would be the counterparts of the German *Entsprechungen*? Equivalences, analogies, counterparts—*pendants, adéquations, équivalents*? Or perhaps correspondents—*correspondances*?

"What fascinated him about the matter was that the spirit and its material manifestation were so intimately connected that it seemed permissible to discover everywhere Baudelaire's correspondences, which clarified and illuminated one another if they were properly correlated, so that finally they would no longer require any interpretative or explanatory commentary."[10] "What fascinated him" refers to Walter Benjamin. In the original German version of her essay, Arendt characterizes Benjamin's writing style through the plural words "*Entspechungen/correspondances*." She uses the word *Entsprechungen* once again in this essay when she sums up his unique way of thinking on "the intellectual and its material appearance" (*das Geistige und seine materielle Erscheinung*)—"*intellectus et rei*"—as follows: "What is so hard to understand about Benjamin," Arendt writes, "is that without being a poet he thought poetically"[11] (*Was an Benjamin so schwer zu verstehen war ist, daß er, ohne ein Dichter zu sein, dichterisch dachte*). To think poetically, to think philosophically, to think politically—what connections, conjunctions, relationships does Arendt open up here surrounding her question whether there is a kind of thought that is not tyrannical?

In the following entry, after she cites the poetic thought of "*Entspechungen/correspondances*," Arendt notes in English, "If Man is the topic of philosophy and Men the subject of politics, then totalitarianism signifies a victory of 'philosophy' over politics—and not the other way round." And she continues: "It is as though the final victory of philosophy would mean the final extermination of philosophers. Perhaps they have become 'superfluous'" (*D* II, 16:43). "Superfluous," like "counterparts" in the preceding entry on the "plurality of languages," is set in quotes. For what reason? No other English word is thus marked in the surrounding entries on the problem of totalitarian regimes—where "the omnipotence of Man corresponds to the superfluousness of Men" (*die Allmacht des Menschen der Überflüssigkeit der Menschen entspricht*) (*D* II.21.53). Where does this quoted "superfluous" come from?

"Superfluous were the Sun/When Excellence be dead," begins a poem by Emily Dickinson. It was written in the same year as "Up life's hill with my little bundle." In the *Complete Poems*, the two are neighbors (No. 999 and No. 1010). "Superfluous were the Sun" was published in a 1950 edition that Arendt owned. It is a poem that presents the absence, indeed the death of an all-seeing majesty, and also deals with one presumed dead: "dead/said" is the rhyme of the first strophe. Arendt juxtaposes the internally rhyming "final victory of philosophy" with the potential "final extermination of the philosophers." Would it be the assassination of a tyrant or rather his suicide? Would this mark the end of the time of philosophical thought? How could one continue to write in such an era? The iambs of the last verses both narrow it down and open it up:

> Upon His dateless Fame
> Our Periods may lie
> As Stars that drop anonymous
> From an abundant sky.[12]

Which "periods" are falling from the sky here? Eras, punctuation marks? Which conjunction(s) could stand between them? And they drop "as stars"—the time when the stars were brought to the earth was a time of Revolutions. Constellations of tides, times, terms—characters, signs?

One could call Arendt's system of writing in the *Denktagebuch* creating constellations: It is a collection and juxtaposition of notes, excerpts, reflections, fragments, quotes, poems; assemblages that establish connections and leave them open, because they are being questioned; or figurations, whose traces are reworked in Arendt's texts, from *The Origins of Totalitarianism* (1951) to *The Life of the Mind* (1977). This characteristic of Arendt's writing remains, up to today, largely without response. To accept "Homelessness for Home," as Dickinson writes, can thus also be read in relation to Arendt's barely answered way of writing.

It might *not* be a coincidence that it was a poet who responds to Arendt's way of scrutinizing the questions "Is there a way of thinking which is not tyrannical" and "how one can avoid swimming in the tide" most precisely. In her novel *Das zweite Paradies* (Second Paradise), Hilde Domin gives the following line to an Arendt-voice: "'*Auf dem Atlantik,*' sagte eine, '*bau ich mein Haus. Beide Kontinente sind unmöglich. Ich lebe zwischen Ihnen,*'" ("I'll build my house in the Atlantic," she said. "Both continents are impossible.

I'll live between them").[13] It is a moving and apt image for Hannah Arendt's "place" between different languages, audiences, and traditions, and it is the emerging outline of a thinker of conjunctions and relations.

In the "Postscriptum" to *Thinking*, at the end of the first section of *The Life of the Mind*, the question of a way of thinking that is not tyrannical resurfaces. Here this "distinct capacity of our minds" is closely associated with another: the capacity of "judging."[14] In "contradistinction" to the intellectual activities of thinking and willing, "judgments are not arrived at by either deduction or induction," Arendt says, "in short, they have nothing in common with logical operations."[15] While the sonorous voice of consciousness confers its commands to action on the basis of generalization, the quiet praxis of judgment is constantly concerned with uniquenesses. Arendt, in agreement with Kant, characterized judgment as "a peculiar talent which can be practiced only and cannot be taught." Correspondingly, Aristotle recognized that scientific rules could not be applied to ethical matters; rather, moral actions are situationally determined, in individual cases and according to particularities. Any discussion of matters of ethics and action he adds, echoing ethics and aesthetics, "cannot be more than an outline and is bound to lack precision."[16]

In order to be able "to arrive at a halfway plausible theory of ethics," according to Arendt, it is important to separate judgment from other intellectual capacities and to grant it its own modus operandi.[17] For the question of whether a person is able to make this distinction, Arendt devises an interesting litmus test. How does one understand the relationship of judgment and history? Does one accept with Hegel and Marx that history is the tribunal of the world and that questions of ethics are essentially questions of development and progress? Or does one believe with Kant in human autonomy, in the ability to spontaneously start a series from the beginning?

Arendt has a characteristic way of dealing with such questions of the development of traditions and possibilities of thinking, in which she dives down to the moment in the past when a common word was transformed into a concept, when the crystallization of a concept happened. She thereby recreates a moment of undecidedness, and therefore the possibility of deciding. With the word "*Geschichte*/history," she starts her reflections at its Greek stem *historein*. The word once had several meanings: to see, to know, to report, to investigate and question an eyewitness, to evaluate testimony like an impartial judge. While Arendt understands the will as a sense of the future, she understands judgment as a capacity for dealing with the past. "If judgment is our faculty for dealing with the past, the historian is the inquiring man who *by relating it* sits in judgment over it."

How should this emphatic "by relating it" be read? The decisive aspect, the place where the judgment becomes manifest, seems to be the (way of) presenting (the story/history). The English expression "by relating it" has a double meaning here: the process of telling, and a way of relating things, of putting them in relation to each other. Which relationships are created here? Which capacities are addressed? How is the relationship that Arendt invokes between Homer and Herodotus—authors that fall somewhere between writers of history and poets—to be understood? Why does Arendt focus on the relationship of judgment (to writing, and) to history? What door does the insertion of the phrase "by relating it" open in our understanding of judgment? What grammars (English, German, Greek) are folded into each other here, what plurality of ways of thinking are introduced to the reader?[18]

In the "Postscriptum" to the first volume of *The Life of the Mind*, Arendt had already decided and announced that her investigation of judgment would come at the end of the second volume, which is dedicated to willing. That *Judging* should become its own—however unwritten—book, was at that point unforeseeable. In the last section of *Willing*, we again encounter the constellation that is introduced in the "Postscriptum." Here again she talks about the turning point in the traditional understanding of history: of the modern conception of historical progress, which is connected with Hegel and Marx, as well as its counterpart in Kant's thinking on freedom.

But here Arendt tells the story a bit differently, and with a surprise: with John Donne. In the seventeenth century, as a new scientific understanding of history was already emerging, John Donne, who was not a scientist, but a poet, wrote an astounding observation "in immediate reaction to what he knew was going on in the sciences" in 1611. Without a colon, which would demote what follows to the status of an illustration, but rather with a new, indented paragraph that interrupts and resets the discursive text, Arendt says what she has to say at this moment in her train of thought with another voice, namely the voice of John Donne's poetry:

> [Donne] did not have to wait for Descartes, or Pascal, to draw all the
> conclusions from what he perceived.
> And new Philosophy calls all in doubt,
> . . .
> 'Tis all in pieces, all cohaerence gone;
> All just supply, and all Relation:

Prince, Subject, Father, Sonne, are things forgot. . . .
And he ends with lamentations that needed roughly three hundred years
to be heard again. . . .[19]

Arendt sets in motion all John Donne's conclusions, reached independently of Descartes and Pascal, whose ideas are still formative today, by picking up on precisely this word—"all." In this way a plurality of sentences emerges from all-embracing completeness. Arendt's and Donne's observations do not seem complete, but instead offer possible combinations. Arendt's "all the conclusions" is posed as an echo of Donne's "all in doubt" and "all in pieces." The verses diagnose a state of affairs: "all cohaerence gone . . . and all Relation." What follows is a string of powerful entities— ruler, subject, father, son—that have been forgotten: That is to say, their relationships to each other must be reconsidered. The only conjunction in this poem is "and": conclusive connecting particles like "because" or "thus" are absent. The verses she cites begin with "and," and it is with "and" that Arendt continues her text. Arendt's passage deals with history, with the oscillation between "all" and "and," and seeks "to draw all conclusions" from history "by relating it."

In this mode of "relating," philosophy, poetry, history, and politics come into relation with each other. In Notebook XX of Arendt's *Denktagebuch* there is a passage of about twenty pages (477–496) notable because of the density with which poetry, philosophy, history, and politics are brought into relation, and because of the density or urgency with which at the same time she questions their relationship to judgment.[20]

Those who know Arendt's later writings will hear hints of judging already at the beginning of Notebook XX: one with "*common sense* 'argues,'" because otherwise he would have no way of ordering particular sense-data in the common world. This 'common sense' always works with *working hypotheses* that serve to control the particular in reference to its 'general validity'" (*D* XX.1.477). Although "judging" is not specifically mentioned, the use of expressions like "common sense" (as "*gesunder Menschenverstand*" and as "*Gemeinsinn*"), with which Arendt was to develop her reflections on judging over the next two decades, shows that it is already clearly under consideration here. This early passage from the *Denktagebuch*, in which the "particular" is twice mentioned, and its relationship to "general validity" emphasized seems directly echoed by the end of Arendt's *Kant Lectures*. "In conclusion," she writes there, "The chief difficulty in judgment is that it is 'the faculty of thinking the particular' [Kant, Section IV of the Introduction to *KdU*]; but to *think* means to generalize, hence it is the faculty of mysteriously combining the particular and the general."[21]

The keyword of Notebook XX appears right at the beginning in entry 2: *athanasia*, the Greek word for immortality, for deathlessness, imperishability, which can also be understood as persisting or living on. In the polis, glorious deeds were helped toward immortality and their heroes made deathless by being told over and over again, so that they remained a vital element of life in the polis, the political sphere. Arendt confronts this ancient understanding of history, according to which "the polis was the site of 'historicity' and so politics was 'the medium of history,'" with a modern way of thinking about history as a *Prozess*, as a process or trial, according to which history was seen as the medium of politics (*D* XX.6.480). If one accepts the modern conception of nature and history as a process of development and progress, history is in the position to be understood as "produced," which results from a quasi-mechanical understanding of the making of history. For our traditional conception of *athanasia*/deathlessness, Christianity also plays an important role. "In antiquity, man is perishable, but the world is not," according to Arendt's aphoristic distinction, and "in Christianity the world is perishable but man is not" (*D* XX.7.482). In modernity meaning is won for individual deeds and lives from their arrangement in a universal design, while in antiquity the history of men and deeds was given meaning in relation to a specific, unique occurrence.

"What the concept of process implies is that the concrete and the general, the single thing or event and the universal meaning have parted company," Arendt writes in her essay "The Concept of History" at the beginning of the section on "History and Earthly Immortality": "The process, which alone makes meaningful whatever it happens to carry along, has thus acquired a monopoly of universality and significance."[22] While this understanding of history as a universal meaning-creating process has its representatives in Hegel and Marx, Arendt invokes the author of the *Histories* in her consideration of the other conception of history. Herodotus "never would have doubted that each thing that is or was carries its meaning within itself and needs only the word to make it manifest," according to Arendt in the same passage: "Everything that was done or happened contained and disclosed its share of 'general' meaning within the confines of its individual shape and did not need a developing and engulfing process to become significant."

It is astounding, this sentence in which Arendt concretizes Herodotus's concept of history. "The flux of his narrative," she writes, "is sufficiently loose to leave room for many stories, but there is nothing in this flux indicative that the general bestows meaning and significance on the particular."[23] Herodotus's writing style, the *presentation* of his *Histories*, is what makes the difference. This way of writing makes distinctions that open possibilities; it creates relationships without subordinating. It is able to think the particular *by relating it*, which characterizes the capacity of judging, according to Arendt and Kant. Is it a sufficiently loose flow of presentation to deal with the question of "how one can avoid swimming in the tide at all"?

How does Arendt deal with the relationship between history, politics, presentation, and judging in the German version of her essay? In the closing of *Geschichte und Politik in der Neuzeit*, she turns her criticism of history-making decisively on the present; in the English version this is presented in an epilogue. The monstrous destruction that characterizes the "political experiences and catastrophes of the 20th century," according to Arendt in a 1957 text, "arose from the disposition" to see politics as a process of production.[24] Understanding politics as the consequent product of a given aim ultimately took away the meaning of politics as an action of freedom that includes incalculabilities. The "totalitarian regimes, the tyrannies and dictatorships of our century" would in fact "ultimately aim to achieve this." When people are forced into an inescapable, inevitable course, there is no room to jump out of this line and begin a new sequence. According to Arendt what is set in motion through action cannot be controlled, since its interaction with the actions of others is unforeseeable. Not only are the outcomes of acting (together) unpredictable, but even their general tendencies cannot be clearly determined. The vectors of political action, which consolidate into history, do not have a definable direction; rather, they move in a space of time, which points into "an endless future and an endless past." Herein lies the foundation of an experience of history as related moments, which is strictly distinct from history as development. This former experience rather questions the way relationships are formed, it asks about the mode of "relating." How can the experiences of such a "potential earthly immortality" be written?

Arendt addresses this question with four lines of a poem by Rainer Maria Rilke from the tenth poem in his cycle "From the Remains of Count C.W." In Arendt's copy of the published edition of this "poem cycle," which is preserved in her library at Bard College, the afterword notes that Rilke said precisely these four lines aloud to himself as if in passing one evening, and subsequently remarked "in astonishment" that these verses "are not written by you."[25] With a mixture of strangeness and familiarity, Arendt puts these verses in both the German and English versions of her essays on "The Concept of History." There—as later John Donne's words would in *The Life of the Mind*—they continue the thought process of the essay without a colon, transitioning to the German original also in the English version of her essay, simply beginning a new paragraph:

Berge ruhn, von Sternen überprächtigt;
aber auch in ihnen flimmert Zeit.
Ach in meinem wilden Herzen nächtigt
obdachlos die Unvergänglichkeit.[26]

Here the Greek *athanasia* has disappeared from the world; it no longer lives in the public retellings of men, presented in the bright light of the polis. The "immortality" is relocated to the darkness of the human heart. It is a process of internalization through which "earthly immortality" loses its shelter and becomes homeless in the world. Rilke's verses are not the inspiration for Arendt's criticism of a now-dominant understanding of history as the result of a process of development, in which context this inward retreat occurred. The lines' purpose is not exhausted in serving as a quotation. They host something independent. They stand for themselves—as *verses*.

Rilke's verses describe a phenomenon that Arendt called the reversal of the Greek relationships between man and the world. Whereas in antiquity man was the only perishable entity in the boundless immortality of the world, in modern times he has become the last refuge of immortality. Arendt's text presents the *reversal* of this relationship in *verse*. The poetry here does not propose an eternal truth. Rather, it invokes that endangered immortality (*athanasia*) that accompanies the experience of a political action, pointing "into an endless future and an endless past." It is for this purpose that Arendt interrupts the linear development of her essay and opens it to the turns, the phrasings of this poem. The presentation of this reversal of discourse (the reversal of the relationships between man and world) and this performative reversal (the interruption of the progression of the text and insertion of verse) is resolved neither into discourse nor into rhetoric. Arendt puts these particularities in relation to each other without predetermining their relationship (without grammatical subordination, for example, and without proposing a resolution).

Even in the English version, Arendt quotes the verses in the original German, since "their perfection seems to defy translation."[27] Rilke's lines do not fundamentally resist translation, for Arendt provides the reader with a prose version in the notes to her essay.[28] Nonetheless, the gesture of interrupting the discursive text is made particularly explicit here, as the change of mode of writing is accompanied by a leap into another language. It is a gesture that acknowledges the singularity of the fact that only in German can "*flimmernde Zeit*" be rhymed with "*obdachlose Unvergänglich-keit*," and that "*Nacht*" can neither be made into a verb ("*nächtigt*") in English nor echoed with a confusingly clear neologism like "*überprächtigt*." In

other words, Arendt's writing offers an experience of how the particular is
not replaceable and cannot be rendered into a general meaning. In this way
Arendt extends her observation of the capacity of judging in Herodotus's
Histories, "that the general [does not] bestow meaning and significance on
the particular," and that instead the author sits in judgment of history "by
relating it."[29]

Judging describes a mode of "mysteriously combining the particular and
the general," Arendt writes.[30] Her method of combining, her constellating
mode of writing has a somewhat less mysterious effect in the *Denktagebuch*,
since one can ascribe this structure of the writing to the genre of the notebook. How does the particular character of the *Denktagebuch* comment on
the capacity of judging in Arendt's writing in general? How do the different spaces of writing relate to each other?

"Book," Arendt notes in the XX Notebook in April 1953: "Possibly three
essays: Forms of government—Vita Activa—Philosophy and Politics" (*D*
XX.9.482). Such entries are rare. Arendt seldom reaches beyond the concrete moment of thought or reading notes and plans future publications in
the *Denktagebuch*. Nonetheless, she remained faithful to the plan sketched
here, and it previews her writings of the next twenty years. Arendt began
writing "Forms of Government" a bit later as "Introduction to Politics,"
an unchanged project that became the nucleus of her attempts at and varia-
tions on rethinking the political. "*Vita Activa*" was the title she originally
considered for her 1958 book *The Human Condition* in English and the one
she actually chose for the 1960 German edition, which revolves around the
human activities of labor, work, and action in modern times. Many consider it her "most philosophical" book. In the United States it is as good as
canonized as such. But what would it mean to read *Vita Activa*, in contrast
to its canonization as a philosophical monograph, as an "essay," in agreement
with her earlier note from the *Denktagebuch*?

Arendt elaborated on the third project of her plan: "Philosophy and
Politics. Including 'common sense' (Hobbes) and history as 'Ersatz' for the
polis" (*D* XX.9.483). If one adds to this an entry written shortly before, it
becomes clear that these few lines essentially outline Arendt's entire project.
Hobbes transformed common sense into its logical conclusion—"reckoning
with consequences" (*D* XIX.44.473). Arendt challenges this tradition with
her question of the possibility of nontyrannical thought. Her question likewise challenges Hegel, whose speculative reason was inspired by Hobbes
through a dialectical-conclusive process-thinking. According to Arendt,
Hegel's universal theory of history had dismissed the praxis of the Greek
polis, which understood history as the remembrance of continually retold

deeds of great heroes. This is the context, Arendt writes in parentheses, of "Hegel's contempt for Kant's power of judgment." In this way the early entries, which opened up a line of thought that associates history and judging, once again establishes a relationship to Arendt's late writings.

The side question about the temporality of thought raised by the relationship of thoughts in Arendt's early and late writings stretches out another "rainbow of concepts" than the one Arendt mentions near the end of the second volume of *The Life of the Mind*. With one of Nietzsche's words, she speaks of the "rainbow bridge of concepts" by which so many modern thinkers attempted directly to reach the ancient world. It is a harmonization that glosses over ruptures. Arendt was not able to cross this bridge, saying that she was "not homesick enough."[31] Here in the *Denktagebuch* the rainbow bridge of concepts, which helps to think about and address the ruptures of the twentieth century, seems to lead not only to Herodotus but also to thinkers like Kant and Goethe.

In the same passage of the *Life of the Mind* where the "rainbow bridge of concepts" appears, Kant and Goethe are referred to as thinkers who resist a totalizing tendency toward idealism. This tendency attempts to harmonize the diversity and contradictions of history, whether in the form of personifications like Adam Smith's "invisible hand" or in metaphors of humankind's collectively fostered design like Hegel's "Cunning of Reason." Arendt opposes this with the "dismal reign of chance" with which Kant described the turmoil of history in his *Idea for a Universal History from a Cosmopolitan Point of View* (1784) or Goethe's remark on history as "mishmash of error and violence" (*D* XX.21.488). "Do not think that I ramble, that I versify,/Look and find me in a different form!" Goethe writes in a rare poetological quatrain of his late collection of aphorisms *Zahme Xenien/Tame Xenia* (1820–24): "Church history/is a mishmash of error, outrage, and force."[32] Arendt takes the liberty of extracting and varying the fragment that she finds useful. These verses allow this room for play. They share a core quality with other fragment collections by authors Arendt quotes in the same section of her *Denktagebuch*—Pascal's *Pensées*, Nietzsche's *Will to Power*, and not the least the epitome of the genre, Novalis's collection of fragments *Blossom-dust (Blütenstaubfragemente)* from 1800: These fragments stand only for themselves; they do not lead to an all-encompassing framework of meaning. To encounter them in any way other than to recognize their particularity is pointless; it is from this very pointlessness that they derive their power. In the same year *Zahme Xenien/Tame Xenia* was published (1827), Goethe wrote: "The view that every creature exists for its own sake and that, for example, the cork tree does not grow so that we may stop our bottles, is something Kant and I have in common."[33]

Arendt cites Goethe yet again in the context of these passages in Notebook XX of her *Denktagebuch*, in fact this time she cites from a work that the poet of the era himself declared to be fragmentary: Goethe's *Farbenlehre/ Theory of Colors* (1810). This book is also a thinking notebook, if you will, it was written over decades, a collection of experiments, attempts, observations and reflections, accompanied by a scattering of poems from across the four decades of its creation. "Goethe's Theory of Colors" (*Goethes Farbenlehre*) is the title of a poem noted by Arendt in the *Denktagebuch* (496):

> Gelb ist der Tag.
> Blau ist die Nacht.
> Grün liegt die Welt.
> Licht und Finsternis vermählen
> sich im Dunkeln wie im Hellen.
> Farbe lässt das All erscheinen,
> Farben scheiden Ding von Ding.
>
> Wenn der Regen und die Sonne
> ihrer Wolkenzwiste müde
> noch das Trockene und das Nasse
> in die Farbenhochzeit einen,
> glänzet Dunkles so wie Helles—
> Bogenförmig strahlt vom Himmel
> Unser Auge, unsere Welt.

> The day is yellow.
> The night is blue.
> The world lies green.
> Light and darkness marry
> in shadow as in daylight.
> Color allows all cosmos to appear,
> Colors separate thing from thing.
>
> When rain and sun,
> tired of their cloud-strife
> unite the dry and the wet
> in a wedding of the colors,
> dark will shine like brightness—
> beaming in a bow from heaven
> our eye, our world.

Right from the beginning, there is a plurality of colors. The world lies in the mixture of day and night, light and darkness. When the singular "color" appears in the poem, it is quickly followed by "all," the same universal from which John Donne drew his conclusions: the all-encompassing coherence is past, dissolved in a multiplicity of relationships. According to Goethe in his *Theory of Colors*, colors never exist in the world as absolutes, but rather always in relation to the other colors that exist with and around them, surrounding and bordering them. "Colors," now plural again, "separate thing from thing" according to the poem, they correspond to judgment. In other words, they are capable of separating out particularities and setting them in relation to each other. It is a capacity of judgment that "our eye, our world" comprehends both actively and passively when it beams from heaven in the form of a bow. When it is able to separate "thing from thing," like the power of colors, like another rainbow of concepts. Which rainbow "Goethe's Theory of Colors" crossed over to arrive as a poem in Arendt's *Denktagebuch* remains an open question. A reference in Goethe cannot be proven, and it does not fit into the archipelago of poems by Arendt in her notebooks. A gem, a fragment of thought, a curiosity, a phenomenon of uncertain origin?

According to Arendt, Goethe's *Urphänomen* (essential phenomenon) was central to Benjamin's way of thinking—a thinking that she connected with the gift of thinking poetically. Understood in this way, Goethe's essential phenomenon is not an idea and cannot be deduced from any philosophical or theological theory, but rather material and concretely traceable, in that "word and thing, idea and experience collapse" (*Wort und Ding, Idee und Erfahrung zusammenfallen*).[34] The word "*zusammenfallen/* collapse" is a remarkable choice, since it can be read in the sense of "coincide" as well as in the sense of "break down." It formulates an echo of the opposition and relation of destruction and crystallization with which Arendt outlined Benjamin's gift of thinking poetically. In his fragments for the *Arcades Project*, he sought to trace the essential phenomena of history, which were comprehensible to him only because the "breakdown of tradition had exposed the 'prehistoric moments' of all history." Quotation and thought-fragment are key phenomena that are exposed here. Poetic thinking, as it exists in Benjamin, has a "strange power to settle down, piecemeal, in the present," and to deprive "the mindless peace of complacency" from transmitted authority.[35] Quotation and/as thought-fragment describes two capacities: both to "interrupt . . . the flow of presentation" and "to assemble together what is presented." Is it a mode of presentation and of thinking that could deal with avoiding "swimming in the stream at all"? Ways of reading that could be associated with Herodotus's "flux of narrative," in order to investigate the possibility of a way of thinking that is not tyranni- cal? Attempts to think our ability "of mysteriously combining the particu- lar and the general" to judge, for example, or to present "by relating it"?

Translated by Anne Posten

NOTES

1. Hannah Arendt, "The Aftermath of Nazi Rule: Report from Ger- many," *Commentary* 4 (1950): 343. Reprinted in Hannah Arendt, *Essays in Understanding, 1930–1954: Formation, Exile, and Totalitarianism*, ed. Jerome Kohn (New York: Schocken Books, 1962), 249.

2. Ibid., 248ff.

3. Ibid., 250.

4. Ibid., 251.

5. Ibid., 249.

6. Ibid.

7. Hannah Arendt, *Vita activa oder vom tätigen Leben* (Munich: Piper Verlag, 1981), 156.

8. Hannah Arendt, "Von der Menschlichkeit in fisteren Zeiten. Gedan- ken zu Lessing," in *Menschen in finsteren Zeiten*, ed. Ursula Ludz (Munich: Piper Verlag, 1989), 38ff; for the English version, translated by Clara and Richard Winston, see Hannah Arendt, *Men in Dark Times* (New York: Har- court, Brace & World, 1968), 22ff.

9. Arendt, *The Origins of Totalitarianism* (New York: Schocken Books, 2004), xiii.

10. Hannah Arendt, "Walter Benjamin: 1892–1940," trans. Harry Zohn, in *Men in Dark Times*, 163. The German original reads: *"Was ihn an der Sache faszinierte, war, grob gesprochen, daß das Geistige und seine materielle Erscheinung sich miteinander verschwisterten—und zwar so innig, daß es erlaubt schien, überall Entsprechungen, 'correspondances', zu entdecken, die sich gegenseitig erhellten und illuminierten, wenn man sie nur richtig einander zuordnete, so daß sie schließlich keines deutend-erklärenden Kommentars mehr bedurften."* Hannah Arendt, "Walter Benjamin: 1892–1940," in *Menschen in finsteren Zeiten*, 200ff. See also my book on Arendt and German postwar writers: Thomas Wild, *Nach dem Geschichtsbruch. Deutsche Schriftsteller um Hannah Arendt* (Berlin: Matthes & Seitz, 2009), 14ff.

11. Arendt, "Walter Benjamin" (English), 166; (German), 204.

12. Emily Dickinson, *The Complete Poems*, ed. Thomas H. Johnson (Bos- ton: Little, Brown, 1960), 464:

> Superfluous were the Sun
> When Excellence be dead

He were superfluous every Day
For every Day be said

That syllable whose Faith
Just saves it from Despair
And whose "I'll meet You" hesitates
If Love inquire "Where"?

Upon His dateless Fame
Our Periods may lie
As Stars that drop anonymous
From an abundant sky.

13. See for this and the preceding quotes Hilde Domin, *Das zweite Paradies. Roman in Segmenten* (Munich: Piper Verlag, 1968), 73. See also Domin's letter to Hannah Arendt from January 20, 1960, in Hannah Arendt Papers, Library of Congress, Container 08/08, page 005730.

14. Hannah Arendt, *The Life of the Mind, Vol. 1: Thinking*, ed. Mary McCarthy (New York: Hartcourt, Brace Jovanovich, 1977), 215.

15. Ibid., 213, 215.

16. Aristotle, *Nicomachean Ethics*, trans. Martin Ostwald (Englewood Cliffs, N.J.: Prentice-Hall, 1999), 35.

17. Arendt, *Thinking*, 216.

18. See Arendt on the plurality of languages, ways of thinking, and truths in *Denktagebuch*, 42.

19. Hannah Arendt, *The Life of the Mind, Vol. 2: Willing*, ed. Mary McCarthy (New York: Harcourt, Brace Jovanovich, 1977), 159.

20. At the same time, passages 1–34 in volume XX are notable for their multiplicity of literary references: Chekov (17), Tolstoy (18), Goethe (21), Hölderlin (28), Brecht (29), Novalis (31), and Goethe (33); in addition, there are poems by Arendt herself (3, 30). Other thinkers we read about here include Pascal (14), Nietzsche (17), Kant (21), and, in contrast, Descartes, Hegel, and Marx.

21. Hannah Arendt, *Lectures on Kant's Political Philosophy*, ed. Ronald Beiner (Chicago: University of Chicago Press, 1982), 76. The traces of many entries in the XX notebook of the *Denktagebuch*, however, also lead to writings by Arendt from around the same time. A large portion of the entries are related to the essays "Natur und Geschichte" and "Geschichte und Politik in der Neuzeit," which Arendt published in the volume *Fragwürdige Traditionsbestände im politischen Denken der Gegenwart* (Frankfurt: Europäische Verlagsanstalt, 1957) as well as to the essays "History and Immortality" (*Partisan Review*, 1957) and "The Modern Concept of History (*Review of Politics*, 1958) which were originally written in English and published together under the

title "The Concept of History: Ancient and Modern" in Arendt's essay collection *Between Past and Future* (1961). The versions differ from each other significantly in many places, as Ursula Ludz pointed out in her edition of the German version in *Zwischen Vergangenheit und Zukunft*; the English differs between the versions published in magazines and the book version, significant differences are in addition to be found between the English and German versions (the latter translated by Charlotte Beradt and reworked and largely rewritten by Arendt). A comparative reading of the German and English version merits a separate inquiry.

22. Hannah Arendt, "On the Concept of History: Ancient and Modern," in *Between Past and Future* (New York: Viking, 1968), 64.

23. Ibid. Aristotle characterized Herodotus's writing style of placing things next to each other (*léxin eiroménen*) as the mode of presenting his *Histories*; Wolfgang Schadewaldt remarked that in Herodotus's prose the most heterogeneous becomes associable; and Henry Immerwahr formulated elements of syntactical coordination for each action (and/but/as well as), whose relationship in Herodotus was organized more by fractures than by connection; their primary function was "to build a large unified work out of a mosaic of small elements." Florian Klinger picks up on this reading in his recent book *Urteilen* and emphasizes that in Herodotus *historía* is "articulated through tensions, even on the smallest level, as essentially no distinction, no matter how slight, was to be implied by or assimilated into another distinction." Klinger continues: "The grainy/rough contrasting of elements whose independence is as broadly protected as possible gives the text an inner resistance which keeps it from collapsing into subordinating relationships, in which individualities run the risk of being structurally assimilated by their respective unities." Florian Klinger, *Urteilen* (Berlin: Diaphanes, 2011), 94 and 97ff.

24. Hannah Arendt, "Geschichte und Politik in der Neuzeit," in *Zwischen Vergangenheit und Zukunft*, ed. Ursula Ludz (Munich: Piper Verlag, 1994), 109.

25. Rainer Maria Rilke, *Aus dem Nachlass des Grafen C.W. Ein Gedichtkreis* (Wiesbaden: Insel Verlag, 1950), 38. See also Wout Cornelissen's considerations about the "singing poet" in his essay in this volume.

26. Arendt, *Between Past and Future*, 44; *Zwischen Vergangenheit und Zukunft*, 76. Arendt quotes the following prose translation granted to her by Denver Lindley: "Mountains rest beneath a splendor of stars, but even in them time flickers. Ah, unsheltered in my wild, darkling heart lies immortality" See Arendt, *Between Past and Future*, 285.

27. Arendt, *Between Past and Future*, 44.

28. Ibid.

29. Ibid., 64.

30. Arendt, *Lectures on Kant's Political Philosophy*, 76.

31. Arendt, *Willing*, 158.

32. Johann Wolfgang von Goethe, *Werke*, Hamburg edition, 1:334, "Zahme Xenien, IX," late work 1820–27, after the Xenias he wrote with Schiller in 1796, which ironically attacked the literary industry.

33. Ibid., 1:645. Cf. corresponding citations from Arendt in the *Denktagebuch*, but also in her essay "The Concept of History" as well as in *Willing*.

34. See this and the following quote in Arendt, *Menschen in finsteren Zeiten*, 199ff.

35. Ibid., 229ff.

CHAPTER 4

Thinking in Metaphors

Wout Cornelissen

What connects thinking and poetry [*Dichtung*] is metaphor.
In philosophy one calls concept what in poetry
[*Dichtkunst*] is called metaphor.
Thinking creates its "concepts" out of the visible,
in order to designate the invisible.

—HANNAH ARENDT, *D* XXVI.30.728

Thinking without Contemplation

The *Denktagebuch* is a strange "book."[1] In fact, it cannot be read as a book just as any of or next to Arendt's "other" books, such as *The Human Condition* or even *The Life of the Mind*, for it does not contain any single theory or a coherent set of propositions it argues for. Perhaps it is better to be considered as a collection of "thought fragments" (*Denkbruchstücke*), a term used by Arendt in her essay on Walter Benjamin. By this term, she refers to a peculiar use of quotations within a text, as having "the double task of interrupting the flow of the presentation with 'transcendent force' . . . and at the same time of concentrating within themselves that which is presented."[2] A thought fragment is not so much to be considered as a piece of knowledge, the final outcome of a thought process, "a nugget of pure truth to wrap up between the pages of your notebooks and keep on the mantelpiece forever" (Virginia Woolf).[3] Rather, interpreting and quoting is to have "witnesses, also friends" (*D* XXVII.7.756), as Arendt suggests toward the end of the *Denktagebuch*. We might say that each fragment serves as a witness attesting to some aspect of, or a particular perspective on, a specific matter of interest. Arendt's *Denktagebuch* consists of many such perspectives, the correspondences and contradictions between which may provoke us to think a matter through by and for ourselves, as if we were drawn into a conversation with friends.

In fact, the fragmentary form of the *Denktagebuch* makes us more attentive to the fragmentary aspects of her published work as well. Usually, *The Human Condition* is read as a plea in favor of the *vita activa*, as embodied in the Greek *polis* especially, over and against the *vita contemplativa*, as embodied in "the Socratic school" and especially by Plato. More specifically, Arendt is often taken to defend (the founding of) the *polis* as "the Greek solution" to "the frailty of human affairs" over and against the philosopher's remedy of "the traditional substitution of making for acting," the latter of which had resulted in the replacement of politics—as acting and speaking in concert—by rule.[4]

We may doubt, however, whether it is in fact the case that Arendt *advocates* one such theory or proposal over the other. Foremost, she tries to *understand* adequately the phenomenon of politics—or, rather, "to think what we are doing," as she states in the prologue of *The Human Condition*.[5] In order to do so, she needs to liberate our understanding of action from the allegedly superior perspective of contemplation. Hence, her aim is not so much to *reverse* the traditional hierarchy of the two ways of life—raising politics above philosophy—but rather to liberate us from the interpretative framework that is implied in this traditional hierarchy and which has blurred our understanding of the proper distinctions between the diverse range of human activities—including the activity of thinking itself.

Against this background, it is perfectly understandable why Arendt devotes the penultimate paragraph of *The Human Condition*—or of *Vita Activa*, as she initially intended to title her book—to thought, about which she says: "if no other test but the experience of being active, no other measure but the extent of sheer activity were to be applied to the various activities within the *vita activa*, it might well be that thinking as such would surpass them all."[6] In the introduction to *The Life of the Mind* Arendt explicitly admits that the term *vita activa* itself remains too much tied to its traditional polemical counterpart, the *vita contemplativa*. Thought had been conceived of as a mere means to lead up to the end of contemplation: "thinking aims at and ends in contemplation, and contemplation is not an activity but a passivity; it is the point where mental activity comes to rest."[7] As a result of this interpretation, the specific nature of thought's being an activity had been forgotten. Analogously to *The Human Condition*'s aim "to think what we are doing," in *The Life of the Mind* Arendt asks: "What are we "doing" when we do nothing but think?"[8] In order to answer this question, she needs to liberate our understanding of thought from the perspective of contemplation—the distinction between which had already been introduced by her in *The Human Condition*—that is, from conceiving of thinking as nothing but a process strictly obeying the rules of logic, a mere means in service of the higher end of contemplating the truth.

Accordingly, Arendt draws a distinction between thought on the one hand and knowledge or cognition on the other, the former of which has always been interpreted after the model of the latter, and the latter of which has always been interpreted after the model of seeing—contemplating—the truth. In fact however, Arendt claims, the "end" of thought is not truth, but *meaning*. Whereas cognition establishes what something is and whether it exists at all, thought asks what it means for something to exist. The function of thought is "to come to terms with" whatever we may experience: "The sheer naming of things, the creation of words, is the human way of *appropriating* and, as it were, disalienating the world into which, after all, each of us is born as a newcomer and a stranger."[9]

In other words, *both* acting *and* thinking have been understood after the model of the experience of making (*Herstellen*). To be more precise, whereas acting and speaking together have been instrumentalized and then substituted by fabrication, the activity of thinking has been instrumentalized and then substituted by contemplation. In her *Denktagebuch*, Arendt already expressed this in 1953:

> All making [*Herstellen*] rests upon contemplation and violence. Thus, in the western tradition, by taking its cue from the experience in making, everything has been split into contemplative thought, in which the "Ideas," the ends, etc. are given, and into violent action, which realizes these contemplated ends by violent means. Our concepts of theory and praxis are equally oriented on making. (*D* XIII.20.305)

While fabrication implies the use of mute violence, contemplation is reached in a state of speechless wonder. What contemplative thought and violent action have in common, therefore, is that they are both *speechless*, that they both entail a loss of language.[10] As a result, we may conclude, the element of "speech" has disappeared not only from our conception of action, including of politics, but also from our conception of thought, including of philosophy. According to Arendt, however, thought without speech is inconceivable: "Our mental activities . . . are conceived in speech even before being communicated."[11]

In this essay, I will address the question how Arendt conceives of the activity of thinking without the model of making (*Herstellen*). Thus, I believe, an answer can be found to the pressing question she raises in one of the earlier entries in the *Denktagebuch*, a question to which Thomas Wild also directs our attention elsewhere in this volume:

> The question is: is there a thinking that is not tyrannical? This [is] really Jaspers' effort, without him completely knowing it. For communication, in contradistinction to discussion—"advocatory" thinking—, does not wish to ascertain itself of the truth by the superior weight of argumentation. (*D* II.20.45)

Three Motifs of Thinking

In order to offer some orientation, I will first introduce three different motifs of the activity of thinking which can be traced throughout Arendt's oeuvre. All three center on a specific term or set of words, which at some point occur for the first time, and then keep recurring throughout her work, although sometimes in different but still related constellations. These motifs may be characterized as "thought fragments" too: condensed meanings, wandering through her writings.

The first and best-known motif used by her is that of "dialectical" thinking, of the solitary and soundless dialogue between me and myself, the inner "two-in-one." It is introduced already in "Ideology and Terror" (1953), included in *The Origins of Totalitarianism*,[12] and remains present throughout her entire oeuvre, including in *The Human Condition* and in *The Life of the Mind*. Arendt links it to the exemplary figure of Socrates especially, who engaged into friendly dialogues on the essence of concepts like justice, courage, etc. Although it is the single motif that stays around from the beginning to the end, and although she sometimes seems to identify dialectical thinking with thinking per se, there are two other distinct motifs that can be found within her work.

The second receives a name for the first time in her essay "The Crisis in Culture" (1960), where she speaks of "representative thinking." It is linked especially to the notion of "enlarged mentality" (*erweiterte Denkart*) from Kant's *Critique of the Power of Judgment*. Whereas dialectical thinking presupposes a duality, the "two-in-one," representative thinking attempts to "represent" the plurality of perspectives that are present in and constitute the public realm, in order thus to prepare the formation of opinions and judgments about future projects and past events.

The third motif that can be found in her work receives a name only in her essay on Walter Benjamin (1968), where she speaks of "thinking poetically."[13] What it fundamentally refers to is the recognition that thought is conducted in language, and that language is essentially metaphorical. In *The Life of the Mind*, Arendt devotes two full chapters to metaphor. By thinking in metaphors, that is, by "transferring" (*metapherein*) words we use to grasp visible experiences within the external world of appearances to invisible concepts within the internal world of the mind, we may establish or reestablish some form of correspondence between ourselves and the world. Since it may seem that Arendt's attention for the importance of metaphor is restricted to these two later texts only, it is worthwhile emphasizing that she already attests to its importance in the *Denktagebuch* as early as 1950, in an entry on "Metaphor(s) and Truth":

> How a phrase is changed back into a word, how out of metaphor truth
> again arises, because reality has disclosed itself. How without this
> being-turned-into-word one could not sustain the shock of reality. In
> this moment, where reality discloses itself and a word comes into
> being in order to capture it and make it bearable for man, truth comes
> into being. Perhaps this is indeed what underlies the "adaequatio rei et
> intellectus." (*D* II.25.48)

As we have indicated above, in her later work Arendt will no longer speak of "truth" being the end of thought, but of "meaning." But apart from this terminology, her reflections on metaphor remain remarkably consistent. As she explains in *The Life of the Mind*, traditionally the *"adaequatio rei et intellectus"* had been interpreted as the correspondence of knowledge with its object, and this "adequacy" had been understood as being analogous to the correspondence of vision with the object it sees.[14] Metaphor, by contrast, opens up an entirely different understanding of the nature of this correspondence.

Directly following her explanation of the function of metaphor in *The Life of the Mind*, Arendt asks whether we may find a metaphor for the activity of thinking itself, that is, whether, and, if so, how we may understand this invisible, mental activity by taking recourse to a visible, worldly experience. Traditionally, the activity of thinking had been interpreted after the model of cognition, that is, of seeing or beholding the truth. When proposing a different metaphor, Arendt claims that it should do justice to the fact that thinking, in contradistinction to cognition, is an endless activity. She therefore suggests that there is a correspondence of thinking to "the sensation of being alive," as well as to cyclical motion, both metaphors of

which she derives from Aristotle.[15] Yet, she readily admits that these metaphors are not entirely satisfying, as they "remain singularly empty."[16]
Rather than search for an alternative metaphor, however, Arendt directs
our attention away to a different kind of question: "What makes us think?"

I have always found this a rather abrupt shift. At least it could be asked
in what sense the suggested metaphors are "empty." For, as we have seen,
what had vanished from our understanding of philosophy interpreted after
the model of the speechless beholding of the truth is not only the endless
character of the activity of thinking, but foremost its intrinsic connection
to speech. It is precisely this element that is missing in the two Aristotelian
metaphors mentioned. I would like to suggest that our understanding of
the activity of thinking should somehow orient itself on or "correspond to"
the phenomenon of speech.

Correspondences Between Thinking and Political Speech

On several occasions in the *Denktagebuch*, Arendt indicates that just as science (as a form of cognition) is related to doing (making), thinking is
related to acting: "Philosophy, or free thinking, is related to acting as science [*Wissenschaft*] is related to doing [*Tun*]" (*D* XII.19.283). In addition, in
several entries she claims that there is a "correspondence" (*Entsprechung*)
between thinking and acting (*D* XIV.30.340). In her Benjamin essay, she
uses the same word, "correspondence," to signify the metaphorical relation
between two concepts.[17] In agreement with this, we will now turn to the
activity of speaking (as a visible, audible experience) in order to understand
the activity of thinking (as an invisible, soundless activity).

To this end, we will first need to acquire an understanding of Arendt's
notion of speech. In *The Human Condition*, it is most clear that acting and
speaking somehow coincide. Yet, it is notoriously difficult what is exactly
meant by that. Arendt refers to Aristotle, who characterized Greek *polis* life
as "a way of life in which speech and only speech made sense and where the
central concern of all citizens was to talk with each other."[18] Yet, what *kind*
of speech is referred to here? At first sight, what characterizes the *polis* is
the art of rhetoric, or of persuasion (*peithein*): "To be political, to live in a
polis, meant that everything was decided through words and persuasion
and not through force and violence."[19]

Yet, Arendt says, political speech in this sense presupposes a separation
between action and speech, which in the pre-polis experience still belonged
together:

speech and action were considered to be coeval and coequal, of the
same rank and the same kind; and this originally meant not only that
most political action, in so far as it remains outside the sphere of violence, is indeed transacted in words, but more fundamentally that
finding the right words at the right moment, quite apart from the
information or communication they may convey, is action.[20]

In a similar vein, Arendt characterizes speech as "the specifically human
way of answering, talking back and measuring up to whatever happened or
was done."[21] What this means becomes clearer in the section of *The Human
Condition* entitled "Action." Here, she claims that the "revelatory quality of
speech and action comes to the fore where people are *with* others and neither for nor against them—that is, in sheer human togetherness."[22] In
addition, what they talk *about* or what they are *concerned with* in their speech
is what lies between them, that is, "the matters of the world of things in
which men move, which physically lies between them and out of which
arise their specific, objective, worldly interests."[23] In other words, people
do not only speak *about* something, that is, about the "objective" world
which lies between them (*inter-est*) and which "interests" them, but they
also speak *to* one another, out of which results the "in-between" world of
human relationships.

Interestingly, the *Denktagebuch* has something to offer in further clarifying
this. Most helpful is a motif which runs through it and which may give us
some guidance: *legein ti kata tinos*. This fixed set of Greek words is originally
derived by Arendt from one of Heidegger's lectures on the question "What is
called thinking?" that she attended in 1952.[24] Literally, it means "to say something about something." Yet, Arendt gives it a twist: not merely (as in Heidegger's explanation) to say something about something—a predicate and a
subject which should somehow correspond to each other—but in her case it
comes to signify: to talk *with* (or to) others *about* (*über*) something or *with a
view to* (*im Hinsicht auf*) something. In her terminology, the "dative" case
(speaking with or to others) is combined here with the "accusative" case
(speaking about or with a view to something).

Just as in *The Human Condition*, in the *Denktagebuch* the first type of
speech that appears as political speech (*politeuein*) is persuasion (*peithein*).[25]
Politeuein as such is characterized by Arendt as "to bear the fact that each
thing has multiple sides (not just two; that is already a logical attitude)" (*D*
XVI.20.390–391). *Peithein* is characterized by her as "to push one's own
aspect through" (*D* XVI.20.391). Yet, we now gain a clearer view than in

The Human Condition of the reasons for this type of speech being somehow derivative. For, insofar as persuasion consists in presenting one's own aspect—"it appears to me" (*dokei moi*)—as the *only* aspect—the "absolute"— under which something is to be considered, it becomes "demagogical" (*D* XVI.20.391). For, in this case one person isolates himself from the *legein* (speaking with others) in which he had his own specific *kata* (about) and presents his own aspect *against* the multitude (*die Menge*) (*D* XVI.21.393).

We will now ask how, if at all, the first motif of thinking, that is, "dialectical" thinking, can be said to "correspond" to speech, to talking (*Reden*) in the aforementioned sense of the *legein ti kata tinos*. Arendt continues the entry I quoted at the beginning of this section in the following way: "Because [free thinking], as dialogical-being-with-itself, is from the outset involved with others, it has to be communicative—which science does not need." (*D* XII.19.283). This passage resonates her answer to her initial question whether there is a thinking that is not tyrannical, and in which she said that thinking ought to be "communicative" rather than "advocatory." In Plato's *Gorgias*, dialectics is conceived of as the counterpart to rhetoric.[26] We will pay special attention, therefore, to aspects of dialectical speech that remain somehow polemically tied to certain aspects of rhetorical speech, most notably to the latter's advocatory opposition to the multitude.

Usually, dialectical thought is characterized by Arendt as "to speak a matter through with oneself" (*D* XIV.21.392) or "to express and speak something through for and with oneself" (*D* XIV.30.340). In both cases, it is contrasted with acting as "to speak about something with others (*legein ti kata tinos*)" (*D* XIV.30.340), or "to talk about something with a view to something . . . : *legein ti kata tinos*" (*D* XIV.21.392). The contrast is clearly twofold. In the first place, in the case of dialectical thought, talking *about* something is replaced by talking something *through*. In the second place, in dialectical thought, a *plurality* (talking with my fellow human beings) is replaced by a *duality* (talking with myself).

Regarding the first point, in the case of dialectics (*dialegesthai*), the object (the "about," the accusative) is absolved from the in-between (the "with," the dative), and hence ends up in direct accusative relation to the subject (*D* X.19.246).[27] In this sense, Arendt says, thinking is related to "doing" (*Tun*) (in the sense of "making") rather than to "acting." For, here the subject holds on to the object it thinks through, and both the subject and the object become isolated from the "in-between" of the public realm within which people talk with each other about something. The subsequent step, that is, the opposition to the multitude (*die Menge*) is equally present in rhetoric (*pei*-

thein), and from this point on, *both* rhetoric *and* dialectics may be characterized as "advocatory: "Who wants to show more than one's own aspect, turns
into a demagogue or (Platonically) into a tyrant." (*D* XVI.20.391). Or, as
Arendt explains most clearly in an earlier entry:

> If one wishes to avoid the "about," then one forces the other into one's
> own thinking; here the coercion of someone else's thinking arises.
> What is thus given up, is precisely that which I have in common with
> the other in the form of the "about." One enforces a false identifica-
> tion. The coercion exists in treating the other as one's own alter ego.
> Without the form of the "about," there is no conversation. What is
> expressed in the "about" is that we <u>have</u> the world in common, that we
> live on the earth <u>together</u>. (*D* IX.19.214).

In the second place, insofar as the inner "two-in-one" is indeed a duality, it seems thus to be a form of plurality, of talking with another, yet
limited to only *one* "other." Accordingly, one might say that one experiences the self as "another friend." By contrast, when Aristotle calls the
friend "another self," Arendt suggests, he inverses the order. For, in her
view one is capable of talking with oneself precisely *because* one has had the
experience of talking with others. Yet, even if this is true, she states that the
presence of the inner dialogue between me and myself, of the "two-in-
one," is "<u>not</u> yet <u>thinking</u>," but it is rather "the political side of all thinking:
that plurality expresses itself even in thinking" (*D* XX.13.484). It may be
doubted, however, whether the two-in-one may be called "political" in the
full sense, for she usually claims that true plurality requires the presence of
at least three.[28]

If all this is the case, it seems that the correspondence of "dialectical"
thinking to speech in the sense of *legein ti kata tinos* is rather limited. The
analogy between this type of thinking and speech is in fact a disanalogy.
We will therefore turn to the second motif of thinking we traced, that of
"representative" thinking. Clearly, this type of thinking represents the
plurality of the world in a fuller way. For, when we are thinking in this way,
we "represent" a conversation between more than two citizens (all citizens
who happen to be present) about or with a view to a matter that interests
us all. Hence, in this case, "talking" (*Reden*) does indeed "correspond" to
this type of thinking. In the *Denktagebuch*, Arendt links it to Kant's notion
of "*erweiterte Denkungsart*" (introduced at *D* XXII.19.570, in 1957). Yet, she
testified to this kind of thinking already in the following entry from 1953,
although without yet giving it a name:

In politics, <u>understanding</u> never means: to understand <u>others</u> . . . but [to understand] the common world as it appears to others. If there is a virtue (wisdom) of the statesman, then it consists in the capability of viewing <u>all</u> sides of a certain thing, i.e., to view it as it appears to all participants. (*D* XIX.2.451)

The logical law of noncontradiction (agreeing with one's other self) is replaced by thinking in the place of others (agreeing with one's fellow-citizens). Thus we seem to have found a way of thinking that truly "corresponds" to acting in the sense of talking with others about something. Representative thinking, rather than dialectical thinking, "corresponds" to acting and speaking together.

Correspondences Between Thinking and Poetic Speech

Yet, if this "political side" of thinking is "not yet thinking," as Arendt suggested, how is thinking in the sense of "thinking something through" to be understood? We will now need to investigate the third motif of thinking we traced, "poetic" thinking. In this case we are confronted with a serious difficulty, however. In the first place, poetry seems to be intrinsically linked up with the activity of making (*Herstellen*), as Arendt makes clear in *The Human Condition* and as is clear in the etymological relation between "poetry" and *poièsis*. By understanding thinking from the model of poetry, or of the poet who is "making" poetry in his or her room, isolated from his or her fellow human beings, we run the risk of bringing the elements of mute violence (which is inherent in the organization of means to a certain end) and of speechless contemplation (which is inherent in seeing the idea or blueprint) back in. Indeed, in *The Human Condition*, in Chapter 23, entitled "The Permanence of the World and the Work of Art," Arendt claims that writing poetry involves "the same workmanship which, through the primordial instrument of human hands, builds the other durable things of the human artifice."[29]

In the second place, the poet is usually presented by Arendt as a *rival* of the *polis*, and hence also as a rival of (the aspirations of) the kind of speech belonging to the *polis*, the *legein ti kata tinos*.[30] It is important to understand the nature of this rivalry correctly, however. In her essay "The Crisis in Culture," Arendt draws a distinction between two aspects of making or work: "The chief reason of the distrust of fabrication in all forms is that it is utilitarian by its very nature. Fabrication . . . always involves means and ends."[31] It is precisely this *instrumental* aspect of work—organizing material as means to fabricate an end product—which threatens the durability of the *polis*, the world. However, Arendt suggests, the conflict vanishes as soon as we take into account the *product* of art, which becomes part of the world, both in its material appearance and in the fact that it is being talked *about* by the public. By adding beauty to it, art in fact fortifies the *polis*, the world.[32]

We may ask however, whether the latter qualification is of much help. In my view, it is no coincidence that Arendt does not mention any of the *performative* arts, let alone poetry, as an example here. Moreover, she shifts her attention to the "representative" thinking that is meant to prepare the judgments of taste of the public about the works of art. Instead, therefore, I propose to turn to a fascinating passage in the *Denktagebuch* in which Arendt says of the "singing poem" that it can "absolutize" without having the same problems as the "absolutization" that is committed either by making (its use of violence) or by philosophy:

> The <u>accusative</u> of violence, as of love, destroys the in-between, annihilates or burns it, leaves the other without refuge, robs itself of its refuge. Opposite is the <u>dative</u> of saying and speaking, which confirms the in-between, moves within the in-between. And then there is the accusative of the singing poem, which absolves and releases what is sung about from the in-between and its relations, without confirming anything. If poetry, and not philosophy, absolutizes, there is salvation. (*D* XVIII.11.428)

Clearly, poetry—that is to say, "the singing poem"—is distinguished not only from philosophy (of the contemplative sort), but also from talking with others about something (*legein ti kata tinos*). In my view, the crucial element of this fragment consists in Arendt's suggestion that it is the poem insofar as it is *sung* which distinguishes it from philosophy and from talking. In fact, this element is also present in several other entries in the *Denktagebuch* addressing poetry, for instance when the poet—in his capacity as rival of the *polis*—is pictured as a *singer* (*D* XX.10.483) and when it is implied that in poetic speech "there is neither thinking *dialegesthai* nor speaking-about," because people, insofar as they are poets, "do not talk [*reden*], and they do not speak [*sprechen*], but they resound [*ertönen*]" (*D* IX.19.214). We may say that in all these cases, Arendt conceives of poetry primarily as being a matter of oral linguistic expression, though of a different kind than of talking with others about something. It is this kind of speech that is capable of "absolving" the "about" from the "in-between," yet "without confirming anything," or, we might say, without being "advocatory," that is, without "ascertaining itself of the truth by the superior weight of argumentation."

In order to further determine the peculiar nature of poetic speech, we will turn to the passage from the *Denktagebuch* that I chose as epigraph to this essay. In it, Arendt explicitly speaks of a correspondence between thinking and poetry, and between their use of concepts and of metaphors respectively:

> What connects thinking and poetry [*Dichtung*] is metaphor. In philosophy one calls concept what in poetry [*Dichtkunst*] is called metaphor. Thinking creates its "concepts" out of the visible, in order to designate the invisible. (*D* XXVI.30.728).

In order to illuminate the conceptual activity of thinking, Arendt makes use of the analogy with poetry's use of metaphors. When we combine both aspects—the emphasis on the singing poem and the use of metaphorical language—suddenly *other* aspects from the section in *The Human Condition* just mentioned manifest themselves. For, Arendt calls music and poetry "the least "materialistic" of the arts because their "material" consists of sounds and words"—note her use of quotation marks here—and she adds that the workmanship they demand is "kept to a minimum."[33] Moreover, after having suggested that the durability of a poem is not so much caused by the fact that it is written down, but by "condensation," she speaks of poetry as "language spoken in utmost density and concentration." The German word for condensation is "*Verdichtung*" and for density "*Dichte*." While being absent in the English expression of "making poetry," both words clearly resonate in the German verb "*dichten*."

Although Arendt does not draw any explicit connection between the activity of *Verdichtung* (condensation) and the use of metaphor, she may have had it in mind. For, one page earlier, she calls "the human capacity for thought" "the immediate source of the art work,"[34] and she says that thought transforms the "mute and inarticulate despondency" of feeling so that it is "fit to enter the world and to be transformed into things, to become reified."[35] She calls this reification "more than a mere transformation," a "transfiguration," a "veritable metamorphosis in which it is as though the course of nature which wills that all fire burn to ashes is reverted and even dust can burst into flames."[36] Hence, a work of art is *more* than a matter of "making" in the ordinary sense. Arendt illustrates this by citing a poem of Rainer Maria Rilke, "Magic," which is worthwhile quoting here in full. Consider especially the second stanza of this poem, which simultaneously articulates and performs the power of metaphor in using the visible in "calling" the invisible:

From indescribable transformation flash
such creations—: Feel! and trust!
We suffer it often: flames become ash;
yet, in art: flames come from dust.

Here is magic. In the realm of a spell
the common word seems lifted up above . . .
and yet is really like the call of the male
who calls for the invisible female dove.[37]

We are reminded here again of the entry in which Arendt praises the capability of metaphor to turn a phrase back into a word again, and thus to (re)establish a "correspondence" between our inner mind and the outer world.

To conclude this essay, we will return to the question of how Arendt conceives of the activity of thinking without contemplation. In accordance with her account of "poetic" thinking, we have searched for an adequate metaphor. Thus we have found that, in contradistinction to "dialectical" thinking, only "representative" thinking can truly be called "communicative," because of its analogy to speaking in the sense of *legein ti kata tinos*, of talking with others about or with a view to something. Yet, "poetic" thinking seems to be the only one of the three motifs that enables us to truly "appropriate," "make sense of," or "come to terms with" the conceptual activity of thinking itself, of thinking something *through* by making distinctions, that is, by distinguishing metaphors which offer a "correspondence" between concept and experience from metaphors which do not. Moreover, the analogy works both ways, in the sense that by illuminating thinking by the model of poetic speech, we have also been able to draw attention to a crucial aspect of poetry itself that has hitherto remained less visible in Arendt's work, but that subtly shapes her own thinking and writing.

NOTES

1. All translations of German fragments from the *Denktagebuch* are my own unless otherwise indicated.

2. Hannah Arendt, "Walter Benjamin: 1892–1940," in *Men in Dark Times* (New York: Harcourt Brace, 1968), 153–206.

3. Virginia Woolf, *A Room of One's Own* (London: Penguin Books, 2000), 5.

4. Hannah Arendt, *The Human Condition* (Chicago: University of Chicago Press, 1998), Chapters 27 and 31.

5. Ibid., 5.

6. Ibid., 325.

7. Hannah Arendt, *The Life of the Mind* (New York: Harcourt Brace & Company, 1971), 1:6.

8. Ibid., 1:8.

9. Ibid., 1:100.

10. Arendt, *Denktagebuch*, XV.1.345–346.

11. Arendt, *The Life of the Mind*, 1:32.

12. Hannah Arendt, *The Origins of Totalitarianism* (New York: Harcourt, 1976), 476.

13. Arendt, "Walter Benjamin," 205.

14. Arendt, *The Life of the Mind*, 1:122.

15. Ibid., 1:124.

16. Ibid.

17. Arendt, "Walter Benjamin," 166.

18. Arendt, *The Human Condition*, 27.

19. Ibid., 26.

20. Ibid.

21. Ibid.

22. Ibid., 180.

23. Ibid., 182.

24. Martin Heidegger, *What Is Called Thinking?* (New York: Perennial, 2004), Part II, Lecture IV (148–157). Arendt attended the fourth session of the second part of Heidegger's course in Freiburg on May 30, 1952.

25. Arendt, *The Human Condition*, 26.

26. Ibid., 26 n. 9; Arendt, *Denktagebuch*, XVI.1.381: "Socrates draws a distinction between *technè rhètorikè* and *dialegesthai*: clearly that rhetoric is the art to talk *about* something to others (and as such belongs to politics), whereas *dialegesthai* speaks something *through* with oneself or others."

27. Cf. Arendt, *Denktagebuch*, IX.19.214, XIII.4.298.

28. Arendt, *Denktagebuch*, IX.26.220.

29. Arendt, *The Human Condition*, 169.

30. Ibid., 197; Hannah Arendt, "The Crisis in Culture," in *Between Past and Future: Eight Exercises in Political Thought* (New York: Penguin Books, 1993), 197–226, at 217; Arendt, *Denktagebuch*, XIX.21.461; XX.10.483–484.

31. Arendt, "The Crisis in Culture," 215.

32. See Patchen Markell, "Arendt's Work: On the Architecture of *The Human Condition*," *College Literature* 38, no. 1 (Winter 2011): 16–44.

33. Arendt, *The Human Condition*, 169.

34. Ibid., 168.

35. Ibid.

36. Ibid.

37. Rainer Maria Rilke, *Rilke on Love and Other Difficulties*, translated by John J. L. Mood (New York: Norton, 1975), 89. Arendt cites the German original only (*The Human Condition*, 168 n. 39): "*Aus unbeschreiblicher Verwandlung stammen / solche Gebilde—: Fühl! und glaub! / Wir leidens oft: zu Asche werden Flammen, / doch, in der Kunst: zur Flamme wird der Staub. / Hier ist Magie. In das Bereich des Zaubers / scheint das gemeine Wort hinaufgestuft . . . / und ist doch wirklich wie der Ruf des Taubers, / der nach der unsichtbaren Taube ruft.*"

CHAPTER 5

The Task of Knowledgeable Love: Arendt and Portmann in Search of Meaning

Anne O'Byrne

> When striving to re-form the pattern of our own way of life, we often invoke Nature as our great teacher, seeking to justify man's actions by arguments based on what happens in nature.
>
> —ADOLF PORTMANN, *Forms and Patterns of Animals*

> Grammatology must pursue and consolidate whatever, in scientific practice, has always already begun to exceed the logocentric closure.
>
> —JACQUES DERRIDA, *Positions*

> The natural sciences . . . have done the "unthinkable," and now use thinking to try to grasp what they have done.
>
> —HANNAH ARENDT, *D* XXIV.58.643

In 1966, notes begin to appear in Arendt's *Denktagebuch* about the Swiss zoologist Adolf Portmann and his studies of morphology, the appearances of animals.[1] One of his early studies, *The Beauty of Butterflies* from 1936, concerns the variety in the size, shape, and color of butterflies, and the book's title already suggests that this is an unusual scientist.[2] His work evidently begins in wonder and remains suffused with it throughout. Instead of submitting the phenomenon of this variety—and for him butterflies are just one terrifically flamboyant example—to the demands of natural and sexual selection as the mainstream of evolutionary theory would have it, Portmann identifies in pattern and color an Aristotelian desire to appear. Functionalism, the approach dominant in his discipline, would require him to ask why there should be such variety. What purpose does it serve? How does it further the evolutionary development of the species? What is its function? What is expressed in these colors? He insists, though, on speaking of beauty and remaining at the level of appearance.

By this point in her career, Arendt had long been concerned with appearance: Rahel Varnhagen's appearance in high society; Pericles's appearance before his fellow Athenians; the appearance of each of us as natal beings.

She has also long been attuned to the work of scientists, whether on the Sputnik project or on splitting the atom or in basic research. What is new here is the fact that Portmann is a biologist, and that, for him, appearance is interesting specifically as the appearance of the natural world around us. His studies extend from butterflies to Mediterranean sea snails, and his examples include tulip poplars, wild carrots, tawny owls, and embryos of many species of mammal. His theory and practice of morphology became an unorthodox strand within evolutionary theory. In addition, he developed the thought of human neoteny in a work devoted to the various morphologies of the first year of human life.

As a result, the *Denktagebuch* entries on Portmann turn out to be entrances onto the realm of life or, more to the point, onto a distinctive and dynamic thinking of life. What can this mean for Arendt, for whom life was another long-term, troublesome interest? What drew her to Portmann's work? Sometimes life is for her a matter of *zoe*, the merely living existence that threatens to take over the sphere of human action and freedom, and sometimes it is *bios*, the worldly life of human beings. Sometimes it is both; natality, for example, is for Arendt a matter of our natural mammalian emergence from our mothers' bodies but also the signal of our capacity for the highest, most distinctively human actions. But the *bios/zoe* distinction is hardly relevant to Portmann, who regards his work as biology *and* zoology and eventually also as anthropology. Given this, what status can Arendt grant the insights he offers? Are they the incontrovertible, compelling truths of scientific knowledge (*D* XXIV.14.622) or the more speculative—and therefore more politically and philosophically interesting—claims of a human science? Are they the cognitive products of empirical study or the worldly manifestation of thought? Are they a matter, in Kantian terms, of *Verstand* or of *Vernunft*? Are they contributions to our knowledge of the functioning of bodies or to our appreciation of the intensities of life?

Philosophers who approach the sciences—and indeed other disciplines within the humanities—sometimes proceed as if they know more than they do, or as if their capacity for metalevel analysis equips them to understand what they find going on among the scientists. They may even behave as if their theoretical point of view makes it unnecessary to understand the detail and technicality of what they see, which might be part of the reason why Arendt, despite her philosophical training, refused to describe herself as a philosopher. She took seriously the need to avoid philosophical hubris by educating herself as any member of the reading public would; in the case of biology, this meant reading Portmann's books, among others. Yet, while she may have turned to him as a popular scientist, to be appreciated for his ability to translate his research into layman's terms, she engages his work as a fellow thinker of the human condition, a fellow member of the reading and writing public. Passing through her *Denktagebuch* notes and *The Life of the Mind* to his thinking of life leads us to their meeting place in the question of meaning.[3] There we find both the thinker of political life and the observer of sea sponges, the student of the totalitarian system and the critic of technological thinking, the professor who urges us to love the world enough to take responsibility for it and the one who leads us back to a childish love for a zebra's stripes, both of them reaching for a love of the shared world that must be both knowledgeable and thoughtful.

The Circle of Thought and the Metaphor of Life

The Life of the Mind, originally envisioned as a sequel to *The Human Condition*, begins with a volume on thinking, which in turn begins with a section on appearance. The book was first published in 1978, having been presented as part of the Gifford Lectures at the University of Aberdeen in 1973, but the connection between thinking and appearing emerged earlier in Arendt's thought and was concisely formulated in a *Denktagebuch* entry made in November 1968:

> Re: volume II of *Human Condition*: All that lives strives to appear (see Portmann). All functions show themselves—but not the *silent* dialogue of thinking, not the will and also not judgment. They *are*, without necessarily coming into appearance.
> "Being shows itself as thought" (Heidegger, *Identity and Difference*, p. 48). And how does thinking show itself? (*D* XXVI.1.701)

The note captures the phenomenological sensibility that is evident throughout her work, not only with the quotation from Heidegger but also with the reference to Portmann's morphology. Portmann is mentioned in the *Denktagebuch* between 1966 and 1968, in the period when the thinking that would come to light in the 1973 lectures was under way—*whatever that might mean*. This is Arendt's question.

After all, we each appear into a world and it is not a matter of mere appearing or a mode of existence that is somehow second best. We are the sort of beings who see and are seen and for whom appearing is active, a vital element of existence. For us, being is appearing. As living beings we are not accidentally located in the world but belong to the world even as it belongs to us. It was old when we arrived in it, and it will persist even when we have gone, so our experience of time and finitude is shaped by the arc of life between birth and death, that is, our appearance on the earth and eventual disappearance from it. Our first appearing presupposed a spectator, so our being in the world is never in the singular; we exist here in the plural. Also, seeing and sentience are not abstractions; the world appears to us in the ways made possible by the specific bodies and senses we have. Arendt writes: "Seen from the perspective of the world, every creature born into it arrives well equipped to deal with a world in which Being and Appearing coincide."[4] Without mentioning its source, she sets about correcting Heidegger's assertion that animals are poor in world by celebrating a diversity of rich human and nonhuman worlds. She writes:

> Nothing perhaps is more surprising in this world of ours than the almost infinite diversity of its appearances, the sheer entertainment value of its views, sounds and smells, something that is hardly mentioned by the thinkers and philosophers. . . . This diversity is matched by an equally astounding diverseness of sense organs among the animal species, so that what actually appears to living creatures assumes the greatest variety of form and shape: every animal species lives in a world of its own, [though] all sense-endowed creatures have appearance as such in common, first, an appearing world and second . . . the fact that they themselves are appearing and disappearing creatures.[5]

There is an important train in Arendt's thought that stretches from *The Human Condition*, with its thinking of world and worldly action as appearance, to the late *Lectures on Kant's Political Philosophy*, where attention is turned to the actor/spectators who together sense and make sense of the appearing world.[6] The abiding image of the first is of Pericles—statesman and general—addressing his fellow Athenians, while the image that endures from the second is that of the uninvolved spectators on the events of the French Revolution, whose watchful participation "make the event at home in the history of the world."[7] In those late lectures, the spectators' participation relies on a distinctive human capacity, the *sensus communis* or *Menschenverstand*, the common understanding of man.[8] As this thought train passes through *The Life of the Mind* and the question of how thinking appears, we will see Socrates emerge as the revelatory figure. Yet here, at the point early in *The Life of the Mind* where her thinking encounters Portmann's, what is important is that appearances are *sensed*, and that sensing is the province of all sentient beings. Arendt now has the occasion to consider the material specificity of every point of view; the world—any world—is the product of distinct, species-specific body forms. Beetles' eyes give them a rich world quite different from ours. We do not share their world—we don't have the eyes for it—but we appear in it and they appear in ours. Indeed, they appear to us in a variety of sizes, shapes, and colors that confirms Arendt's insight that the flood of appearances, in all its diversity and abundance, is endlessly entertaining to us. If there is a figure to accompany this stage in her thought, it is that of the natural scientist observing the living world.

Elsewhere, when Arendt is concerned with the work of scientists, her examples are physicists, and the scientific projects that appear on the pages of her works are typically the great physics projects of the mid–twentieth century that culminated in splitting the atom and the technological development of the atomic bomb. The worldly moment that opens *The Human Condition* is the launch of Sputnik, while the image of scientific work that concludes the book is of scientists working together to initiate a new process in nature. Biology could readily provide the model, but for Arendt the release of atomic energy into nature remains paradigmatic. This is not surprising. World War II and the Cold War meant that the work of Meitner, Hahn, Straussman, and Frisch would quickly surge to political significance and public consciousness; they discovered nuclear fission in 1938, and in 1945 Hahn was awarded the Nobel Prize. In that same year the United States dropped atomic bombs on Japan. Crick, Watson, Wilkins, and Franklin discovered the structure of DNA in 1953, and the discovery earned the Nobel Prize in 1962. The emergence of biotechnology happened rather more slowly, and the significance of the changes underway in the science of life— so present to us now—drew public attention more gradually.

Yet, since Arendt is a thinker concerned with the life conditions of natality and mortality, we could reasonably expect her to be attuned to changes in the understanding of life. After all, Sputnik was significant for our human condition not because of the engineering and rocket science that brought it into being but because its launch promised to change the human condition of living on Earth and sharing the planet with all other humans. In fact, Arendt was clearly interested in biology. Her library holds several volumes, with marginalia in her hand, of contemporary works in popular biology including *What Is Life?* by Erwin Schrödinger, *Man and the Living World* by Karl Von Frisch (not to be confused with the fission physicist Otto Robert Frisch), and *The Language of Life: An Introduction to the Science of Genetics* by George and Muriel Beadle.[9] In addition, she followed Hans Jonas's prescient work on bioengineering, and, as we have seen, she owned and read several volumes of Portmann's work.

What these have in common is a commitment to the scientific mode of encountering the world, paired with an appreciation of its limits. Arendt notes a passage where Schrödinger, writing about the physics of life, states:

It is the four dimensional pattern of the "phenotype," the visible and manifest nature of the individual, which is reproduced without appreciable change for generations, permanent within centuries—though not within tens of thousands of years—and borne at each transmission by the material structure of the nuclei of the two cells which unite to form the fertilized egg cell. That is a marvel—than which only one is greater, one that is intimately connected with it, yet lies on a different plane. I mean the fact that we, whose total being is entirely based on a marvellous interplay of this very kind, yet possess the power of acquiring considerable knowledge about it. I think it possible that this knowledge may advance to little short of a complete understanding—of the first marvel. The second may be beyond human understanding.[10]

The distinction Schrödinger couches in mystical terms is the distinction between knowledge, which holds out the promise of completeness, and the being of the knower, which inevitably exceeds knowledge and confounds all efforts at completion.

When Beadle and Beadle describe the process of genetic mutation and its workings in evolution, they, too, run up against a limit. Arendt marks this passage: "One gasps a bit on contemplating the exquisite timing that was necessary—not to bring us into being but just to make us *possible*. Nature must have made mistakes by the millions."[11] The gasp comes when we realize the scale of the universe and the fact that our existence depends on contingency upon contingency, but embedded in this experience is the additional realization that nature, which science must approach as though it were a rule-governed system, must have deviated from those rules many times in order for our existence to be even possible. Not only are we incapable of accounting for our having come into being, but it is also beyond knowledge. Our existence as the beings we are could not have been predicted. What's more, genetic mutation is only part of the picture. In Portmann's *Neue Wege in Biologie*, Arendt marks this passage with an exclamation mark: "One of the most reliable arrangements there is for the regular occurrence of new combinations is that curious game that biologists call *sexuality*."[12]

What we gain from scientific encounters with the world is truth, but the gap between knowing and being—indicated by Schrödinger, hinted at by Arendt in the closing pages of *The Human Condition*, and indeed worked through by Kant in the Transcendental Aesthetic—persists, and generates the distinction between truth and meaning. Along with a desire to know, we have a need for meaning, which is pursued through the activity of thinking.[13] Cognition not only cannot give us meaning, but it also disguises that fact by covering over the gap even as it uncovers truth. The science of life, and indeed our everyday way of knowing, approach the living organism as capable of full appearance in the course of its short life; it suggests that nothing bars our way to complete knowledge of it and, if knowledge is true and complete, why should there by a need for meaning?[14] In contrast, Arendt argues that the living body does not give itself unreservedly to the observing eye; the constant changes that are part of metabolism, growth, and aging mean that any state of a living body is a passing state, and the condition of being alive does not allow living bodies to be revealed in the ways that dead matter can be. The incompleteness of our knowledge of living beings is constitutive rather than incidental or merely temporary. Thus science runs up against its limits, opening the space where the question of meaning arises.

Philosophy is apt to occupy this space, but Arendt resists philosophy's metaphysical tendency—established by Plato—to construe it as the gap between two worlds. Invariably, the otherworldly cause of appearance is granted more reality than the appearance itself—think not only of Plato's forms but also Descartes's causal argument from the Second Meditation— so that appearances must be penetrated in order to get to their ground and therefore their meaning. More surprisingly, she regards modern science as giving new life to this old tendency.[15] Science keeps its eyes turned toward this one world, but it persists in delving behind appearance in search of truth, privileging the base of appearance above the appearance itself. This is what happens when the colors of a bird are understood only in reference to the evolutionary function that they serve, that is, when the wealth of appearance is reduced to the life process.

This move beyond appearance is not our only alternative. Indeed, for Arendt, it is no alternative at all, since we must live in the world of appearances. The choice between appearance and reality is a false dilemma that, in its modern version, has its roots in the failure to grasp the distinction between Kant's *Verstand* or Intellect, which allows us to know, and *Vernunft* or Reason, which drives us to pursue meaning. The former gives access to the world that appears to our senses; the latter has been understood as leading us to ask for the meaning *behind* appearances. But what Kant does when he discerns a world where the things in themselves *are* as we *are* in our world of appearances is identify a semblance of reason or an authentic semblance. Earlier, Arendt cited Portmann's distinction between authentic appearances, that is, appearances that *present themselves*, and inauthentic appearances, which are forced into view as an animal's inner organs are brought to light by dissection. Now, applying the language of authenticity and inauthenticity to semblance and tracing Kant's discovery to the experience of thinking, she hones her thesis to a fine point:

> Hence, in our context the only relevant question is whether the semblances are inauthentic or authentic ones, whether they are caused by dogmatic beliefs and arbitrary assumptions, mere mirages that disappear upon closer inspection, or whether they are inherent in the paradoxical condition of a living being that though itself part of the world of appearances, is in possession of a faculty, the ability to think, that permits the mind to withdraw from the world without ever being able to leave it or transcend it.[16]

Does such worldly thinking appear? As we saw in the *Denktagebuch* note, the form that Arendt's question for *The Human Condition II* took in 1968 was "How does thinking show itself?" In the course of these early sections of *Life of the Mind* she struggles to find a way to think about thinking, and the formulations of the question accumulate, each one supplementing rather than supplanting its precursors. The initial version "What is thinking?" persists as an expression of the philosophical desire for an analytic starting point; "Why do we think?" is entertained briefly, suggesting a hope for existential insight into internal motivations; later, "What makes us think?" acknowledges the impossibility of grasping internal processes and looks instead for the external circumstances that provoke the activity of thinking. Behind all three lingers the *Denktagebuch* formulation, reminding us that whatever habits of thinking we develop, and however insurmountable the requirement that thinking be conducted in withdrawal from the world, we continue to *live* in the world of appearances. Thinking is an activity of *living* beings. Thinking about thinking must somehow bridge the gulf between the visible and the invisible, the world of appearance and the thinking ego, and it cannot do this using either empirical study or dialectical philosophical speculation, that is, what Arendt describes as Hegel's "speculative cognition."[17] Rather, thought is carried across such gulfs by metaphor. But which metaphor? Arendt considers and rejects the traditional model of sight, which remains too firmly tied to the *sense* of sight and therefore to cognition, before concluding, "The only possible metaphor one may conceive of for the life of the mind is the sensation of being alive. *Without the breath of life the human body is a corpse; without thinking the human mind is dead.*"[18]

She embraces this metaphor. Just as the life process turns in a circle, so—citing Aristotle, Hegel, and Heidegger—she finds thinkers insisting on the circular motion of thought. If thinking were identical with cognition, it would share its rectilinear trajectory from the quest for the object to cognition of that object; instead, thinking has an "unceasing motion, that is, motion in a circle" that has no end and no product (Aristotle). Certainly the trajectory of an individual life is rectilinear, stretching from birth to death, but it is also inevitably folded, with the birth and death of successive generations, into the natural cycles of the life process.

Yet, for all that, she pronounces the metaphor empty.[19] "It obviously refuses to answer the inevitable question, Why do we think?, since there is no answer to the question, Why do we live?"[20] Quickly—precipitously— she abandons it and changes the question, quoting the Wittgenstein of the *Philosophical Investigations*:

> How can we find out why man thinks? Whereupon he answers: "It often happens that we only become aware of the important *facts, if we suppress the question 'why?'.* . . . It is in a deliberate effort to suppress the question, *Why* do we think? that I shall deal with the question, *What* makes us think?"[21]

It is true that we cannot answer the question of why we live, but this alone does not render the metaphor useless. Moving more slowly and drawing on other resources in her thinking, it becomes clear that Wittgenstein's strategy can be applied to the question of life too, leading us to give up "Why?" in favor of "What is life?" or "What is it, to live?" Indeed, even though at this point at the end of the "Appearance" section of *The Life of the Mind*, Arendt moves away from the metaphor of life toward the model of Socrates, life will soon emerge again in her specific attention to the *life* of Socrates. Moreover, by this same point, she has also made it possible to explicitly pursue the question of life in deeper and more revealing ways. In the course of her engagement with Portmann, she has implicitly mobilized a distinctive form of scientific thinking that is ready for these questions and committed to pursuing them hermeneutically in the world of appearances. It may turn out that thinking about thinking still requires models, but perhaps, along with the familiar model of Socrates, we can also have Thales, and Aristotle, and indeed the young Socrates. If Plato's Socrates rarely ventured outside the walls of Athens and devoted his passionate attention to human affairs, Thales looked at the stars and Aristotle thought not only about politics and metaphysics but also the parts and generation of animals.[22]

The Intensification of Life

Portmann, whose career as a zoologist, biologist, and public intellectual stretched from the 1920s into the 1970s, saw himself as engaged in a shift in the sciences that reoriented our relation to the natural world. This was not a paradigm shift, nor indeed a change that was distinctive to the twentieth century or even to modernity, and it was not a change that would eventually be carried through and brought to completion; rather it happened in every epoch, to all peoples, and indeed in the course of each human life. What he described was a move from the primary, *urprimitiv* experience of being in relation to the world, on the one hand, to the secondary, scientific worldview on the other. "This drama renews itself in every experience of becoming," he wrote in 1960.[23] The form it took in his field, in his time, was a move away from the observation and description of forms of life as they appear, and towards those investigations in physics, chemistry, and biology that delve into the unseen, reaching for their evidence beyond what is available to the naked eye or indeed made available by the microscope. Why should subatomic physics and molecular biology come to dominate as they did? Because, according to Portmann, they are propelled by the conviction that it is in the realm of the unseen that the key to the mastery of nature lies.

The critique is not unfamiliar. Feminist philosophers took up a version of it in the 1980s as they reread early modern philosophers and found them deploying a masculinist, objectivist worldview that would turn out to destroy the intimacy of our relation with the mothering natural world.[24] It would also have been familiar to Portmann's audience in another version, Goethe's botany, which was a study of the observed forms of living plants. As we have seen, Arendt shares this sensibility in her affirmation of appearance and her rejection of otherworldly sources of meaning. Portmann, for his part, had no illusion that his style of morphological research would or should supplant the predominant form of scientific research. He had a clear view of the forces that drove science to focus on questions involving the general functions of life and to pursue the most general laws of biology, but, in *Animal Forms and Patterns* (1948), he sketched them in a way that was far from celebratory.[25] Certainly, the scientific knowledge that had been amassed using this method had been put to work healing the sick and making us more productive, but also simply exerting power over material things and developing technologies of destruction.[26] This was three years after the liberation of Auschwitz and the destruction of Hiroshima and Nagasaki.

He dramatized the distinction between the primary and secondary views of the natural world over the course of many works, and argued for the primitive view as a corrective to the dominant scientific approach. At some moments the arguments are epistemological. In *Animal Forms*, he notes that "the search for the general laws of life has produced more facts than we can yet grasp."[27] Borrowing a metaphor from the biologist J. von Uexküll, he describes this blizzard of facts as initially allowing us to look at the world anew but soon hiding and immobilizing a great wealth of detail under a blanket of frozen truths. The sheer abundance of facts begins to hinder our attempts to understand them. Portmann writes:

> By aiming all the time at discovering the laws of nature, it has been completely overlooked that, in doing this, one of the most important general laws has been utterly forgotten, one of the most universal phenomena of all: the constant production in the course of the earth's history of new organic life.[28]

In the face of the ever-changing, ever-expanding, frankly troublesome variety of manifestations of life, laws of nature that promise constancy—or at least relative stability—are certainly appealing. As Arendt might put it, they provide the banisters that could help scientists toward true claims about the world. As Portmann does put it, they help produce scientific knowledge that can be deployed in "the many utilitarian tasks which are associated with the building up of human civilization and the control of natural forces."[29] The problem comes when, falling between the two stools of abundant, uninterpretable facts and elusive general laws, we forget the value of looking attentively at the things in the world as themselves a source of meaning.

It is not a matter of just any sort of looking. When we allow function to provide the context for what we see, our observations turn out to reinforce the evolutionary principles of natural and sexual selection. Thus, the shape of a dolphin is the right shape for a fast swimmer; the long legs of the antelope are appropriate for an animal that runs on grassland; the wing of a bird is perfectly adapted to flight. Portmann writes: "This utmost purposiveness, this perfect agreement between form and function, is considered to be the way in which Nature really works."[30] But this is backward thinking. It directs our attention almost exclusively to these technical forms of life, constantly reinforcing the significance of whatever coincides with function and allowing us to neglect "the immense field of animal forms which mean little or nothing to our technical sense."[31] For Portmann, this is at least dissatisfying, at most a dangerous dismissal of other organisms that show a less compelling form-function relationship as "rabble or vermin, monsters or abortions, worm or maggots, a collection of monstrosities from which just a few groups are separated off to receive a one-sided aesthetic respect."[32] Remember: This work is from 1948. The critique is immanent to the theory of functionalism, but the moral impulse is undisguised.

In Arendt's thinking, this same resistance to instrumentality springs from a political impulse. If the political sphere is the place for activities that can only be understood in terms of means and ends, it can no longer be the realm of action. Action escapes this schema since it is an open-ended process that exceeds any purpose or use. For the Greeks, action and speech served no end beyond themselves; they were only in actuality and were therefore the highest activities of the political realm. Like healing, flute playing, and playacting, speech and action are activities where the product is identical with the performance, and performance needs spectators, those who know how to look without looking for means and ends.

For Portmann, it is not a matter of contrasting overdetermined, technological looking with a pure, naive looking that lets the world simply show itself. When we turn our careful attention to the living world, we will make sense of it only if we bring categories of some sort to bear. Without them, we are forced to resort to *life itself* as the sole value, which (1) amounts to producing a biology with no *logos* and (2) reinforces the rise of *animal laborans* that Arendt regards with such dismay and marks the destruction of political life. Portmann does not resist taxonomy or indeed hierarchy but, crucially, he does not endorse the hierarchical relationship between appearance and a hidden reality. Rather, the significant difference is between the dim life of simple marine animals on the one hand and "the higher type of existence" on the other, and the relevant gauge is the intensity of living, specifically, the intensity of communal life. He writes:

> Barnacles which colonize the inter-tidal zones of the rocky shores in dense crowds . . . form a poor and dumb sort of animal association compared with the schools of fish or better still, with a noisy colony of breeding birds in which the living together shows many of the features which we meet in the life of the higher animals, as well as in our own human society.[33]

The argument is open to the objections Portmann himself made to the functionalists: if we choose technical efficiency as the relevant value, we will get a hierarchy of functional forms; if we choose communal intensity as our value it will be a hierarchy of community life. Portmann was surely aware of this but does not allow it to dismantle his position. He proposes his alternative taxonomy in the spirit of liberal dissent, offering it as a point of resistance to the hegemony of instrumental thinking that subjects scientific research to the aims of technology. There is room enough for both. Yet this is not a matter of dissent alone. Portmann's preference for intensified life springs from a positive desire for a "fuller, richer concept of living forms."[34] Despite his use of aesthetic language, and despite the fact that we will soon see him translate his view into economic, social and political terms, this emerges as a distinctly scientific value. He argues that "research has various aims, not only that of controlling the forces of nature, the one most intensively sought after and promoted at the present time."[35] A richer concept allows us to know more, and has the salutary effect of bringing us to the limits of knowledge. Scientific research leads us to mystery, and the humility forced on us in the experience of that limit is the antidote to the hubris that comes with technological prowess.[36] From the point of view of technology, this is useless. In the Kantian terms Arendt uses in *The Life of the Mind*, functionalism presents itself as a matter of Reason (*Vernunft*) generating an account of the meaning of appearances, but in fact it never reaches beyond knowledge and perception (*Verstand*). In contrast, and counterintuitively, it is Portmann's insistence on the value of patterns and surface, precisely on the value of appearance, that is the work of Reason.[37]

For Portmann, technological uselessness is to be celebrated. At the end of *Animal Forms*, the scientist emerges as social critic and issues his clarion call:

> As soon as the powers of production are no longer organized and
> increased so overwhelmingly with a view to destruction, as soon as
> there is a real opportunity for the many to have free, true leisure, then
> the unquenchable urge for work will turn also towards those spheres
> where there are only "useless" values to be gained; where it is not only
> that feeling of power which comes from domination that will deter-
> mine what shall be sought out, but it will be rather the awe that sur-
> rounds the mysterious.[38]

If the deepest value is the intensification of life in communal living, we find ourselves gazing at the world as an artist might, allowing ourselves to be moved by the realization all around us of possibilities of existence that are different from our own, and experiencing something "which seems at times to be like the bonds of brotherhood, albeit one which it is difficult to grasp."[39]

All of this is available to us thanks to appearances. Arendt does not share Portmann's inclination toward fraternity or the mysterious but she does want the knowledge gathered from looking at the world in the way Portmann does to be brought to bear on our human condition. She writes in the *Denktagebuch*: "Whatever part of us is appearance is, among other things, 'a broadcast meant to be picked up by receivers' (Portmann), that is, it indi-

cates a with-world [*Mitwelt*]. We are 'social' beings, insofar as we appear"
(*D* XXIV.64.647).

In *The Human Condition*, first birth, the biological event of appearing in
the world, was the *signal* of our second birth, that is, our capacity for spontaneous action. Now appearance *indicates* the with-world. It is not a matter
of biology providing a metaphor for understanding our existence. Nor is it
a matter of scientific research producing incontrovertible truths that simply compel affirmation. Nor is it a matter of substituting Thales for
Socrates as a model of thinking. Rather, what is at work here is something
more like Heidegger's practice of formal indication. When Heidegger
uses the phrase in his lecture courses of 1919 and the early 1920s, what he
has in mind is the need for his students to reach into their own experience
in search of the initial pointers that will get phenomenological research
under way. (Arendt began to study with him in 1924.) Rather than take
the world as merely given in its laws and its details, and rather than launch
immediately into abstraction, they must examine their experience and set
about describing it in ways that will lead to truth, phenomenologically
understood.[40]

For Arendt and Portmann, this approach produces a hermeneutic phenomenology, a way of looking at the world that engages and transforms
the viewer. It is at work in *The Human Condition* and *Eichmann in Jerusalem*, the two works Arendt cites as having prompted the questions that set
The Life of the Mind under way.[41] For Portmann, our experience of the
variety of butterfly colors opens up reflection on the seen and the one who
sees, moving us from the naïve—childlike—enjoyment of the colors to
questions of what each one in particular means and what the very fact of
their variety can mean. What might it mean for butterflies, and what
might if mean for us? In Heidegger's terminology, this is the shift from
ontic information to ontological meaning, and this shift happens repeatedly as we move around the hermeneutic circle, never quite arriving back
at the point from which we started because who we are has undergone its
own changes along the way. We can imagine Portmann on his journey
around the circle. Driven by the curiosity he describes himself as having
felt from an early age, he turns his attention to the natural world and is
struck by an awe that inspires him to keep looking ever more carefully and
attentively. He accumulates knowledge, becomes an expert in certain
marine life forms of the Baltic Sea, looks some more, and then more, and
so on. The appearances continue to appear and the growing understanding of them is not a matter of penetrating beneath the surface to the hidden depth or of surpassing mere appearance on the way to the essence of

the thing. Rather, it is a matter of learning to see. It is also a matter of learning to love.

Conclusion: Love and Knowledge

Arendt's highest hope for thinking is that it should prevent the thinker doing evil, and that we should be able to require it of everyone. It is no accident that, once the question "How does thinking appear?" brought her to the thought of life, the model life she identifies would be the one that most perfectly fulfills these hopes. Socrates was convinced that no one could knowingly commit evil, and his life was spent requiring thinking of everyone he met. This was not a matter of prescription. In the *Apology* he describes himself as having spent his life reproving his fellow Athenians, and indeed the final favor he asks of them is that they do the same for his sons "if they value riches or anything over virtue or if they think they are something when they are nothing."[42] The requirement to think is not, then, a law to be enforced but a practice to be cultivated in the course of an education and a life lived in the polis.

To be sure, Arendt's appeal to the model of Socrates's life is immensely productive for her investigation of the life of the mind: It opens up a discussion of thinking as the conversation of the two in one; the Socratic *daimon* provides a model of conscience; his habit of spending his time in the agora brings thinking to—if not exactly *into*—public life, where it becomes something we can all participate in, just as we all participate in the life of the city. Socrates devoted himself to thinking, yet refused to think of himself as possessed of any expertise, with one exception. As Arendt points out, he acknowledged that he did know something about love: "By some means or other I have received from heaven the gift of being able to detect at a glance both a lover and a beloved."[43] Yet how does love appear? The dialogue—in good Socratic fashion—delivers no definition of love or friendship, preferring to leave the readers and listeners more puzzled at the end than they were at the beginning. But throughout the conversation we are shown love in the glances that pass between the men, the blushes, the whispered conversations, the gaze that Hippothales turns on the beloved Lysis, in a word, the attention that love pays. And no one is more attentive than Socrates.

In "The Crisis in Education," Arendt describes education as the point at which we decide if we love the world enough to take responsibility for it.[44] The world she has in mind is the human world, the one made by the work of our hands, and what we are asked to be responsible for is the accumulation of human history that has made it as it is. The educator shows this world to the new generation, asking the newcomers to attend to it and, in taking joint responsibility, to also tend to it. Socrates is a superbly worldly figure in this sense. The object of his attention, the focus of his questioning, and the object of his lifelong examination was life as it is lived by humans in the polis. Arendt's writing on Portmann invites us to imagine a Socratic naturalist, someone who extends his attention beyond the affairs of the city to the natural world, a thinker for whom the examined life involves an examination of the lives of nonhuman living beings with whom we share the planet. It invites us to imagine a Socratic mode of encountering those beings that does not rely on either a Platonic theory of forms or an Aristotelian understanding of teleologies, but on a phenomenological practice of looking.[45]

Portmann was himself such an educator and such a naturalist. His colleague at Basel Karl Jaspers described the task of the university teacher as bringing about in the student an internal turn (*Umkehr*). Portmann, speaking on the same occasion—the five hundredth anniversary of the founding of the University of Basel—concluded his lecture, "Natural Science and Humanity," with this glance toward the future:

> This, then, is my wish for the future working of our university: that the young people who come here seeking what they need for their development, on the one hand, and their instructors, on the other, will never lack the spirit that is essential if we are to bring the paradoxical mosaic of our life into the service of the tasks before us: what I mean is the great gift of knowledgeable love.[46]

NOTES

1. My thanks to Roger Berkowitz and Jeff Champlin for their very helpful comments on an earlier version of this work.

2. The volume contains twelve color drawings, an introduction by Julian Huxley, and an "introductory text" by Portmann. *The Beauty of Butterflies* (Oxford: Oxford University Press, 1936).

3. Hannah Arendt, *The Life of the Mind*, vol. 1, *Thinking* (New York: Harcourt Brace Jovanovich, 1971).

4. Ibid., 20.

5. Ibid.

6. Hannah Arendt, *Lectures on Kant's Political Philosophy*, ed. Ronald Beiner (Chicago: University of Chicago Press, 1982).

7. Ibid., 65.

8. Ibid., 70.

9. Erwin Schrödinger, *What Is Life?* (Garden City, N.Y.: Doubleday, 1956); Karl Von Frisch, *Man and the Living World*, trans. Elsa B. Lowenstein

(New York: Harcourt, Brace and World, 1963); George Beadle and Muriel Beadle, *The Language of Life: An Introduction to the Science of Genetics* (Garden City, N.Y.: Doubleday, 1966).

10. Schroedinger, *What Is Life?* 32.

11. Beadle and Beadle, *The Language of Life*, 45.

12. Adolf Portmann, *Neue Wege der Biologie* (Munich: Piper Verlag, 1960), 45. My translation.

13. Arendt, *The Life of the Mind*, 15.

14. Ibid., 22.

15. Ibid., 25.

16. Ibid., 45.

17. Ibid., 123, 124.

18. Ibid., 123.

19. Ibid., 124.

20. Ibid., 125.

21. Ibid.

22. Note that the young Socrates was possessed of an extraordinary passion for natural science (Phaedo 96a).

23. Adolf Portmann, "Naturforschung und Humanismus," *Basler Universitätsreden*, vol. 43 (Basel: Helbing & Lichtenhahn, 1960), 55.

24. See Susan Bordo, *The Flight to Objectivity* (Albany: State University of New York Press, 1987).

25. Adolf Portmann, *Animal Forms and Patterns*, trans. Hella Czech (New York: Schocken Books, 1967).

26. Ibid., 202, 216.

27. Ibid., 202.

28. Ibid., 203.

29. Ibid., 202.

30. Ibid., 210.

31. Ibid.

32. Ibid.

33. Ibid., 183.

34. Ibid., 218.

35. Ibid., 216.

36. Ibid., 220.

37. Hannah Arendt, *The Life of the Mind*, 57.

38. Portmann, *Animal Forms and Patterns*, 216.

39. Ibid., 220.

40. See Søren Overgaard, *Husserl and Heidegger on Being in the World* (Dordrecht: Kluwer, 2004), 84 "Being thus almost devoid of descriptive con-

tent, the initial indications can be called formal—they are not descriptive but are more like signposts that tell us where to look for description."

41. Arendt, *The Life of the Mind*, 3–7.

42. *Apology*, 41e.

43. *Lysis*, 204b–c, cited in Arendt, *The Life of the Mind*, 178.

44. Hannah Arendt, "The Crisis in Education," in *Between Past and Future* (New York: Penguin Books, 1977), 173–196.

45. As noted, the Socrates that appears in Plato's *Phaedo* was once a student of the natural world (96a–100b), and the Socrates Aristophanes presents in *Clouds* appears to offer his students knowledge of everything from insects to stars. The one is a Socrates on his way from the question of causation to a theory of forms, the other a charlatan on his way to showing young men how to escape their debts.

46. Portmann, "Naturforschung und Humanismus," 56. My translation.

CHAPTER 6

Vita Passiva: Love in Arendt's *Denktagebuch*

Tatjana Noemi Tömmel

Heaven's Sovereign saves all beings but himself
That hideous sight,—a naked human heart.

—EDWARD YOUNG, *Night Thoughts*, Night iii, 226

Hannah Arendt's *Denktagebuch* is certainly the richest source for her thoughts on love, richer even than her dissertation about the concept of love in Augustine.[1] Here, all loose ends converge, waiting to be tied up—it turns out in vain. Some of them go back to her earlier, even the earliest works, others appear here for the first time. In June and December 1952, for example, she comments on Rilke's "abandoned lovers,"[2] a topic she had already discussed in an essay written with her first husband Günter Anders in 1930. In 1952 and in 1969, she quotes Heidegger's *volo ut sis* and reflects on its ambiguous meaning. Plato's myth of the spherical creatures makes an appearance; and of course, Augustine, her "old friend and benefactor,"[3] and his concept of charity show up time and again to be criticized. We find her thoughts on passion and *eros*, on friendship and sexuality, on marriage and faithfulness. Many, but not all, of these "thought threads" will find their way into the works to come.

As Barbara Hahn has pointed out, one entry in the *Denktagebuch* suggests especially that love will play a superior role in her philosophy of plurality: "In this realm of plurality, which is the political realm, one has to ask the old questions—what is love, what is friendship, what is solitude,

106

what is acting, thinking, etc., but not the one question of philosophy: Who is Man, nor the *Was kann ich wissen, was darf ich hoffen, was soll ich tun?*[4] The three Kantian questions, which all come down to the one question "Who is man?" are not compatible with Arendt's notion of plurality, which is so closely linked to her understanding of politics. The "old questions," however, have lost nothing of their dignity; they have to be asked again and answered anew; and yet, there is no such thing as a "*vita passiva*." Arendt does not write a book on love and friendship in addition to her works on the *vita activa* and the *vita contemplativa*. In May 1955, she noted in her *Denktagebuch*: "Philosophy, which sees everything from the perspective of 'contemplatio,' cared neither about 'actio' nor 'passio.' In the modern age, both step into the center of thinking, not for the sake of their own dignity, but because man is thrown back onto himself, tossed out of the common world. But then 'actio' is precisely misunderstood as work and 'passio' in the sense of desire."[5]

One can hardly doubt that Arendt's oeuvre as a whole is oriented at remedying philosophy's neglect of *actio*. When she noted these lines, she was lecturing at Berkeley about *amor mundi* and thereby about the dignity of the active life, for which the highest activity is not labor or work but action. But what about the category of *passio*, which philosophy equally neglected?

In this essay, I claim that Arendt did not neglect the personal and intimate life, as it has often been suggested even if it is true that Arendt's main works concern the active life and the life of the mind; and although love does not fit in with labor, work, or action—or with thinking, willing, and judging—love plays an important role in Arendt's thinking.

In her preliminary work for *The Human Condition* for example, love features among the fundamental modes of life for a while, but is left out later.[6] However, remarks like the one that desire is not the authentic form of *passio* point to the fact that Arendt was not indifferent toward the "heart." Against Marx, for example, she claimed that the "elementary relation between humans" was not based on coercion but on need (*dem Bedürfen*), that it was, hence, essentially "Eros"· "Men get together as persons because they need each other (love)."[7] The fundamental forms in which humans encounter each other, are neither labor, an isolated activity, nor production, in which one man sets himself up as a creator god, but action and love.

The *Denktagebuch* makes clear that the *vita passiva* must be understood as an independent mode of life. In the first half of the 1950s, we find several lists about the "elementary human activities," the "*active* modes of being alive" (*die* tätigen *Modi des Lebendigseins*), sometimes in relation to their "political indications,"[8] sometimes as "modifications of plurality."[9] Arendt sketches as it were a landscape of the *conditio humana*, assuming that the fundamental modes of life (normally, she counts labor, work, action, thinking, and suffering among them), are assigned to specific spaces like the public, the social, or the intimate sphere, and specific relational forms like solitude, solidarity, or friendship. She supposes these assignments to be in the nature of the activities themselves.

But what does she mean by the odd activity of "suffering" (*leiden*)? Its meaning encompasses "being passive," "enduring" in contrast to "acting" in the wider as well as the *perturbationes animi*, the passions of the soul, in the narrower sense.[10] Related to suffering, *pathein*, is love, which Arendt sometimes calls the only true passion, because all other "passions" were really desire.[11] Sometimes she gives the impression that love as desire was the inauthentic form, while passion was the authentic form: "Passion is always connected with love; the man of action—Achilles—knows love only as desire, and it then plays a minor role. Ulysses, the much enduring one, knows love as passion; the gods play on him."[12] Other entries however show that Arendt did not simply identify love with passion; she mentions forms of love, which are not passion, and forms of passion, which are not love.

Although her lists are still in a state of flux, they already show the basic structure of *The Human Condition* with its threefold division of the active life; in the book, however, she dedicates just a few paragraphs to thinking and suffering, not whole chapters or parts. What is left from her extensive reflection on love in the *Denktagebuch*, is the claim that love was "by its very nature . . . unworldly," "the most powerful of all antipolitical human forces."[13] I would like to argue that this somewhat undercomplex concept of love in *The Human Condition* is challenged by some of her entries in the *Denktagebuch* as well as other texts. There is more to love than just being a worldless passion.

What is love according to Arendt? What are we doing when we love? Where are we if we are neither alone with ourselves nor equally bound to all other people but entirely focused on one person?

Although it is not possible to fully reproduce the richness and originality of the thoughts and themes that appear, reappear, morph, and develop, throughout the *Denktagebuch*, there are fundamental ideas, which allow a coherent reconstruction of her concept(s) of love. In the following, I will give an overview of these core thoughts. Though her notes on love are comprehensive, the scattered and sometimes fragmentary remarks cannot always be understood without contextualizing them within her published works and correspondences. I take Arendt's ambiguous relation between *love* and the *world* to be the Ariadne's thread that will help lead a way through the labyrinth of Arendt's voluminous notes. Given Arendt's claim that love was "apolitical," her notion of *amor mundi* (or love for the world) has been called "surprising," "mysterious," and "highly paradoxical."[14] The *Denktagebuch* helps to illuminate such seemingly contradictory claims. I would like to suggest that Arendt's ambivalent, partly paradoxical thinking about love emerges from a—never systematic—differentiation between various *forms* of love. It is possible to distinguish three or even four different concepts of love in the *Denktagebuch*. The characteristics of these different kinds of love may partly intersect, but they cannot be subsumed in a single, consistent concept of love:

1. Probably the best-known concept is love as a worldless *passion*. This is the same notion of love we find in *The Human Condition*.
2. A less influential concept is love as *eros* in the sense of Aristophanes's speech in Plato's *Symposium*, namely, as a *desire* of what one is not. The precondition for *eros* or desire is plurality, yet it is completely different from politics.
3. In 1955, Arendt makes notes about her plan to write a book called *Amor Mundi*. With it we find a third notion of love, which at first seems completely unconnected to the form of love that affects humans: the *love for the world*.
4. The forth notion of love we find in Arendt is love understood as *unconditional affirmation*, and its main source is the Augustinian (or Heideggerian) quote *volo ut sis*.[15]

I will, however, focus in the following almost exclusively on the first and the last concept. Compared to "passion" and "affirmation," "desire" is systematically less relevant for Arendt's philosophy. And although *amor mundi* is a very important notion for Arendt's political theory, discussing it here in detail would go beyond the scope of this chapter. Given that it has a different "object" than the other forms of love, the decision might be justified.

With regard to the first concept of love, love as passion, I will argue that the separation between love and the world is not as absolute as Arendt sometimes suggests. Arendt sees love as a creative force, one that while it is politically destructive nevertheless is generative of human plurality. Furthermore, I will argue that the forth notion, love as *unconditional affirmation*, sheds some light on the seemingly paradoxical relation between love and the world.

Love as Divine Power and Worldless Passion

"What I want to tell you now is nothing but, at heart, a very sober portrayal of the situation. I love you as I did on the first day—you know that, and I have always known it, even before this reunion. The path you showed me is longer and more difficult than I thought. . . . The solitude of this path is self-chosen and is the only way of living given me. But the desolation that fate has kept in store not only would have taken from me the strength to live in the world, that is, not in isolation; it also would have blocked my path, which, as it is wide and not a leap, runs through the world."[16]

Arendt's claim that love is "worldless" is certainly the best known of her theses about love. Even in this early letter to Heidegger (actually her earliest extant letter to him), Arendt speaks about the conflict between love and living-in-the-world, and closes with the lines: "And, if God exists, I shall but love thee better after death."[17] Decades later, she adds an interpretation to these verses by Elizabeth Barrett Browning, which Rilke had translated into German: "and not, namely, because I don't 'live' anymore, and am therefore maybe able to be faithful or the like, but on condition that I continue to live after death and have lost in it only the world!"[18]

Since working on her dissertation *Der Liebesbegriff bei Augustin* (1929), Arendt abhorred the idea of founding a community on love, because Augustinian charity would turn the world into a desert, and not into a homeland. The believer does not love his neighbor for his own sake, but instead to lead him toward God. In her later works, too, Arendt claims that whereas the "world" as a space for politics was the "product of *amor mundi*,"[19] love for another person was a *passion*, in which we suffer the "power of the universe"—as if under a divine spell. As did Heidegger, Arendt does not understand "passion" in modern, psychological terms, but as an overindividual power:[20] Although love nests in man's heart, she writes in the *Denktagebuch*, the heart is neither its origin nor its "home:"[21] "As a universal power of life, love does not really have a human origin."[22] No one, she writes, can escape this power, which makes us a part of the "living universe." To turn the divine event of love, which man can only endure, into a feeling or a friendship means to evade the power of love, to deny it.[23] Insofar as it takes power over the heart but does not originate from it, Arendt distinguishes between love as an event and as a mere feeling or emotion:[24] "*Passions* degenerate into feelings . . . because we cannot stand to be purely seized by passion (the *pathos*), and fall back on feelings (under the pretense of internalization)."[25] The difference between "passion" and "feeling" for Arendt is that feelings are always connected to a subject, while all subjectivity is dissolved through passion: "To differentiate: I have feelings, but love has me."[26] The widely held assumption that love was a relation between subject and object originates in the dominating experience of productive work. But love is as far from working as thinking or acting. *Homo faber* is neither capable of "thinking—namely being purely active—nor of loving—namely being purely passive."[27]

This last quotation from the *Denktagebuch* undergirds Arendt's stance toward the *vita passiva*, insofar it shows that in addition to thought and action, love can be counted among the pure activities, which are assigned the highest dignity. Although she writes "Passion is the exact opposite of action,"[28] Arendt also points out that "'enduring' in the sense of *pathein* is only the other side of acting, in the sense of *prattein*. The opposite of *pathein* is *poein*."[29] Action and endurance belong together, and they are both a far cry from production and its categories: subjects and objects, means and ends.

As early as in *Rahel Varnhagen*, the book in which Arendt discusses the nature of passion for the first time, it becomes clear how closely her notion of love is connected to a certain notion of *time*. Love is a sudden irruption of an event that transforms one's existence for good.[30] In the *Denktagebuch*, too, Arendt claims, that love was "always a 'coup de foudre,'"[31] in stark contrast to friendship, which needs duration: "a two weeks old friendship does not exist."[32] As love is already accomplished in the "sublime moment"[33] of its beginning, its duration is not crucial, but the event alone—"out of which can emerge a story or fate" (*aus dem eine Geschichte werden kann oder ein Geschick*).[34]

For this reason, *faith* has a different meaning in love than in friendship. "Being faithful" does not necessarily mean to spend a life together, but to let the common story or the common fate evolve freely, "without all guarantees and faithful only in not forgetting what happened and what was sent [by fate]."[35] Because all institutions have the tendency to consume events, passion can only be destroyed by marriage, which, subject to divorce, is no longer a real institution. As the "institution of love," marriage makes love "completely and utterly homeless and defenseless."[36]

The passion of love in its extreme intensity belongs certainly to the greatest experiences man can have: "Who has never endured this power, does not live, does not belong to the living."[37] But this does not mean that love for Arendt is (as for Heidegger or Augustine), a reliable source of knowledge:

Love is not blind and makes not blind; rather the opposite is true; but love dedicates itself to the darkness of the heart, which lights up and illuminates itself . . . for moments only. . . . The venture of love, its "blindness," is that it does not reckon with deceit and cannot reckon with it. Therefore it is true: "*Wer sich der Liebe ergibt, hält er sein Leben zu Rat?*" [Who yields to love, does he spare his life? (Goethe)][38]

Love and philosophy belong together, insofar they both "flee the world, are apolitical and antipolitical,"[39] but they belong to each other only in this regard. While lovers are close to each other up to the point of symbiosis, thinking shifts its object in a distance to be able to look at it.[40] Moreover, while thinking creates plurality through its inner dialogue, love inversely turns two people into one. By the "absoluteness of a relation, which is not a relation anymore, because one does not relate anymore, but one *is*,"[41] the common realm between people disappears. This realm between people normally is the medium to relate to and understand others, whereas if we understand each other directly, without relation to anything that lies between us, we love.[42] The thunderbolt of passion disrupts all human relations and opens up an experience of an absolute, which is not communicable. The intensity of a passion seems to make love an embodiment of life itself, and, by the same token, an antagonist of death: "[Love] is the power of life and guaranties therefore its progression against death. This is why love 'overcomes' death."[43]

From this point of view, the loss of the world in love is by no means only a privative state, because it brings man's specific humaneness, "man as such," as it were, to the fore. In "consuming" the world, love unveils the human being behind the persona, which always is, at least in part, a mask: "If [love] seizes humans, it becomes the most 'humane' [quality] that humans have, namely a humaneness that exists worldless, objectless (the beloved one is never object), spaceless."[44] Love reveals the specifically human element in the universe, because it shows that humans are more than the world they create: "as *lovers*," she writes, "every human being is—in a unimaginably ironic way—also the *human being as such* [*der Mensch*]."[45]

But politically speaking, the experience of such an absolute is a form of death within the world, because there must not be any interfering of the "divine" within politics, that is, there must not be an absolute measure.[46] "In politics," Arendt wrote to James Baldwin in an unpublished letter, "love is a stranger. . . . Hatred and love belong together, and they are both destructive; you can afford them only in the private."[47] Time and again Arendt warned not to mix love with politics, because in the heat of passion "the world between us, the world of plurality and homeliness, goes up in flames."[48] In *The Human Condition* and in *On Revolution*, she emphasizes that introducing love into politics will inevitably change even the most authentic feeling into hypocrisy. The verses by William Blake: "Never seek to tell thy love,/love that never told can be" were for her a credo.[49] Love for the *world* (and not of *mankind*) can be the motif for political engagement, but it must neither be functionalized as a political argument nor regarded as the proper relation between people acting *in concert*. With these claims, Arendt does not want to debase private phenomena. She only fights against any mixing of the private with the public: "Whenever we have souls in politics, we are perverted. Whenever we are soulless in private life, we are perverted."[50]

Creativity and Tragedy

For a long time, we had little reason to question that "worldless passion" was Arendt's main, if not her only concept of love. But with the posthumous publication of her correspondence and, most notably, her *Denktagebuch*, the wall she raised between the private and the public realm has revealed some cracks. When we look closer, we find a more complex model of how love and the world relate to each other. Although she repeatedly refers to love as apolitical, insisting that love has no role to play in politics, there are other passages where the *positive* and creative interaction between love and the world comes to the fore.

Arendt makes it clear that the state of worldlessness described earlier cannot last. As a life in the absolute is impossible, because it creates its own relativity,[51] so too love without the world has no constancy: "the pure sounding of love urges one always back into communication, in which one shares something common with the other. The thou of the I becomes the other—if all goes well, the one closest to oneself."[52] From this perspective, there are only two possibilities for lovers: Either they try to conserve their passionate yet worldless symbiosis and live in eternal remembrance, or they return into the world. One possible way of returning is for Arendt "symbolized in the child," who at the same time separates and connects his parents. But the return to the world as the only "happy ending" of love is at the same time the end of love.[53] As the *Denktagebuch* testifies, Arendt did not only discover the kernel of human freedom in the phenomenon of birth, but also reflected on the symbolic meaning of the act of love that precedes it: The union of two people, by which a new person is created, is a double metamorphosis from duality to unity, and from unity to plurality: "It could be possible that mankind arises, because the two, having become one, ebbs away into plurality . . . but in a way that the principle of life (which is the pure vitality of two becoming one), must necessarily survive even within plurality for the sake of mankind's continuation."[54]

But if the loving unification of two people is the dynamic mediation between singularity and plurality, the separation between love and the world cannot be absolute. In 1953, Arendt notes in her *Denktagebuch*: "From the absolute world(=space)lessness of the lovers, a new world has its source, symbolized in the child. To this *new* in-between, the new space of a beginning world, the lovers belong from now on, and they are responsible for it. . . . Love *is* living without a world. As such, it proves to be world-creating; it creates, engenders a new world. Every love is the beginning of a new world; that is its greatness and its tragedy. Because in this new world in so far as it is not only new but also world, it perishes."[55]

I must admit that I am always struck by Arendt's claim that *every* love was the beginning of a new world. To my knowledge, the *Denktagebuch* is the only source where Arendt discusses the creative force of love at such length. Love might be "worldless," even world-destructive—but it is also "world-creating." And yet, passion does not survive the act of birth, which forces the lovers to act, no matter if the lovers literally have a baby or accept another challenge in the world. For Arendt, love, like pregnancy, seems to be a state of transition only, an ephemeral process, the sense of which seems to be nothing else than to create something new—as if love was "only necessary to make a beginning at all."[56]

Consequently, the relation between love and the world is not simply that of mutual exclusion or destruction—it is, first of all, a *dialectic* or a *tragic* relation. "Tragedy" must be understood here in the Hegelian sense: The conflict between love and the world is tragic, because both are equally justified and yet cannot coexist. One principle has to yield, but in its negation, it is still there; abolished, but also preserved and elevated.[57] Love creates a world as a result of which it perishes, but in sacrificing itself for the creation of a new world, love becomes immortal. As such, love is not simply a destructive force; it is a catalyst of togetherness and plurality in the *world*.

A World in Miniature

If I am right and the tragic relation between love and the world raises questions about the prejudice that Arendt did not assign much value to private love, it remains questionable how convincing her conception of the creative force of love is. Why should love perish with the return into the world; more important, why should it "be transformed into another mode of belonging together"? Until now, it seemed as if love and the world, although intimately connected, could not coexist. But love is not only the complementary side of the world. There is also another generative idea of love as a world in miniature that Arendt explores in some of her letters and other less "official" texts.

After the death of her husband, Heinrich Blücher, Arendt wrote to Heidegger: "Between two people, sometimes, how rarely, a world grows. It is then one's homeland; in any case it was the only homeland, we were willing to recognize. This tiny microworld where you can always save yourself from the world, disintegrates when the other has gone away."[58] This rare passage gives us a glimpse into how Arendt thought the relation between a *long-lasting* love and the world. Here, love is not a stranger in or an enemy to the world—it is "a" world, in addition to "the" world. But what is this little world—is it simply the oasis Arendt speaks of in *Introduction into Politics*, a refuge where one can hide from "the" world? Why does she call it a "world" at all?

In a *laudatio* for Karl Jaspers, Arendt described love as a space where the integrity of a person can endure in dark times:

> It was thanks to good fortune that Jaspers could be isolated in the course of his life, but could not be driven into solitude. That good fortune is based on a marriage, in which a woman who is his peer has stood at his side ever since his youth. If two people do not succumb to the illusion that the ties binding them have made them one, they can create a world anew between them. Certainly for Jaspers this marriage has never been merely a private thing. It has proved that two people of different origins—Jaspers' wife is Jewish—could create a world of their own. And from that world in miniature he has learned, as from a model, what happens or what could happen in the world.[59]

In this passage, Arendt abandons—as a tribute to Jaspers's notion of love or out of conviction—her strict distinction between public and private, *oikos* and *polis*, love and the world. Here, the space love creates is not ephemeral. Arendt contemplates togetherness as a form of playground providing the possibility of preparing *for* the world. But she makes it very clear that this kind of love can only occur under certain conditions—one of them being the renouncing of complete symbiosis. If two people are too close, there is no space between them for the world to appear, as it were.

Already in her earliest remark on love, which can be found in an unpublished letter to Erwin Loewenson, Arendt emphasized the importance of *equality* in love. A loving relationship demands, she writes in 1927, "that the phenomenon of serfdom which obliterates the one person and thus makes love impossible, does not appear."[60] Given a relationship of equals, love can overcome being only an ephemeral state or a protecting oasis, and transform itself into quite the reverse: At its best, love creates a space where two people can open up in complete frankness and interact with each other in a way that Jaspers beautifully called "a loving struggle." In this sense, love is neither passion nor a "life-giving source," but a space where one can exercise political virtue such as dialogue. Thus, the *laudatio* continues: "Within this small world [Jaspers] unfolded and practiced his incomparable faculty for dialogue . . . the constant readiness to give a candid account of himself . . . and above all the ability to lure what is otherwise passed over in silence into the area of discourse."[61]

While Arendt normally emphasized that lovers understand each other immediately and therefore talk *without* relating to objects, the relationship here is plural and thus worldly. Arendt followed Jaspers in considering debates as essential for personal relationships because arguments are the condition for recognizing someone as equal. Thus, the dignity of a friendship or a love does not depend on the unanimity with the alter ego but on a complete mutual trust, which can never occur in public. It may well be this trust that is expressed in the loving word as the absolute affirmation: *amo: volo ut sis.*

Volo ut sis: *Love as Unconditional Affirmation*

It is hardly an exaggeration to say that the phrase *amo: volo ut sis*—"I love you, I want you to be"—was Arendt's lifelong companion. Heidegger had sent her the words in a letter in May 1925, attributing them to Augustine.[62] While he understands the phrase as the will to the other's being, a will that lets the other be and thus transforms the other's existence, Arendt rejects the Augustinian idea of love in her dissertation as a form of domination or denial.[63] Later, however, in her *Denktagebuch*, she is more ambiguous about its meaning. In 1952, she notes that *volo ut sis* could be related to one's essence, the authentic being of someone, and as such would not be "love, but imperiousness, which, under the pretense of affirming, subjects the other's essence under the own will. But it can also mean: I want you to be—whatever you eventually will have been. That is to say, knowing, that no one is 'ante mortem' who he is, and trusting that it will have been just right in the end."[64] In contrast to her middle period, in which she characterizes love above all as worldless passion, Arendt comes eventually to discuss love in the context of willing and judging; in these texts, she discovers in love the supreme form of affirmation.

In 1969, she notes, "The highest form of recognition is love: *volo ut sis*."[65] In *The Life of the Mind*, too, Arendt repeatedly refers to love as the strongest and "unconditional acceptance."[66] "There is no greater assertion of something or somebody than to love it, that is, to say: I will that you be—*Amo: Volo ut sis*."[67] Love in this sense is the free choice of the other person comparable to the act of *willing*. It is the affirmation of the other who is loved for his own sake and not as an object of desire: "The willing ego, when it says in its highest manifestation, '*Amo: Volo ut sis*,' 'I love you; I want you to be'—and not 'I want to have you' or 'I want to rule you'—shows itself capable of the same love with which supposedly God loves men, whom he created only because He willed them to exist and whom He *loves without desiring them*."[68] In Arendt's understanding, "I want you to be" is not the will to the other person's future possibilities, her potential, but the affirmation of her present reality and givenness.

Although Arendt sometimes labels *volo ut sis* as a form of "recognition," the Hegelian overtones of this notion and its association with struggle are not what Arendt implies. In contrast to other forms of affirmation or appreciation, love is the pure gift of the lover to the beloved. Unlike for rights, for example, it would be absurd to fight for this gift. Therefore, love is the complementary side of other, less exclusive forms of recognition like law, respect and solidarity. In this regard, love itself is not political, but it becomes clear that the political or public sphere would be incomplete without the intimate realm. It is love's specific humaneness to show and value that every person is more than what she creates and accomplishes:

> The human being who has lost his place in a community, his political status in the struggle of his time, and the legal personality which makes his actions and part of his destiny a consistent whole, is left with those qualities which usually can become articulate only in the sphere of private life and must remain unqualified, mere existence in all matters of public concern. This mere existence, that is, all that which is mysteriously given us by birth and which includes the shape of our bodies and the talents of our minds, can be adequately dealt with only by the unpredictable hazards of friendship and sympathy, or by the great and incalculable grace of love, which says with Augustine, "Volo ut sis (I want you to be)," without being able to give any particular reason for such supreme and unsurpassable affirmation.[69]

What Arendt discusses here, in the chapter about the right to have rights in *Origins of Totalitarianism*, is that aspect of every person that cannot be recognized by the public, because it is not based on words and deeds, on achievement and excellence, but ultimately on something unspeakably individual and contingent. Love in this sense is not a divine power, it is a "confirmation of the sheer arbitrariness of being: We have not made ourselves, we stand in need of confirmation. We are strangers, we stand in need of being welcome. *I want you to be*."[70]

Fame and honor, the recognition of the public, can never be a substitute for this pure gift of love. It is this affirmation of the other that forms the basis for unreserved dialogue. In discourse, the world of politics enters the small world of the lovers, as the example of Jaspers shows. The world inhabited by the lovers is an object of their common care. Speaking seems to be that titration point in which the inwardness of thinking and feeling can become acting in the world. Thus, the world *en miniature* represents and relates to "the" world where the totality of mankind is assembled. Arendt therefore agrees with Lessing in considering personal relationships as the foundation for humaneness:[71] As discourse gives intimate relationships a political meaning, it introduces humaneness into politics, a humaneness that teaches to prefer people to principles. And from this point of view, love as affirmation would have an indirect influence on the political sphere.

Moreover, I claim that Arendt's *amor mundi* can only be adequately understood by taking into account her understanding of *volo ut sis*. When she talks about the love for the world, she is not referring to a passion, but to love understood as unconditional affirmation. With her conceptualization of love as affirmation, Arendt bases love and love for the world on a common conceptual ground. The concept they have in common is love as an engaged, but in the Kantian sense disinterested affirmation of the beloved, of his dignity and autonomy. The *amor mundi* is a "disinterested interest in the world,"[72] a lively engagement for the worldly *inter homines esse*, which is not based on self-interest. For "a true lover of this world"[73] politics are "sui generis,"[74] not a means to an end, but an end in itself.

Affirmation can be a stance towards the world as well as toward other people, and Arendt actually used the quote in both contexts alike. She did not only summarize the highest affirmation of other people, but also the fulfilled relation of men toward the world in these very words, as, among others, the manuscript for her seminar *Kant's Political Philosophy* proves, on the margins of which she wrote in capitals "AMO UT SIS"[75]: The "politically minded"[76] *dilectores mundi* do not only love the world, because it *is*, but because they *want* it to be, they love in order to create it.

By this concept of love, which is unrelated to passion, the concept of *amor mundi* is not only saved theoretically, but love for men and love for the world can also be combined practically. He, who experiences in private that the dignity and autonomy of the other is not only unimpeachable, but also does not diminish one's self-love, but on the contrary, nourishes it, may universalize this experience in forms of friendship, respect, solidarity or love for the world.

Conclusion

With Lessing, Arendt once said that she was not obliged to resolve the difficulties she raised. The following conclusion is my attempt to deal with these difficulties. I am quite sure that the implicit differentiation between several forms of love did not simply happen to Arendt. Arendt embraced contradictions and regarded them as characteristic of great thinking. She thought dialectically, in her very own way, not through a Hegelian dialectic but with a certain "vividness" of her concepts. Her notions are never carved in tablets of stone as it were, because they react to new events and experiences and they do always implicate a process.

I do not advocate here blurring distinctions Arendt made. We should take her warning to keep the private and the public sphere separately very seriously. But while we should not blur her distinctions, neither should we overestimate the importance of each and every one of her notions. Instead, we should keep the diversity of her concepts and the liveliness of her thinking. It is the variety of forms of love, which must not be given up in favor for a logical system, because it corresponds to the different modes of human existing. Arendt's response to the perils of love she diagnosed throughout her work (the world-fleeing *égoïsme à deux* or the metaphysical love for principles) can be found in the diversity of her concepts of love. It is the *plurality* of love that guarantees the mutual protection of the public and the intimate sphere. We need them both to turn a desert into a world.

NOTES

1. For Arendt's use of the epigraph, see *D* XXIII.12.609.

2. *D* IX.19.215; *D* XII.13.279. Unless stated otherwise, all translations are mine.

3. Arendt in an unpublished letter to Erwin Loewenson from October 27, 1927. Deutsches Literaturarchiv Marbach, Signature: A: Arendt 76.955/3.

4. *D* XIII.2.295. See Barbara Hahn, *Hannah Arendt. Leidenschaften, Menschen und Bücher* (Berlin: Berliner Taschenbuch Verlag, 2005), 51ff.

5. *D* XXI.35.529: "*Die Philosophie, die alles aus der Perspektive der 'contemplatio' sieht, hat sich weder um 'actio' noch um 'passio' gekümmert. Im modernen*

Zeitalter treten beide ins Zentrum des Denkens, nicht um ihrer eigenen Würde willen, sondern weil der Mensch auf sich zurückgeworfen, aus der gemeinsamen Welt herausgeschleudert ist. Aber da wird dann eben 'actio' als Herstellen und 'passio' im Sinne des Begehrens mißverstanden."

6. Dieter Thomä, "Verlorene Passion, wiedergefundene Passion. Arendts Anthropologie und Theorie des Subjekts," *Deutsche Zeitschrift für Philosophie* 55, no. 4 (2007): 627–647, here 630ff. Thomä's excellent essay about love in the *Denktagebuch* is an important source for my own analysis.

7. *D* IX.3.203: *"Menschen finden zueinander als Personen, weil sie einander bedürfen (Liebe)."*

8. *D* XII.26.289f.

9. *D* XIX.17.459.

10. *D* XIV.19.334.

11. *D* XI.1.250.

12. *D* XXI.31. 525.

13. Hannah Arendt, *The Human Condition* (Chicago: University of Chicago Press, 1998) 242.

14. Thomä, "Verlorene Passion, wiedergefundene Passion," 627; Véronique Albanel, *Amour du monde. Christianisme et politique chez Hannah Arendt* (Paris: Les Éditions du Cerf, 2010), 327, 403.

15. In this essay, I will not discuss the much-debated origin of the quotation, cf. Tatjana Noemi Tömmel, *Wille und Passion* (Frankfurt: Suhrkamp, 2013).

16. Arendt to Heidegger on April 22, 1928, in Hannah Arendt and Martin Heidegger, *Briefe 1925–1975*, ed. Ursula Ludz (Frankfurt: Klostermann, 2002), 65ff. I slightly modify Andrew Shield's translation; cf. Hannah Arendt and Martin Heidegger, *Letters 1925–1975*, ed. Ursula Ludz (Orlando, Fla.: Harcourt, 2004), 50.

17. Arendt and Heidegger, *Briefe*, 66. Rainer Maria Rilke's translation of the 43th Sonnet from the Portuguese by Elizabeth Barrett Browning differs from the original; he writes "*Und wenn Gott es gibt*" (And if God exists) while Barrett Browning writes "And if God choose."

18. *D* XVI.3.373: *"und zwar nicht, weil ich dann nicht mehr 'lebe' und darum vielleicht treu sein kann oder dergleichen, sondern unter der Voraussetzung, daß ich nach dem Tode weiterlebe und in ihm nur die Welt verloren habe."*

19. Hannah Arendt, History of Political Theory, lecture course at University of California, Berkeley 1955. The Hannah Arendt Papers at the Library of Congress. Subject File, 1949–1975, Signature: 024090.

20. Martin Heidegger, *Phänomenologische Interpretationen zu Aristoteles. Einführung in die phänomenologische Forschung. Gesamtausgabe* vol. 61 (Frankfurt: Klostermann, 1994), 138; Martin Heidegger, *Was ist das—die Philosophie? Vortrag vom 28. August 1955 in Cerisy-la-Salle/Normandie* (Pfullingen: Neske, 1963), 39.

21. *D* II.26.49.

22. *D* XVI.3.373.

23. Cf. *D* II.26.49; *D* III.6.59, *D* IV.2.83; *D* XVI.3.373.

24. *D* XVI.3.372.

25. *D* III.6.59: "*Leidenschaften degenerieren zu Gefühlen . . . weil wir das reine Ergriffensein von der Leidenschaft (das pathos) nicht aushalten und ihr ins Gefühl (unter dem Vorwand der Verinnerlichung) ausweichen.*"

26. *D* II.26.51: "*Zur Abgrenzung: Gefühle habe ich; die Liebe hat mich.*" See Martin Buber, *Ich und Du* (Leipzig: Insel Verlag, 1923), 22.

27. *D* XI.1.250: "*weder denken—nämlich rein tätig sein—noch lieben—nämlich rein leiden.*"

28. *D* XXI.31.525.

29. *D* XII.19.283.

30. Heidegger to Arendt on February 21, 1925, in: Arendt and Heidegger, *Briefe 1925–1975*, 13.

31. *D* II.26.51.

32. Ibid.

33. Hannah Arendt, *Rahel Varnhagen. Lebensgeschichte einer deutschen Jüdin aus der Romantik* (Munich: Piper Verlag, 1981), 73.

34. *D* II.26.49.

35. *D* II.26.50: "*ohne alle Garantien und treu nur in dem Nicht-vergessen des Ereigneten und Geschickten.*"

36. Ibid., 49.

37. *D* XVI.3.373: "*Wer nie diese Macht erlitt, lebt nicht, gehört nicht zum Lebendigen.*"

38. *D* VI.3.127: "*Liebe ist nicht blind und macht nicht blind; das Gegenteil ist eher wahr; aber Liebe verschreibt sich der Dunkelheit des Herzens, das auch ihr sich nur augenblicksweise erhellt und erleuchtet. . . . Das Wagnis der Liebe, ihre 'Blindheit', ist, daß sie mit dem Betrug nicht rechnet und nicht rechnen kann. Darum stimmt: 'Wer sich der Liebe ergibt, hält er sein Leben zu Rat?'*" The quote within the quote is from Goethe's Elegy "Amyntas" and could be translated as, "Who yields to love, does he spare his life?"

39. *D* XIX.25.464.

40. *D* XXVII.79.793.

41. *D* XXVI.33.729.

42. *D* XVIII.12.428.

43. *D* XVI.3.372: "*Sie ist die Macht des Lebens und garantiert seinen Fortgang gegen den Tod. Darum 'überwindet' die Liebe den Tod.*"

44. *D* XVI.3.373: "*Wenn sie Menschen ergreift, wird die Liebe allerdings zum 'Menschlichsten' der Menschen, nämlich zu einer Menschlichkeit, die welt-los, objekt-los (der Geliebte ist nie Objekt), raum-los besteht.*"

45. *D* IX.3.204: "*Und als Liebende, die als Eine die zwei brauchen, um sich von der Natur die Drei usw. schenken zu lassen, nämlich aus der Einzigkeit sofort in*"

die Mehrheit, aus dem Singular in den Plural müssen, [sind die Menschen,] ist jeder Mensch—auf eine nicht auszudenkende ironische Weise—auch der Mensch."

46. *D* XII.12.276.

47. Hannah Arendt, "The Meaning of Love in Politics: A Letter to James Baldwin, November 21st, 1962." HannahArendt.net, Journal for Political Thinking, www.hannaharendt.net/index.php/han/article/view/95/156 (last accessed June 15, 2015).

48. *D* XIX.39.470. See the German edition of *The Human Condition*: Hannah Arendt, *Vita activa oder vom tätigen Leben* (Munich: Piper Verlag, 2007), 309, where the image of the destroying powers of love seems more drastic.

49. Hannah Arendt, *Responsibility and Judgment* (New York: Schocken Books, 2003), 9ff.

50. Arendt, Contemporary Issues, Seminar University of California, Berkeley 1955. The Hannah Arendt Papers at the Library of Congress. Subject File, 1949–1975, Signature 024160.

51. *D* XXVI.33.729.

52. *D* IX.19.215: *"drängt das reine Ertönen der Liebe immer wieder in die Mit-teilung, in der man mit dem Anderen ein Gemeinsames teilt. Aus dem Du des Ich wird der Andere—wenn es gut geht, der Nächste."*

53. Arendt, *The Human Condition*, 242.

54. *D* III.8.61: *"Es könnte sein, dass das Menschengeschlecht dadurch entsteht, dass die Eins gewordene Zwei in die Pluralität . . . abebbt, aber so, dass das Prinzip des Lebens: das die reine Lebendigkeit des Eins-werdens von Zwei ist, zur Fortdauer des Menschengeschlechts notwendig auch in der Pluralität erhalten bleiben muss."*

55. *D* XVI.372ff: *"Aus der absoluten Welt(=Raum)losigkeit der Liebenden entspringt die neue Welt, symbolisiert im Kinde. In dies neue Zwischen, den neuen Raum einer beginnenden Welt, gehören nun die Liebenden und für ihn sind sie verantwortlich. . . . Als solche zeigt sie sich als welt-schöpferisch; sie erschafft, erzeugt eine neue Welt. Jede Liebe ist der Anfang einer neuen Welt; das ist ihre Größe und ihre Tragik. Denn in dieser neuen Welt, soforn sie nicht nur neu, sondern eben auch Welt ist, geht sie zugrunde."*

56. *D* XII.13.279: *"als sei sie nur notwenig gewesen, damit überhaupt ein Anfang gemacht werde."*

57. G.W.F. Hegel, *Vorlesungen über die Ästhetik III. Werke*, vol. 15, ed. Eva Moldenhauer and Karl Markus Michel (Frankfurt: Suhrkamp, 1986), 523ff.

58. Arendt to Heidegger, November 27, 1970, in *Briefe 1925–1975*, 206.

59. Hannah Arendt, "Karl Jaspers: A Laudatio," *Men in Dark Times* (Orlando, Fla.: Harcourt, 1983), 78. I changed the translation in the last phrase to be closer to the original.

60. Hannah Arendt to Erwin Loewenson, letter from January 23, 1928, Deutsches Literaturarchiv Marbach, Signature: A: Arendt 76.956/2: *"Dazu*

gehört allerdings gerade, daß das Phänomen der Hörigkeit, die die Person des Einen auslöscht und damit Liebe gerade unmöglich macht, nicht eintritt."

61. Arendt, "Karl Jaspers: A Laudatio," 78.

62. Heidegger to Arendt, May 13, 1925, in *Briefe*, 31.

63. Hannah Arendt, *Der Liebesbegriff bei Augustin. Versuch einer philosophischen Interpretation*, ed. *Frauke Annegret Kurbacher* (Hildesheim: Olms, 2006), 71. See, for Heidegger's interpretation, my book *Wille und Passion*.

64. *D* XII.12.276ff: "*Liebe, sondern Herrschsucht, die unter dem Vorwand zu bestätigen selbst noch das Wesen des Anderen zum Objekt des eigenen Willens macht. Es kann aber auch heißen: Ich will, daß Du seist—wie immer Du auch schließlich gewesen sein wirst. Nämlich wissend, daß niemand 'ante mortem' ist, der er ist, und vertrauend, daß es gerade am Ende recht gewesen sein wird.*"

65. *D* XXVI.69.748.

66. Hannah Arendt, *The Life of the Mind* (Orlando, Fla.: Harcourt, 1981), 2:144.

67. Ibid., 104.

68. Ibid., 136.

69. Arendt, *The Origins of Totalitarianism* (Orlando, Fla.: Harcourt, 1985), 301.

70. Hannah Arendt, Kant's Political Philosophy, Seminar at the University of Chicago, Chicago 1964, The Hannah Arendt Papers at the Library of Congress, Subject File, 1949–1975, Signature: 032288.

71. Hannah Arendt, "On Humanity in Dark Times: Thoughts about Lessing," in *Men in Dark Times*, 3–31.

72. *D* XXII.30. 577: "*interesseloses Weltinteresse.*"

73. Arendt, History of Political Theory, Signature: 024019.

74. Ibid., Signature: 024025.

75. Arendt, Kant's Political Philosophy, Signature: 032295.

76. Hannah Arendt, Introduction to Politics. Lecture course at University of Chicago, Chicago 1963. The Hannah Arendt Papers at the Library of Congress. Subject File, 1949–1975, Signature: 023805.

CHAPTER 7

America as Exemplar:
The *Denktagebuch* of 1951

Tracy B. Strong

The highest laws of the land (America) are not only the constitution
and constitutional laws, but also contracts.

—HANNAH ARENDT, *D* VI.11.131

Arriving in America in 1941 as a European and a refugee, Hannah Arendt
could not but look upon the new country as an outsider. As with other
outsiders from Tocqueville on, she was struck by the difference between
America and the European countries with which she was familiar. In particular, as she wrote to Karl Jaspers, America did not seem to be a *nation-
state* of the kind that was prevalent in Europe. There the state was
understood as the "monopoly of the legitimate means of violence over a
given territory," as Max Weber famously wrote.[1] What was the import of
the differences?

Arendt became an American citizen in 1950. Her scholarly attention
had focused first on making sense of what had happened to her—to the
experience of National Socialism and related contemporary political
developments. Having published *The Origins of Totalitarianism* in 1951, she
now centered her attention on the contrasting environment around her. It
was becoming *her* environment. She starts a sequence of entries in her
Denktagebuch for September 1951 by referring to America as "the politically new"—these are the thoughts that will eventually result in her argument in the 1963 book *On Revolution*.[2]

Her analysis in that book has often been criticized from a historical point of view, especially since she refers to the Constitution as being the first to be established "without force, without ruling (*archein*) and being ruled (*archesthai*)."[3] Whatever the validity of these criticisms, they strike me as missing an essential point of her concerns. Arendt is trying to work out what she a few pages later calls "the central question of the coming [*künftigen*] politics," a problem she sees as lodged in "the problem of the giving of laws" (*D* VI.18.141). Her aim is to describe a political (i.e., humanly appropriate) system that would not rest upon will, and in particular on the will of the sovereign. "That I must have power [*Macht*] to be able to will, makes the problem of power into the central political fact of all politics that are grounded on sovereignty—all, that is, with the exception of the American." I shall return to the question of sovereignty toward the end of this essay.

Her concern in these pages (130–143) centers on what a human society would be that was truly political. Her understanding of what America could or did represent is her entry into this question, for she will argue that it is from the particular American revolutionary experience that one can construct a picture of a truly human political realm. Writing about what is contained in what humans do is not the same thing as writing history—in particular since the actors in question may have only partial understandings of what they are doing. While her work draws upon historical activity, she is precisely not writing history.

What is striking about her discussion in the intervening (and other) pages is that she approaches the question of America explicitly through the lens of *European* philosophy. The point is not to Europeanize America; it is to see if America does not in some manner constitute a potential instantiation of what in Europe had been thought by some over the nineteenth and twentieth centuries. Thus, she is attempting an answer to the question of "can we determine the particular excellence of the American polity by viewing it through the lenses of European thought?"

The range of European thinkers she now invokes is important. She first mentions Marx and then Nietzsche, each of whom she sees as part of, and as makers of, the "end of Western philosophy." Marx is held to have inverted Hegel, Nietzsche to have done the same for Plato. The point of her analysis of Marx and Nietzsche is to assert that they released thought from its bond to the "Absolute." And in the present world, that is a good thing, too; to hold to the idea of an Absolute is to "make possible in the present unjust and bestial behavior" (*D* VI.12.133). As we know, this will be an ever-returning theme in her work. In 1953, she can write: "The bankruptcy of Western political philosophy reduced to the simplest formulation: the re-realizing [*Um-willen*] of the political life collapses with Marx (or with secularization)" (*D* XV.17.357). She expects to find in America the elements of a political that does not rest on an "absolute." America thus provides for her—or can provide for her—an example of what an understanding of politics that does not rest upon any kind of absolute would look like. America provides, as it were, a case study for how to think about the political "without a banister."[4]

To whom might one look to find this vision of a nonabsolute political? For Arendt, Nietzsche provides the opening to an answer. We are to look, however, not to his doctrine of the revaluation of values but to his discussion of promising in the second essay of the *Genealogy of Morals*. She quotes: "To breed an animal with the right to make promises—is that not . . . the real problem of humans?" For Arendt, the foundation of a new "morality" lies in the right to make a promise; the promise makes possible human relations based on contract. And the grounding on contract, as she writes in the *Denktagebuch* (*D* VI.11.131), was for her the particular excellence of the American polity.

When she expanded these thoughts in *On Revolution*, she referred the ability (and the right) to covenant to the power that the settlers had as human beings. Those on the *Mayflower* and later the *Arabella* must have had some apprehension about the world to which they were coming—it was for them the state of nature and clearly outside of what they knew civilization to be. While they of course knew that there was a native population, their sense was that it was relatively small and not organized into substantial settlements. Their feeling was not without some basis in fact; the diseases and weapons that Europeans had brought from 1492 on had reduced the indigenous population by a factor of almost ten.[5] The arriving settlers, unaware and/or unmindful of the holocaust of the previous one hundred and thirty years, could think they were coming to a more or less empty land, as the great cities and trading empires of the pre- and immediately post-Columbian period had vanished.[6] In his 1651 *Leviathan*, Hobbes would thus remark that European settlers in the New World "are not to exterminate those they find there but constrain them to inhabit closer together, and not range a great deal of ground to snatch what they find," thereby showing his sense that there were not too many of "those they find there" and that they were not politically organized.[7] Thus, Arendt writes about the state of mind of the newly arriving Puritans:

> This fear is not surprising. . . . The really astounding fact in the
> whole story is that their obvious fear . . . was accompanied by the no

less obvious confidence they had in their own power, granted and confirmed by no one and as yet unsupported by any means of violence, to combine themselves together into a "civil Body Politick" which, held together solely by the strength of mutual promise "in the Presence of God and one another," supposedly was powerful enough to "enact, constitute and frame" all necessary laws and instruments of government.[8]

As Locke was later to remark, "That, which begins and actually constitutes any political society, is nothing but the consent of any number of freemen . . . to unite and incorporate into such society. And this is that, and that only, which did, or could give beginning to any lawful government in the world."[9]

On Revolution is thus not precisely about "revolution" as that term has come to be understood. There are, as her book makes clear, *two* sorts of events that are called "revolution" and we would do well to keep them separate. The first, and today standard, derives from the French Revolution: the violent overthrow of an existing sovereign and its replacement by another sovereign power. In this, as de Tocqueville would point out, a "revolution" retained some of the much earlier sense of revolution as of a circular motion.[10] The second, and America is her model for this, sees revolution as the institution of a *novus ordo seclorum*—it is a change in how human live with each other.[11] The America Revolution was not to gain freedom *from* oppression so much as it was to gain freedom *for* those who made it. [12] Because of this, accusations that Arendt's history is bad (the Revolution *was* violent; it maintained slavery; suffrage was less than universal, etc.) are beside her point. The question will and must be if the country has realized the freedom for which it made itself.[13]

What are the components of this freedom? Arendt notes that there are two elements to this contracting or covenanting. The first is undertaken "in the Presence of God"—that is as an individual beholden to him or herself alone before God. The second is taken "in the presence of others" and is "in principle independent of religious sanction." In the passage from Nietzsche that she cites, the "presence of God" element is replaced by the breeding to the "right" to make promises. As Arendt is not in any conventional sense religious, she must call upon Nietzsche to instantiate the two elements of promising. The centrality of "others" means that our concerns in political philosophy derive, in a phrase to which she will repeatedly return, from the "fact that not man but men inhabit the earth and form a world between them."[14]

What is the implication of Arendt's claim that contract (or "covenant" or "compact") is the "highest law" and the particular excellence of America? What is involved in this notion of contract? Note that Nietzsche thinks that having the right to make promises is not something that all humans have, as it were simply by fact of existing—it has to be "bred." One answer is revealed by the end of her extended quotation of Nietzsche's *On the Genealogy of Morals*, where he indicates that the person who has the right to make promises can "answer for the future as himself."

I wish first to explore here what Nietzsche means by this phrase and then to compare it with the use that Arendt makes of it. The movement of his text in the first three sections of the second essay in *On the Genealogy of Morals* is a preliminary key.[15] In each of them, Nietzsche describes the possibility of a particular way of being-in-the-world (the right to make promises, the sovereign individual, the acquisition of conscience) and then circles back to give an account of the genealogy of that quality. Thus the right to make promises requires first the development of the concept of calculability, regularity, and necessity.[16] The sovereign individual requires the development of a memory—the acquisition of a temporal dimension to the self. Each of these qualities is what Nietzsche calls a "late" or "ripest" fruit, the coming into being of which, therefore, has *required* ripening.

Nietzsche is quite clear that the earlier developments are the *means to making possible* a "sovereign individual." He refers to this as a "preparatory task" and includes in it what he calls human "prehistory." What is key here is the understanding of history: The past has made possible the present, but has not necessarily monotonically determined it. The resources for a variety of different presents are all in the past, if we can deconstruct the past we have received and reassemble it. The sovereign individual will thus be in some sense a new beginning.

What quality does the sovereign individual—whom I take here to be an individual who has earned the right and capacity to say what he or she is— have? Nietzsche details a number of qualities in *On the Genealogy of Morals* II, §2, all of which sound like or are intended to sound like the *megalopsuchos* of Aristotle.[17] Yet there is a difference between Nietzsche's sovereign individual and the great soul in Aristotle, for the sovereign individual is the result of an *achievement*, a process by which a consciousness has become instinct.[18] What is important here is the insistence that Nietzsche places on the "*right* to make promises."[19]

We are thus dealing with the question of performatives—of which promising is the standard example. To say "I promise" is actually to promise, thus to change one's standing in the world. Likewise, to say "I do" in certain circumstances is to move from being an unmarried person to a married one. This new status must then be "pronounced" by an appropriate institutional representative.

Yet what Nietzsche has done is to make the matter much deeper in two manners. First is the question of having the "right" to make promises. Standard accounts of weakness of will hold that a person who does not keep a promise is incontinent, *ceteris paribus*. They assume that there is no question of one's *right* to make a promise. When Nietzsche asks as to the *right* to make a promise, it is as if the expectation is that I will *not* be able to enact my words, that is, that I will act weakly because I am not fully myself.

In these matters, the important consequence is that for Nietzsche rationality is of no ultimate avail. His point is not so much to oppose rationality as to point out that *rationality is not why we keep promises*. While it may be rational to keep promises, it is not in the nature of promises to be kept *because* one has a reason to do so—I do not need a reason to keep my promise. If you ask, "Why should I keep my promise?" you will find that sooner or later reasons come to an end. If you ask why, you do not know what a promise is.[20] Nietzsche says that promising requires that I have "mastery over circumstances, over nature, and over all more short-willed and unreliable creatures."[21] Those who have the right to promise are like "sovereigns," because they can maintain their promise in the face of accidents, even in the "face of fate." To have the right to a promise is to have taken upon oneself, as oneself, all the circumstances present and future in which the promise may occur. It is to maintain that promise—the requirement that the present extend into the future—no matter what befalls. Thus when Kaufmann translates the key passage, "*für sich als Zukunft gut sagen zu können*," as "able to stand security for his *own* future,"[22] one may pass by Nietzsche's point, which is that one should be able to "to be able to vouch for oneself *as a* future." One must earn entitlement to one's "own."

What this means is that a person who has the right to make promises does not regard his action as a choice between alternatives but as a manifestation of what she or he is, as something she or he *must* do, where there is no gap possible between intention and action.[23] A promise is a declaration of what I am, of that for which I hold myself responsible; because it is not a choice, there is no possibility of what gets called weakness of will. As Stanley Cavell says, "You choose your life. This is the way an action Categorically Imperative feels. And though there is not The Categorical Imperative, there are actions that are for us categorically imperative so far as we have a will."[24]

In this, and despite obvious echoes, Nietzsche's categorical imperative is not identical to Kant's. In the *Grundlegung zur Metaphysik der Sitten* and elsewhere, Kant argues that one cannot break a promise because to do so would in effect deny the point of the entire institution of promising. Kant took this position with its very strong denial of the relevance of goal, because, as he argued, any breaking of a promise or uttering of a lie for contingent reasons (say, as with Sartre, you were being asked by the Gestapo the location of the partisan they were seeking) would mean that you claimed to know precisely what the consequences of your action would be. Since such a claim was epistemologically impossible, it followed that one must be bound by the only certainty one might have, that of one's non–temporally limited reason.

Kant's reason for keeping a promise or not telling a lie was consequent to the interplay of a fixed and actually rational self and an incompletely graspable world. The difference in Nietzsche's analysis of the right to keep promises comes in his insistence that not only is the external world not fixed, but neither is the self. The self is not given for Nietzsche: it is rather the effect of actions undertaken and thus is motile. The self endures for him only as what it has the power to be responsible to. Hence, the binding of the self to a promise can only be rightfully accomplished by a power "over oneself and over fate" and must penetrate below the level of assessment—where it remained with Kant—to become part of the assessor himself or herself, of what Nietzsche calls "*das Unbewusste.*" This means that for me to have the right to it, a promise must be part of what I am. In this sense, it is part of one's present and not one's past.[25] Nietzsche's categorical imperative builds on the actions of those who can be "sovereign individuals"; Kant's "autonomous individual" is a cousin but is built *in terms of* the categorical imperative.

Nietzsche is also clear—now contra Kant and post-Kantians from Rawls to Habermas—that the self that is so committed is committed also to all the pain and all the reversals that will and may occur—pains that can be seen in his exploration of what he calls mnemotechnics. In this, the sovereign individual in Nietzsche will find (as we shall shortly see does Arendt) an instantiation in Weber's person who has the vocation for politics and who can remain true to his vocation, "in spite of all."[26] (I might note here that the insistence on the necessity of the pain and cruelty of existence was already central to the argument in the *Birth of Tragedy*.) Pain and cruelty are endemic to the possibility of life—they are part of what make the sovereign individual possible.

I have spent time laying out my understanding of this part of Nietzsche's phrase because I think that Arendt shares most all of it, in particular the focus on action as opposed to reason. She adds, however, one other important dimension. The people so constituted promise *to each other*—contract, covenant—and in doing so they bring a political space into existence. There is little or nothing of the "to each other" in Nietzsche—his sense of the polis will be consequent rather to a kind of ecstatic spectatorship of the sort that he describes in the eighth section of *The Birth of Tragedy*.[27]

In Arendt's gloss, this means that if in making a contract (which is what a promise is) one pledges to an other that one will remain true to oneself as the person making the contract, then one has made one's own being the foundation for a political space. The question is if one is able to make and hold to such a pledge. Such a grounding or foundation would not be based either on will or on any external absolute. Importantly, this means that for Arendt, much as it had been for Lincoln in the Gettysburg Address, the most important American political document is not the Constitution but the Declaration of Independence. The truths that are "held" to be "self-evident" are grounded on nothing other than that they are held. That they are thus held is a matter, as the signers of the Declaration made clear, made actual by the act in which the signers "mutually pledge *to each other* our Lives, our Fortunes and our sacred Honor" [my italics]. Here—perhaps not a surprise—is the opening for an interesting comparison of Arendt's arguments in *On Revolution* to those of Jacques Derrida in his "Declarations of Independence" where he relates this to the act of signing one's name. There is an immediate difference, however: Derrida writes: "The signature invents the signer."[28] For Derrida writing has precedence over speech. Not so for Arendt.

The second way in which this Nietzschean approach deepens the issue of promising and performatives is this. In Arendt's reading, the American Revolution is not precisely just a performative; more accurately it is what I, working from Nietzsche, have elsewhere called a "hyper-performative."[29] It not only brings something into existence (like being married), but it also seeks to bring a new institutional structure into existence (like the institution of marriage). As noted, when performed in a particular institutional context, a performative is an act that brings something about—as when the appointed person breaks a bottle of champagne at the launch of a ship and says (presumably in Dutch): "I christen thee '*Nieuw Amsterdam*.'" Arendt's analysis of the American Revolution adds a dimension: The Revolution was (and is) an attempt to bring about a new order that in turn will/ should inscribe itself into institutions, as no appropriate institutional context preexisted. It is a founding.[30]

As Jacques Derrida remarks, such an act, what I am calling, although he does not, a "hyper-performative," brings something new into the world and the new, as we know, was for Arendt the touchstone of human action. Such activity takes place on what one might call a horizontal level—it is with others like you and not in relation to a preexisting structure of authority. It is a moment of fraternity—and perhaps of sorority.[31]

And the question will also arise: How and by what means, if any, might this endure and become institutionalized? Temporally speaking, this means that what one did in the past will be transfigured as the reality of the present will annihilate all that was past to it. This matter is complex: Our political present will thereby be tied to the historical, although not, she notes, in a *"weltgeschichtliche"* (world-historical, i.e., transcendental) manner. How might it then be tied? Here Arendt was fond of quoting the French poet René Char: *"Notre passé n'est précédé d'aucun testament*—No will and testament give rise to that which is our past."[32] So what is our relation to that which we have done? This is not a trivial question: if the promise of the American Revolution was that of a new order under the sun, what is to be done about slavery? As Stanley Cavell remarks in a sentence that glosses Thoreau and echoes Arendt: "It was not a war of independence that was won, because we are not free."[33]

Arendt was, I think, aware of these questions. To make the implications of this problem clearer, she immediately turns to a consideration of Max Weber's distinction between the "ethic of responsibility" (which she holds to be the foundation of the pragmatism and genius of American politics) as opposed to his "ethic of conviction," which, she says, allows us to believe and hold to anything since we cannot know "until the day of the Last Judgment" if our conviction be correct. The implication here is that if we base our polity on the conviction of the supposed correctness of our moral judgments (as opposed to our ability to be responsible to ourselves) we will be able to justify anything, as the validation for our claim can be infinitely postponed. (One has but to look at the claims made about bringing democracy to Iraq.) Indeed, Arendt sees "central question of our time" to be a change in our ability to make valid moral judgments, that is to judgments the correctness of which is not postponed indefinitely (*D* VI. 17.138). She writes: "The legitimate distrust of all moralizing [i.e., her distrust] does not arise so much for a distrust of the standards of good and evil (*Böse*), as it does from the distrust of the human capacity for moral judgment, for the judging of our affairs from the point of view of morality (*Moral*). Those who have an ethic of responsibility and those who are pragmatic do not interest themselves in motive, and those who are of the ethic of conviction cannot know them" (*D* VI.17.138).

This is, she says, a dilemma. How is one to make judgments? She now turns to an examination of "three ways out" from this dilemma, paths she identifies with Kant, Hegel and Nietzsche. In Kant, she looks to his elaboration of the categorical imperative as that which is "splendid" in his solution. As we saw in the contrast of the understanding of a/the Categorical Imperative in Nietzsche and Kant, the problem with Kant's solution comes from the fact that with it, "humans are not of any world, but rather dwell in a future" world (*D* VI.17.138). Hegel, she continues, takes over from Kant "the discrepancy between willing and accomplishment" but the result is that in the end "not even God Himself can judge" (*D* VI.17.139). She continues: "When all being is in truth becoming, that all action is a happening in truth (*alles Handeln* [*ist*] *in Wahrheit Geschehen*). It was not Nietzsche but Hegel who abolished morality." She reads Nietzsche here as "following Hegel and ignoring Kant." (*D* VI.17.139) but sees him as replacing the Hegelian unfolding of the spirit with the *"circulus vitiosus deus"* that is, eternal recurrence. A great spectacle without a spectator thus replaces history. After she has worked her way through these partial rejections of the manners in which Hegel, Nietzsche, and the Kant of the *Critique of Practical Reason* respond to this main question, she briefly mentions the *Critique of the Power of Judgment*. That thought is not developed at this time in the *Denktagebuch*, but it will concern her for the rest of her life. She will later argue that Kant's main contribution to *political* (as opposed to moral) philosophy comes in the Third Critique, in particular in the notion of reflective judgment.[34]

If the central problem of politics-to-come is that of the giving of laws (*Gesetzgebung*—legislation), the answer that has been given by the national state (i.e., the European answer) is that the sovereign gives laws and the sovereign is whoever has the power to will. The will to will—she instantiates Heidegger here (*D* VI.18.141)—is the will to power. Interestingly, this is an argument found in Heidegger's Nietzsche lectures, lectures that were not published until 1961—she could not have attended them when they were given in 1936–38. Did Heidegger already speak of this during the time she was around him, or, more likely after they met again after the war?[35] So already here, she identifies the central problem of modern politics as that of the supposed necessity of sovereignty.[36] As Arendt says later: "If men wish to be free, it is precisely sovereignty they must renounce."[37] In *On Revolution*, she notes that "perhaps the greatest American innovation in politics as such was the consistent abolition of sovereignty within the body politic of the republic, the insight that in the realm of human affairs sovereignty and tyranny are the same."[38] Freedom, she will argue, is an accessory not of the will but of doing and acting.[39]

What is striking in these passages is how her approach from European philosophy brings out the importance of what is new in the American experiment. These were concerns that she brought with her from Europe; they will continue to occupy her for the rest of her life and are given concrete form by the American experience. Such was always the promise of America. As Hamilton wrote in the first of the *Federalist Papers*:

> It has been frequently remarked that it seems to have been reserved to the people of this country, by their conduct and example, to decide the important question, whether societies of men are really capable or not of establishing good government from reflection and choice, or whether they are forever destined to depend for their political constitutions on accident and force. If there be any truth in the remark, the crisis at which we are arrived may with propriety be regarded as the era in which that decision is to be made; and a wrong election of the part we shall act may, in this view, deserve to be considered as the general misfortune of mankind.

This passage tends to get passed over. It is, however, of central importance as revealing what kind of account (at least some) Americans gave to themselves as to the nature and import of their founding. Here we have Hamilton invoking a particular historical mission for the new United States. His claim is much like that Heidegger in his supposedly notorious *Rektoratsrede* (a text of which Arendt would certain have been aware) where Heidegger suggests that what happens in his particular country is tied to (what Heidegger was to call) the "spiritual strength of the West."[40] Note that Hamilton's "the people of this nation" is precisely what is meant by *Volk*. Such concerns have been those of the American land even "before it was ours"—this from a line in a poem by Robert Frost.[41] One already found much the same sense at the end of "A Modell of Christian Charitie," the sermon that John Winthrop preached on board the Arabella to the settlers arriving in New England in 1630. Winthrop ended by saying that his company—soon to sign a covenant—was undertaking the following:

> We shall find that the God of Israel is among us, when ten of us shall be able to resist a thousand of our enemies; when He shall make us a praise and glory that men shall say of succeeding plantations, "may the Lord make it like that of New England." For we must consider that we shall be as a city upon a hill. The eyes of all people are upon us. *So that if we shall deal falsely with our God in this work we have undertaken, and so*

cause Him to withdraw His present help from us, we shall be made a story and a by-word through the world. We shall open the mouths of enemies to speak evil of the ways of God, and all professors for God's sake. We shall shame the faces of many of God's worthy servants, and cause their prayers to be turned into curses upon us till we be consumed out of the good land whither we are going.

. . . we are commanded this day to love the Lord our God, and to love one another, to walk in his ways and to keep his Commandments and his ordinance and his laws, and the articles of our Covenant with Him, that we may live and be multiplied, and that the Lord our God may bless us in the land whither we go to possess it. *But if our hearts shall turn away, so that we will not obey, but shall be seduced, and worship other Gods, our pleasure and profits, and serve them; it is propounded unto us this day, we shall surely perish out of the good land whither we pass over this vast sea to possess it.*[42]

What is striking in both Hamilton and Winthrop is the sense that the founding of this new order presents possibilities of extraordinary greatness and the possibility of extraordinary failure—and that the costs of failure will be the loss of a human political possibility. Some nations, for Hamilton, Winthrop, and Arendt, can come into existence with a destiny (what Heidegger called *Geschick*), and they are aware of their *Geschick* when they acknowledge the fate that is that of their nation-in-becoming (Hamilton's what is "reserved to the people of this country").[43]

The particular *Geschick* of America was for Arendt to have attempted a political realm that did not rest on sovereignty. She is struck by the fact that for at least some moments during the American, French, and Russian revolutions hierarchical structures of authority collapsed and that those making the revolution spontaneously organized themselves into which she calls "councils." Such spaces are formed by and can only be formed by those have the qualities that she describes above in her discussion of Nietzsche and promises. As with the seventeenth-century understanding of the basis of a political space that preceded any relation to central authority, these are formed on the basis of a "mutual contract by which people bind themselves together in order to form a community . . . based on reciprocity and equality."[44] The difficulty, as she points out, is twofold. First, such qualities are by their very nature contingent and potentially transitory. Second, while those covenants gave power to those revolting, they did not in and of themselves generate the kinds of structures through which people might continue actually to exercise power. Instead, they tended to be more or less quickly "crushed by the central and centralized government, not because they actually menaced it but because they were indeed, by virtue of their existence, competitors for public power."[45]

Revolutions are therefore in general quickly followed by the reestablishment of a sovereign authority—an authority made attractive because it insures security, is predictable, and has clear limitations. Hobbes was the first to understand this: He applauded the move and argued that, in their hearts, each person desired the assurances of predictability and security and that they would and should thus be willing to tolerate the limited but absolute authority of a Sovereign.[46] In such a view, the "rights" of an individual are conceived of not as integral to his or her political life but as the realm into which political authority may not venture. They are, as Ronald Dworkin argued, "trumps." Arendt's concern with men rather than with *man* means that she has little interest politically in the "rights of man." For her, in a liberal Hobbesian-Dworkinian view the possibility of political action on the part of most citizens is severally and seriously restricted and to a considerable degree made irrelevant. Modern political science has unthinkingly legitimated this development with concepts such as that of "retrospective voting" in which it is held that people do not vote so much as to support a plan of action but to pass a judgment on what the sovereign power has done since the last election.[47] About the only theorist to try to develop an understanding of popular effective power is the concept of plebiscitarian *Führerdemokratie* by Max Weber, a concept that until recently has languished under the associations with the subsequent implications of "*Führer*."[48]

Against this, Arendt suggests that the naturally emerging councils can or might organize themselves into federal hierarchies based on different spaces. "The common object was the foundation of a new body politic, a new type of republican government which would rest on 'elementary republics' in such a way that its own central power did not deprive the constituent bodies of their original power to constitute."[49] The councils are not political parties: "Councils are organs of action, the revolutionary parties were organs of representation."[50] Therefore what councils cannot and should not do, however, is to occupy themselves with what she calls "the management of things," with, that is, "social and economic claims."[51] These considerations in 1963 thus call upon the more theoretical analysis she had developed in her 1958 *The Human Condition*. Failure to keep the world of action separate from the world of work dooms the political.

America, as Arendt analyzes it, gives her an historical example of how authentically political space might come into being and of how it, for at least at some times, has. It is, for her, exemplary. In *Schopenhauer as Educa-*

tor, Nietzsche refers to Schopenhauer as having been an *Exemplar* for him. (One might note here that the standard translation of this word as "specimen" gives an entirely different tone to Nietzsche's point—and a wrong one.)[52] An exemplar is that which serves to call one to something that is one's own but which one is not as yet. If one is enjoined to "become what you are," in the words that Nietzsche takes from Pindar's *Second Pythian* ode, then the exemplar is that which calls one out—it is provocation rather than instruction, as Emerson put it. America was, in Arendt's reading, an exemplar of what the political could be.

But the country itself did not, and does not, always live up to itself. It is important to realize that Arendt was not ever blind to the dangers to political freedom in this country. Nor, for the reasons given above, does she romanticize the American condition. In 1953, at the height of McCarthyism, she can write to Jaspers as to "how far the disintegration has gone and with what breathtaking speed it has occurred. And up to now hardly any resistance." She continues by noting that much of the persecution has come from "ex-Communists, who have brought totalitarian methods into the thing."[53] She will have similar words again and again, notably in response to the Vietnam War and reaction to the release of the Pentagon Papers. And in our present day we may still wonder if at some point what Winthrop called a "wrong election" have not been repeatedly made. Stanley Cavell made the point:

> Since America had a birth, it may die. . . . It has gone on for a long time, it is maddened now, the love it has had it has squandered too often, its young no longer naturally feel it; its past is in its streets, ungrateful for the fact that a hundred years ago it tore itself apart in order not to be divided. . . . *Union* is what it wanted. And it has never felt that union has been achieved. Hence its terror of dissent, which does not threaten its power but its integrity. So it is killing itself and killing another country in order not to admit its helplessness in the face of suffering, in order not to acknowledge its separateness.[54]

Cavell wrote these lines during the time of the war in Vietnam. Arendt said much the same about the same war and about the release of the Pentagon Papers. It breaks one's heart to recognize that the same can be said today about the American role in Iraq and Afghanistan.

NOTES

1. Max Weber, "Politics as a Vocation," in *The Vocation Lectures*, ed. David Owen and Tracy Strong (Cambridge: Hackett, 2004), 22.

2. *Denktagebuch* I.130–143; Hannah Arendt, *On Revolution* (New York: Viking, 1963).

3. See, for instance, E. M. Hobsbawm's critique of *On Revolution* in his *Revolutionaries: Contemporary Essays* (London: New Press, 1973), 201–208. Left-wing readers accused her of downplaying the socialist intentions of the councils. See Bill Lomax, *Hungary 1956* (London: Allison and Busby, 1976), 17.

4. Arendt uses the phrase "thinking without a banister" several places. See "On Hannah Arendt," in *Hannah Arendt: The Recovery of the Public World*, ed. Melvin Hill (New York: St. Martin's Press, 1979), 336. Though she does not say so, she takes the phrase from Nietzsche. See the account in my *Politics without Vision: Thinking without a Banister in the Twentieth Century* (Chicago: University of Chicago Press, 2012), 1, 334, and Chapter 8. See also Heidi Bohnet and Klaus Stadler, eds., *Hannah Arendt: Denken ohne Geländer* (Zurich: Piper Verlag, 2006).

5. William Denevan, ed., *The Native Population of the Americas in 1492*, 2nd ed. (Madison: University of Wisconsin Press, 1992), and Denevan, "The Pristine Myth: The Landscape of the Americas in 1492," *Annals of the Association of American Geographers* 82, no. 3 (1992): 369–385. Denevan estimates the population of North America as around 54–57 million in 1492 and about 5.5 million in 1650. Arendt does not seem to have been aware of the devastation consequent to the arrival of Europeans. See also Richard Ashcraft, "Locke's State of Nature: Historical Fact or Moral Fiction," *American Political Science Review* 62, no. 3 (September 1968): 898–915.

6. Starting in the early seventeenth century, the five (later six) members of the Iroquois League had conquered most of the noncoastal northeast as far west as Illinois. By the time of the American Revolution they retained (in insecure name only) claim only to Ohio, Michigan, Indiana, and parts of Illinois. After the Revolution, retaliation for their alliance with the British drove those who were left to Canada. See Daniel K. Richter and James H. Merrell, eds., *Beyond the Covenant Chain: the Iroquois and Their Neighbors in Indian North America, 1600–1800* (University Park: Pennsylvania State University Press, 2003).

7. Thomas Hobbes, *Leviathan* (Cambridge: Hackett, 1994), 228–229 (Chapter 30).

8. Arendt, *On Revolution*, 166–167.

9. John Locke, *Second Treatise on Government* (Cambridge: Hackett, 1980), section 99. Arendt quotes part of this in *On Revolution*, 168. Arendt suggests that Locke was more influenced by America than was America by Locke. See also Ashcraft, "Locke's State of Nature."

10. Thus Milton (*Paradise Lost*, x, 184): "That fear Comes thundring back with dreadful revolution / On my defenseless head."

11. Arendt cites this motto (*Denktagebuch* I.592) and calls attention to the full passage in Virgil from which it is drawn: "*Magnus ab integro saeculorum nascitur ordo*—a great cycle of the ages is (re)born as it was in the beginning." It is from the Fourth Eclogue, and in context it was understood in the medieval period to prophesy the coming of Christ. Carl Schmitt closes a 1927 lecture with the same quote, as Arendt undoubtedly knew. See my discussion in *Politics without Vision*, 229.

12. After writing this, I was drawn by some unthinking hand to pick up Russell Goodman's edited volume *Contending with Stanley Cavell* (Oxford: Oxford University Press, 2005), and opening at random I came across an essay by James Conant ("Cavell and the Concept of America") in which he makes this point also about Arendt and *On Revolution* (70–71). I had annotated the essay on a previous reading. This seems to me a case of *tolle, lege.*

13. Barrington Moore Jr., in partial recognition of this, has argued that the real American revolution was the Civil War. See his *Social Origins of Dictatorship and Democracy* (Boston: Beacon Press, 1966), Chapter Three. At best, I might say however, the new was only very partially realized.

14. Arendt, *On Revolution*, 174.

15. It is worth noting that most readings of the second essay of the *Genealogie* pass over the first two sections and go immediately to section 3 on conscience. See e.g. Werner Stegmaier, *Nietzsches Genealogie der Moral* (Darmstadt: Wissenschaftliche Buchgesellschaft, 1994), 131ff. He gets to the question of the sovereign individual on page 136, without, however, the sense of the genealogical development that Nietzsche sees.

16. *On the Genealogy of Morals* II, § 1, *Kritische Gesamtausgabe Werke* (Berlin: De Gruyter, 1966), vol. VI–2, 305. Hereafter KGW.

17. See Aristotle, *Nicomachean Ethics* 4.3: "the great-souled" (Ross's translation gives "proud man").

18. See *On the Use and Misuse of History for Life* § 3, KGW III–1, 267: "The best we can do is to confront our inherited and hereditary nature with our knowledge of it, and through a new, stern discipline combat our inborn heritage and implant in ourselves a new habit, a new instinct, a second nature, so that our first nature withers away. It is an attempt to give oneself, as it were a posteriori, a past in which one would like to originate in opposition to that in which one did originate:—always a dangerous attempt because it is so hard to know the limit to denial of the past and because second natures are usually weaker than first" (my translation).

19. One of the very few commentators to focus on this is Randall Havas, *Nietzsche's Genealogy: Nihilism and the Will to Knowledge* (Ithaca, N.Y.: Cornell University Press, 1995), 193ff., who does so with an eye to the move from "animality" to "humanity," which I think misleading. He is on sounder

ground on page 196, where he relates the idea of "right" to that of the
responsibility for intelligibility.

20. See the discussion in Hanna F. Pitkin, "Obligation and Consent, II,"
American Political Science Review 60, no. 1 (March 1966): 39–52.

21. *On the Genealogy of Morals* II, § 2, KGW VI–2 309.

22. In his edition of *On the Genealogy of Morals* (New York: Vintage,
1967), 58.

23. Were there to be—say I was acting out of fear—then I would be acting fearfully and not precisely promising, but also not not promising either.

24. See the discussion in Stanley Cavell, *The Claim of Reason* (Oxford:
Clarendon, 1979), 309.

25. See the discussion in Chapter 10 in the second and third editions of
my *Friedrich Nietzsche and the Politics of Transfiguration* (Champaign: University of Illinois Press, 2000).

26. See Max Weber, *The Protestant Ethic and the Spirit of Capitalism*,
trans. Talcott Parsons (Los Angeles: Roxbury, 1998), 115: "They [i.e., good
works] are the technical means, not of purchasing salvation, but of getting rid
of the fear of damnation. . . . Thus the Calvinist . . . himself creates his own
salvation, or, as would be more correct, the conviction of it. But this creation
cannot . . . consist in a gradual accumulation of individual good works to
one's credit, but rather in a systematic self-control which at every moment
stands before the inexorable alternative, chosen or damned."

27. See my discussion in *Friedrich Nietzsche and the Politics of Transfiguration*, 3rd ed., Chapter 6, and "Philosophy and the Project of Cultural Revolution," *Philosophical Topics* 33, no. 2 (2008), reprinted in Tracy B. Strong, ed.,
Nietzsche and Politics (London: Ashgate, 2008).

28. Jacques Derrida, "Declarations of Independence," *New Political Science* (1986): 7–15, at 10.

29. See Tracy B. Strong and Joseph Lima, "Telling the Dancer from the
Dance: On the Relevance of the Ordinary for Political Thought," in *The
Claim to Community: Stanley Cavell and Political Theory*, ed. Andrew Norris
(Stanford: Stanford University Press, 2005), 58–79, and Verity Smith and
Tracy B. Strong, "Trapped in a Family Portrait? Gender and Family in
Nietzsche's Refiguring of Authority," in *Dialogue, Politics and Gender*, ed. Jude
Browne (Cambridge: Cambridge University Press, 2013), 46–72.

30. See Aletta J. Norval, "'Writing a Name in the Sky': Rancière, Cavell
and the Possibility of Egalitarian Inscription," *American Political Science
Review* 106, no. 4 (November 2012): 810–826.

31. See Kenneth Benne, "The Uses of Fraternity," *Daedalus* 90 (Spring
1961): 233–246; Aristide Zolberg, "Moments of Madness," *Politics and Society*
2 (1972): 183–207.

32. She cites this at least four times, including as the epigraph to Chapter 6 of *On Revolution* (New York: Viking Press, 1963). The translation is mine. See the discussion in *Politics without Vision*, 385–386. The passage is in Char, *Feuillets d'Hypnos* (published 1947, written 1943–1944).

33. Stanley Cavell, *The Sense of Walden* (New York: Viking, 1972), 7. I owe James Conant's "Cavell and the Concept of America" the thought to put this citation here. It is thus an accident (as Conant and Cavell say) that it happens to be on the Fourth of July that Thoreau initiates the seeking of independence from what America has become when he moves to Walden Pond.

34. See the analysis in *Friedrich Nietzsche and the Politics of Transfiguration*, Chapters 1 and 8.

35. I can find only one letter in their correspondence prior to the publication of Heidegger's Nietzsche lectures in which Nietzsche is mentioned (Heidegger to Arendt, February 17, 1952) in *Letters, 1925–1975*, ed. Ursula Ludz (New York: Harcourt, 2004), 111.

36. See here Jonathan Havercroft's excellent *Captives of Sovereignty* (Cambridge: Cambridge University Press, 2011), 15–34.

37. Arendt, "What Is Freedom?" in *Between Past and Future*, 165.

38. Arendt, *On Revolution*, 153.

39. Arendt, "What Is Freedom?" 165.

40. Martin Heidegger, "The Self-Assertion of the German University," *Review of Metaphysics* 38 (March 1985): 467–502.

41. Robert Frost, "The Gift Outright," in *Collected Poems, Prose and Plays* (New York: Library of America, 1995), 316: "The Land was ours before we were the land's. / She was our land more than a hundred years / Before we were her people. She was ours / In Massachusetts, in Virginia, But, we were England's, still colonials, / Possessing what we still were unpossessed by, / Possessed by what we no more possessed. / Something we were withholding made us weak / Until we found out that it was ourselves / We were withholding from our land of living."

42. Online at http://religiousfreedom.lib.virginia.edu/sacred/charity. html. My italics. Note the echo to the Frost poem (about "possessing").

43. See similar remarks in Graeme Nicholson, "Justifying Your Nation," in *Justifying Our Existence: An Essay in Applied Phenomenology* (Toronto: University of Toronto Press, 2009).

44. Arendt, *On Revolution*, 169.

45. Ibid., 249.

46. George Kateb is one of the few to have grasped this understanding of Hobbes. See his "Hobbes and the Irrationality of Politics," in *Patriotism and Other Mistakes* (New Haven: Yale University Press, 2006), 298–333. See also

my "How to Write Scripture: Words and Authority in Thomas Hobbes," *Critical Inquiry* (Autumn 1993): 128–178.

47. While the concept exists in the work of V.O. Key, *The Responsible Electorate: Rationality in Presidential Voting, 1936–1960* (Cambridge, Mass.: Harvard University Press, 1966), the classic contemporary statement is Morris Fiorina, *Retrospective Voting in American National Elections* (New Haven: Yale University Press, 1981).

48. See in particular Weber's "Parliament und Regierung im neugenordneten Deutschland," in *Gesammelte Politische Schriften* (Tübingen: Mohr, 1971). A very impressive elaboration of this theory has been made by Jeffrey Edward Green, *The Eyes of the People: Democracy in an Age of Spectatorship* (Oxford: Oxford University Press, 2010). I owe some prompting to Green's book, in particular the point about retrospective voting.

49. Arendt, *On Revolution*, 271.

50. Ibid, 277.

51. Ibid, 278.

52. Nietzsche's phrase is "*die Entstehung des Exemplars*" (*Schopenhauer as Educator*, 6 in Nietzsche, *KGW*, III–1:383). To read it as "the production of specimens" as opposed to "the emergence of exemplars" makes a considerable difference. Exemplarity is a Kantian concept. See the discussion in Strong, *Politics without Vision*, 43–44, 86.

53. Letter to Jaspers, May 13, 1953, *Arendt-Jaspers Correspondence 1926–1929* (New York: Mariner, 1993), 209. She continues as if flabbergasted: "The president of Brooklyn College, known citywide as an idiot with an important big job and as what people call a 'reactionary' here, said to me in a public discussion that he was born and raised in Iowa and therefore didn't need to think or read anymore to know what was right. He, along with Sidney Hook—a comical team—then told me that it was un-American to quote Plato and that I, just like Tillich, suffered from being Germanic. (Sic!)"

54. Stanley Cavell, *Must We Mean What We Say?* (New York: Scribners, 1969), 345. Conant, too, quotes part of this in "Cavell and the Concept of America."

CHAPTER 8

"Poetry or Body Politic": Natality and the Space of Birth in Hannah Arendt's *Thought Diary*

Jeffrey Champlin

Jean-Jacques Rousseau gives freedom a body when he opens the first chapter of *The Social Contract* with the famous sentence: "Man was/is born free [*est né*] and everywhere he is in chains."[1] His argument draws its force not only from a strong opposition between nature and culture but also from a multivalent temporality. Where English forces a decision, birth, in Rousseau's French, assumes either a historical or an ontological cast depending on how one reads the verb *est*. A first reading transposes the biblical story of the fall into politics, recounting that man *was* born free but is *now* enslaved. A second reading sets freedom against slavery in a battle over the present: man is, now *and always*, born free though he finds himself in the contradictory situation of being subjugated.[2] Read in Rousseau's double valence, birth is both material (in the world and in time) and transcendental (not bound to material, above the world in a way that it can determine it, and outside of time).

"Natality" has become one of the most central concepts in contemporary work on Arendt and her unique renegotiation of ideas of freedom and possibility. Readers of the *Denktagebuch* might hope for more evidence of the concept's development, but she uses the term only once in the years leading up to her major deployment of it in *The Human Condition*. The puzzling, even obscure, presentation of the term in the *Denktagebuch* challenges interpretive protocols that depend on a linear development. Nonetheless, the entry deserves attention because it shows Arendt transforming a political metaphysics of the body through an alternative conception of corporeality. Maintaining Rousseau's attention to the clash of language and ontology, Arendt shows that the body bears a specifically earthly form of freedom.

The weight of Arendt's published works and their scholarly reception tempt the interpreter to approach the *Denktagebuch* from the tradition of Western philosophy broadly conceived. However, understanding what this early entry means for Arendt's concept of natality requires a focus on its specifically literary aspects, understood as the particular ways in which she constructs it through arrangements of language. Within an awareness of both literary form and the conceptual history of philosophy, my question arises from and contributes to the more developed discussion of natality in *The Human Condition*. There, Arendt changes the very definition of politics, describing it not merely as the negotiation of interests between different groups, but of the creation of groups that act together to start something new. Power, in turn, does not preexist but emerges from common endeavor and legitimately endures only as long as it has continuing support. This alternate conception of the political ultimately depends on Arendt's conception of natality: If there is to be the possibility of something truly, radically *new*, there must be a distinctive way for a person to be politically born. This idea allows her to gesture toward a new understanding of authority, tradition, and even temporality by engaging and challenging the notion of a transcendental guarantee of freedom.

Yet, while Arendt repeatedly emphasizes natality's importance, her specific formulations fall short of systematic explication. The introduction of *The Human Condition* offers a typically moving and deceptively lucid statement: "action has the closest connection with the human condition of natality; the new beginning inherent in birth can make itself felt in the world only because the newcomer possesses the capacity of beginning something anew, that is, of acting."[3] On the one hand, Arendt grants natality singular potency: "only" it grants the power of starting the new. It allows a specific kind of novelty that we need to break ties with the past. On the other hand, "because" marks a unidirectional relation. At one level, Arendt highlights birth as a physical event; it announces the emergence of a new distinct being. Beyond this, birth contains possibility; it holds a new start "inherent" in it. From here, it is difficult to discern whether birth in this sense really relates to the body at all, or instead just describes a transcendental principle, a higher power that always exists and makes action possible.

In a similar manner, Arendt later writes that "the faculty of action is ontologically rooted" in natality.[4] However, she does not *use* natality as an anchor, but as a phenomenon, an event in the material world, that offers a spring of hope and forward motion. Backing away from the view that natality might be a purely transcendental or ontological principle, we are thus led to ask if Arendt insists on the body and the figural dimension of language as she works out a way of describing freedom that requires a specific sense of embodiment. In other words, what might seem to be a confusion of philosophical and literary modes of inquiry actually contributes to the hermeneutic richness of her thought. A careful reading of the explicit reference to natality in the *Denktagebuch* and nearby references to figures of birth can help understand how Arendt uses the narrative and poetic dimensions of the idea to expand the philosophical concepts of novelty and change. Natality, as a *condition* in Arendt's sense, is related to, but different than, a concept, an anchor, and an ontological principle. Arendt's natality needs to be shown and, though it will not present itself directly to the senses, it can be approached indirectly through narrative (time) and poetic layout (spacing).

The Space of Power

Entry 21 in Notebook XIX (October 1953, p. 461) contains the *Denktagebuch*'s only reference to "natality." In order to engage Arendt's challenge to foundational thinking, I propose that we acknowledge that the entry gives us not one but two outlines and aligns them in a way that compels us to work out their relation.[5] The *Denktagebuch* presents the opportunity to take the layout of thinking seriously and to read it as it comes to us, spread out on the page. If we look forward to the published works, we know that the two columns into which Arendt divides the entry will need to become one. Yet, the very way that she writes resists a simple binary, one to-one relationship. Taking up the challenge of this entry allows a renewed appreciation of Arendt's thought in its stylistic and conceptual creativity. In their spatial division, order of terms, and employment of symbols, these two columns offer a productive challenge to reading.

The basic features of the entry suggest a provisional intellectual orientation, and I propose describing them on their own terms before entering into wider questions of Arendt scholarship. In the accompanying table, the left-hand column appears to be generally positive, containing the terms equality, assertion, thought, and action, while the right is broadly negative, including fear, loneliness, and loss of reality. The left proceeds from *Singularität* (singularity) to *Mortalität* (mortality) and the right column begins with *Pluralität* (plurality) and ends with *Natalität* (natality). Each of these corner terms ends with what in English would be the suffix "–ity," which grammatically implies that Arendt denotes a state of being. It may seem that the outline offers pure philosophy, pure concepts and terms. In their very purity however, the lists of terms raise the question of motion, relation, and connection.[6]

Editors Ursula Ludz and Ingeborg Nordmann describe the entry as "keywords" (*Sitchwörter*) to Arendt's lectures at Notre Dame in 1954 (1046). Their description makes sense when one reviews how the third part of these lectures develops questions related to the "two-in-one" in a reading of Plato.[7] A small addition should be made to this relation between notes and lectures by pointing out that the note to the right on "Labor"

Pluralität		**Singularität**
Equality—distinction	⇐	Fear if related to plural
in the modus of <u>speech</u>:		Faith ⇒ if in and by itself
= Assertion of human		
condition		
Thought: Solitude	⇐	Labor: metabolism with
= two-in-one = I with		nature = my life
myself = with Humanity		Loneliness if related to
Fabrication: isolation		plurality: One-ness without
= I with human artifice		confirmation by others
		= loss of reality or common
		sense
Action = together with		
<u>Power</u>		
Futility of action = need		
for permanence—		
Poetry or body politic		
Natalität		Mortalität

has clear connections with the Gauss Lectures that Arendt delivered at Princeton University one year before.[8]

If one sees the *Denktagebuch* solely as a sourcebook for ideas to be developed later, it would be enough to be satisfied to explain it as an outline, a spine, or skeleton to be fleshed out in a final product. Those who know *The Human Condition* might see the opening and closing as parallel terms and assume that, beyond the immediate relation to the Notre Dame and Princeton lectures, the entry ultimately moves in a deliberate manner from plurality to natality and singularity to mortality. Arendt extensively develops her sense of plurality in *The Human Condition*, defining it clearly and programmatically as "the fact that men, not Man, live on the earth and inhabit the world."[9] Simply put, Arendt prioritizes multiplicity over conceptual unity. Arendt scholarship has also done a great deal of work on Arendt's reworking of Heidegger's approach to mortality as "being towards death."

With the rich conceptual development the scholars and Arendt herself provide, it is easy to forget that *The Human Condition* itself never systematically explains the function of natality, insisting on the need for a basis for action in plurality but leaving open the question of how this relationship between action and natality works. It seems to be a kind of foundation, except that is more of a spring than a solid base. It refers to the body. Arendt uses it not as the appearance of the body in the merely natural sense, but instead as a mark of the distinctively human, which she consistently resists reducing to the simply biological.

This entry of *The Thought Diary* keeps keys terms of Arendt's thought at a typographical distance. Indeed, its lack of clear transitions demands that we read the space *between* the terms. While temping us to jump to connections and conclusions, it also inserts a mostly blank barrier between concepts. The history of philosophy, while rarely commenting on its own innovations of layout, does offer some guidance in this regard. Specifically, Arendt's intimate familiarity with Kant's three *Critiques*, and her particular training in the German philosophical tradition, suggest a provisional approach through the lens of the layout of early German editions of Kant's antinomies in the *Critique of Pure Reason*. There, in side-by-side columns, he begins with premises beyond the scope of reason and shows that each necessarily leads to its opposite. For example, in one antinomy, Kant offers negative proofs of the proposition that the universe has a fixed area and beginning *and* the proposition that it does not have a fixed area and beginning. In Kant, the division of the columns signals a rift in thinking that cannot be bridged. The empty middle marks an abyss, a void for human thinking. Arendt's text, by contrast seems to offer an apparently logical development from one key term to another on each side. The equal signs even suggest mathematic progression and conclusion. Often they can be translated "I define as." For example: "Action I define as together with." Choosing one such interpretation, though, would be a strong step, since in this specific case there are so many locutions that could as easily be inserted there instead, such as: "relies upon," "is contingent upon," "has something to do with." This is particularly true since Arendt also offers a different connection between the columns in two small arrows that she inserts in the middle pointing from the right to the left.

Despite these differences, contrasting Arendt's columns with Kant's raises the question of how each side develops, and it prepares us to watch for twists in what seems to be straightforward motion. Most important, it reminds us to take the distance between the two columns seriously and sets a high standard for attempts to bridge them. Indeed, the spacing warns us of the danger of hoping to find one answer to this equation rather than accepting the multiple challenges to thinking that the columns open.

Given such a multiplicity of ways to begin reading this entry, perhaps we can start with the most notably distinct feature, the arrows, small marks flying between terms, that imply that Arendt takes singularity as her starting point (following her teacher Heidegger) and tries to work her way out. Since they force us to read from right to left, though, we might have an uneasy sense that we are swimming upstream, working against a prejudice of tradition. The right hand column offers a series of pitfalls, of ways to go wrong, or at least apparent negatives. "Fear," "loneliness," and "loss of reality" stand out. In contrast, one might hope to find a smooth, positive development in the left-hand column. This is not the case, though. "Fabrication" poses a threat to "equality" that "action" does not just conquer. Instead, one slides, stumbles, and gets stuck in the "futility of action."

Natality offers action its energy but cannot be linked to it in a clear way. The two terms stand apart. However, the specifics of the distance are significant. The development of the line of thought hangs up on poetry:

Futility of action = need
for permanence—
Poetry or body politic

The positive movement of the column hits "futility." The interruption implies at least two directions. It might just be a blip in her run of thought, a speed bump, so to speak, built into the human condition itself. Alternatively and perhaps more interestingly, Arendt may be considering an objection, acknowledging the fact that the boldly announced "action" above remains threatened by disappointment, and trying to come to terms with that objection by contending that practical failure leads to a metaphysical need for stability, and acknowledging the fact that the boldly announced "action" remains threatened by disappointment.

The history of political philosophy has long aligned the "need for permanence" with the "body politic," not only since the early modern reinvention of sovereignty, but even much earlier in classical Greek and Roman thought. In her published work, Arendt uses the term "body politic" without inquiring into its conceptual history, but that history does offer a place to start for critical reflection.[10] Traditionally, philosophers use the body to describe a principle of stable organization. This was already true for Aristotle, who insists on an analogy between mind and body and ruler and subject.[11] In his view, such a hierarchy was prescribed by nature and extended in principle to the control of men over animals and free men over slaves.

As Ernst Kantorowicz famously demonstrated, medieval political theology argues for the continuity of the ruler with the idea of the two bodies of the king: a physical body that passes away in his death, and a spiritual body that does not change.[12] The phrase often cited in connection with this idea, "The king is dead, long live the king," employs a paradox that apparently resolves when one realizes the "king" is being uses in two different senses. However, the imperative hides the implicit group of people that project the still living concept of the king in speech. The French phrase "*le roi est mort, vive le roi!*" employs the subjunctive case, and a more literal translation would be "the king is dead, may the king live." The need to add the marker of duration in English ("long") testifies to an anxiety about the stability of this concept as the idea intersects with the body.

Most important for modern thought, Hobbes describes individuals in the state of nature who cede their individual power to the ruler, resulting in a single body that the famous front piece of *Leviathan* pictures as a giant composite of smaller people. Jonathan Hess highlights the move from Aristotle, who sees man as having an intrinsically political nature, to Hobbes's insistence on the artificial body of the state.[13] Hobbes needs to *convert* man from an antisocial animal into a political being. Hess argues, in effect, that when Hobbes combines the social contract with the body politic, the unity of the body wins, since the contract only operates at the moment of forming the leviathan as head of state, who then has the power to make all future decisions.[14] In the terse phrase "poetry or body politic," Arendt shifts our attention away from this rational moment of the contract and toward a different kind of moment altogether, a creative poetic moment.

Born Like Animals, Guided Like Men

Linguistically, "body politic" has a unique currency in Anglo-American thought that deserves comparative examination in light of Arendt's multi-lingual background. In German discourse, the mechanistic *Staatsapparat* (state apparatus) predominates over *Staatskörper* (state body). Arendt's choice to focus on the body rather than the machine marks a difference between her project and that of the structuralist thinkers of the post–World War II period. Most famously, Louis Althusser drew on Marx and structuralism in his elaboration of "ideology and ideological state apparatuses."[15] Rousseau, in line with his preference for figures of nature and the organic, employs *"corps politique"* in *The Social Contract*, but it never took a central place in French debate. In comparison with these thinkers, Arendt's use of the English "body politic" in connection with "natality" assumes the organic figure of the body, but does not associate it with the teleology that it would assume in Rousseau. Likewise, the arrow markers in the two columns of the entry from the *Thought Diary* suggest a logical, perhaps even machine-like functioning. She does not explicitly clarify the meaning of those opera-tors, though, which prevents the system from assuming a sense of closed circulation.

Arendt's revision of the body politic operates through a plasticity of the concept innately related to its figural aspect. Expanding on one of Arendt's notes on Hans Blumenberg, Sigrid Weigel writes, "The same words can be understood as concepts *or* metaphors, yet their designation as metaphor reflects the moment of transmission that is always inscribed in them—at least when it is a question of the designation of the invisible."[16] Weigel connects the moment of categorizing a word as a metaphor with a release of sense and movement of meaning. She is not saying that new meaning arises from nowhere that finally illuminates a previously unseen idea. Instead, an old word, the same word, marks out a new terrain. Beyond Weigel's insight though, Arendt compels us to think of the words "body politic" not just as a concept *or* metaphor, but concept *and* metaphor. In doing so, concepts also become vehicles of transmission that do not just offer new categoriza-tion but also bring forth unseen knowledge.

From the medieval period to the twentieth century, theories of the body politic shared a common emphasis on unity and an organic principle of stability that points to a metaphysical "need for permanence." In the "or" of Arendt's "poetry or body politic," she compels us to consider an alterna-tive to the necessity of assuming that structure. Considering nearby entries of the *Denktagebuch* within the general horizon of the *Human Condition* shows that she does not merely reject the body or its order, but, by demanding continual participation, instead employs the body to talk about political connections in a way that opens political form rather than closing it.

Perhaps surprisingly, given Arendt's emphasis on natality as the basis of radical newness, other figures of birth in the *Denktagebuch* relate not to change, sudden or otherwise, but to consistency and integration. However, the way Arendt describes this maintenance of the world provides a basis that cannot be circumvented for the radical energy that she ultimately grants action. Reading a few key entries around the same time in the *Denktagebuch* shows that the world (i.e., the common realm of living together) needs to be sustained; it does not just exist by itself. In this regard, the phrase "poetry or body politic" indicates that the political body needs to be continually renewed, either through the poetic, or in poetry itself. This renewal has both a conservative aspect and a potential for radical change in action. Each new body does not just fit the higher state-body, but continually maintains the social structure. Without presupposing that higher principle of stability, the common world can then change its entire political structure because it brings with it the possibility of starting something wholly new.

Jürgen Habermas's critique of Arendt's conception of power helps sharpen her challenge to permanence in the political realm in the other entries I wish to examine. Habermas reads her as usefully placing emphasis on the origin of power as opposed to its means of employment. In contrast to Max Weber, who understands power in terms of particular individuals seeking to realize a fixed goal, Arendt separates power from the necessity of a *telos* (end). Habermas names plurality as the condition for communication and then quickly moves from distinctness to connection. The world has a "spatial dimension" in which "multiple perspectives of perception and action of those present" are unified.[17] Insightfully—and provocatively—he complements this description of the spatial dimension of the world with a temporal one: "The temporal dimension of the life-world is determined by the 'fact of human natality': the birth of every individual means the possibility of a new beginning; to act means to be able to seize the initiative and to do the unanticipated."[18] In this description, Habermas references the past in the singular ("the birth of every individual") but allows for action between people. So, in natality, as he describes it, we go from the past to the future and the individual to the group.

The very emphasis on the origin of power, however, raises the question of how it can endure over time. The phrase "temporal dimension of the life-world" points to this problem: How could it be said to "use" power in the future when, as Arendt writes in the *Human Condition*, "power cannot be stored up and kept in reserve for emergencies"?[19] For Arendt, the specter of the Weberian conception of power cannot quite be so neatly sidestepped as Habermas desires. Power should not be seen as capital that can be deployed at the time that a ruler or executive wishes. Arendt suggests instead that it cannot be virtualized, that it in its purest state it exists only in a one-to-one relation with its supporters.

Habermas ultimately accuses Arendt of a sleight of hand in taking refuge in the idea of the contract to solve the problem of her radical conception of action. His quick assertion that Arendt falls back on the "contract theory of natural law" rings false, though.[20] He leaves us little else to support his accusation, and it seems to be a sort of stopgap approach to closing the important questions raised by his description of Arendt's conception of power. He clearly describes both the spatial and temporal aspect of Arendt's concept of power, but saying that she relies on the contract suggests that, as in Hobbes, political agreement exists in order to closes *off* political form. Even before Habermas's challenge, Arendt had already provided a language to understand the stakes of this problem: her distinction between a promise and a contract. The *Denktagebuch* offers other options, though, particularly around the figures of birth that she explores in philosophical notes as well as those that experiment with the narrative genre. An entry from 1955 draws our attention to the difference between animal and human birth: "Heidegger is wrong: man is not 'thrown in the world'; if we are thrown, then—no differently from animals—onto the earth. Man is precisely guided, not thrown, precisely for that reason his continuity arises and the way he belongs appears. Poor us, if we are thrown into the world!"[21]

Despite the stark tone of her objection, Arendt's critique of metaphysics begins with Heidegger, who already writes about existential spatiality instead of the independent existence of subjects who are cut off from the world. In *Being and Time*, Heidegger's idea of "thrownness" (*Geworfenheit*) offers a conceptual hinge between a limitation and expansion of freedom. On the one hand, the thrown *Dasein* (Heidegger's displacement of the subject through spatial "being-there") cannot choose to come into the world, much less into a particular world.[22] Indeed, Heidegger describes Dasein's usual state of thrownness as "fallen," which of course suggests a range of negative connotations starting with the fall of Adam and Eve in Genesis. Heidegger claims that he does not intend a negative value judgment of this starting state, though, which he associates not with a hierarchical shift, but rather a horizontal dislocation. As thrown, Dasein first exists in a confused disorientation among the mix of everyday opinions of other people. Yet, this type of thrownness does not only describe a past or current condition, but it also enables an openness to the future in that Dasein remains "in the throw" (*in Wurf bleibt*). Dasein's thrownness causes original disorientation, but this state at the same time keeps it in play for future development.

On the other hand, once situated in a field of relations, possibilities open that allow Dasein to fashion a sense of the future and self-knowledge. In contrast to Arendt, Heidegger emphasizes individual development at this point. He repeatedly speaks of authentically "being able to be oneself" in a manner that contrasts with the publicity of the inferior social episte-mology of idle talk.

Arendt asks how exactly we are to recognize the original condition of being thrown in such a way that new possibilities open up. Her objection to Heidegger takes a subtle linguistic path that shows how her method of read-ing inflects her philosophical ideas. She actually combines philosophy and linguistics in a subtle terminological challenge rather than hold exclusively to the conceptual development of "thrownness." She says that man is only thrown into the natural "earth," not the humanly made "world." Arendt broadly holds to this division in *The Human Condition*, though she also uses the terms interchangeably at times. In making the distinction in the *Denk-tagebuch*, she draws on Heidegger's essay "The Origin of the Work of Art," which he wrote in 1937 and published in 1950. There he distinguishes the world as a system of relations that creates meaning from the earth as the given, material aspect of nature. This latter dimension has a certain solidity, but it also resists understanding in its pure state.

By inserting this distinction between the earth and the world, Arendt reads *geworfen* not abstractly as "thrown," but concretely. In doing so, she implies that she has in mind the second meaning of the German verb *werfen*, which one uses to speak of animals other than humans giving birth. Such a shift takes Heidegger down a notch and uses his own term in a nearly oppo-site sense. After all, Heidegger's sense of "thrownness" relates to position, chance, and dislocation, along the lines of a throw of the dice. If he does not intent God to be his model, he at least suggests man as one who engages chance. When Arendt gestures instead to animal birth, she points to neces-sity rather than contingency.

From this point of view, it looks like Arendt wants to simply leave the merely animal behind after recognizing it. The German verb *leiten*, which I have translated here as "guided," could also mean to "direct," "to conduct," "to lead," "to govern." Thinking ahead to Arendt's writing on education, one can hear a connection to *begleiten*, which means "to accompany."[23] The guiding that one receives gives a sense of continuing and belonging to a greater world. Heidegger insists that Dasein does not choose to be thrown into a specific world, but is born without choice or input. For Arendt, this is our earthliness, and she emphasizes the difference between the human world and the given earth. With respect to the world, she highlights the connection to others from the start. Since others exist before the entrance of the newcomer, we also assume responsibility for their entry to the world. One must be educated into the world, which is not simply the earth, but the humanly constructed edifice that includes history and memory and the polis.

In "The Crisis of Education" (1954), Arendt writes, "Basically we are always educating for a world that is or is becoming out of joint, for this is the basic human situation, in which the world is created by mortal hands to serve mortals for a limited time as home." She draws powerfully on Shakespeare in her description of the world's disjunction. Facing the command of the ghost, Hamlet laments his task of revealing that his uncle murdered his father to rule Denmark: "The time is out of joint. O cursed spite, that ever I was born to set it right." As the heir to the throne, Hamlet's personal situation is inherently political, and Shakespeare's tragedy stages the premature death of the father as genealogical break that raises the question of succession. Arendt generalizes Hamlet's words in a manner that might appear paradoxical at first: How can the world always be becoming out of joint? The *Thought Diary* suggests that the continual animal-like birth of people challenges the structures that are to assure their entrance into humanity in its fullest, politically empowered, sense. The body comes first because we cannot assume a moment of rest or cohesion from which the disjunction starts.

Arendt's conception of finitude is key here: humans make a world (comprising structures and practices of living together) that lasts for only a set period. In this sense, "home" for Arendt does not offer the permanent refuge that philosophers and poets often long for. The crisis in education that she writes of in the late 1950s is in part one of a particular time and place. She does critique specific pedagogical trends such as an emphasis on play-like activities in the classroom over "the gradually acquired habit of work." In a broader sense, however, the crisis of education actually responds to the crisis in authority that she sees occurring over a long historical arc. While she recognizes the declining power of the parent, teacher, and expert, Arendt does not merely advocate a harsh return to old models. Instead she advocates a "minimum of conservation" that allows the most basic operation of reinterpreting the past based on new conditions. The word "education" derives from the Latin root *educere*, meaning "to lead forth," but for Arendt such a journey could have little confidence in its destination.

Peg Birmingham and Stephan Kampowski suggest that Arendt replaces Heidegger's *geworfen* with *geboren* (born).[24] The earlier passage from the *Denktagebuch* shows the complexity of this substitution and that it works only by changing the context to the world rather than earth. However, while the quote shows that Arendt relegates Heidegger's thrownness to the realm of the earth and body, her own idea of "natality" brings the body back to her thinking of freedom.[25] Being born will have not one but two important senses for Arendt from the *Denktagebuch* to *The* Human Condition. If *werfen* can refer to animals giving birth, Arendt works out a specific way in which *humans* are born, but her intervention in the conceptual history of the body politic emphasizes a first connection that *already* liberates humans from the earth, and then a mode of being born that changes the world rather than just adding to it. If Rousseau's opening of *The Social Contract* says that man is both in time and transcends it, Arendt sees man as both in the body, as an animal, and guided, albeit in the disjunctive rather than organic manner, into the world.

Birth and . . .

Before moving on, or back, to natality, though, another entry must be reckoned with in which Arendt offers a smooth and touching narrative of welcome into the world that not only tells but also shows what she means by being guided into the world. She offers another form of writing, switching into the narrative mode in a way that performs the guidance articulated conceptually in the passage above. Almost a page long, this entry gets started with a drumbeat of the conjunction "and": "We are born into this world of plurality where father and mother stand ready for us, ready to receive us and welcome us and guide us and prove that we are not strangers" (D XIX.39.469–470). Arendt homes in on the connection between newborn and world to establish a relation that at first appears surprisingly untroubled to readers of her later work. She describes the mother and father as being there for the child in four ways. In being "ready," they have prepared for him in advance. They will "receive" him, bringing him to the place that they made. In "welcoming," we might think of additional signs of acceptance that indicate a broader, social incorporation. Further, the parents do not just take in the child at that moment but also offer to "guide" him, accompanying him for a time in the world.

The parents do all of this to show that the child belongs, but Arendt's repetitions reveal an awareness of the difficult kind and amount of work this requires. Moreover, in the "we," the reader sees not just another reference to the child but to the parents as well. The repeated welcome affirms the place of the parents *and* child. Beyond the content, however, the passage compels a switch from a critical philosophical mode of analysis to an embrace of narrative. Arendt moves along with the story. Invited, welcomed by this switch in style, readers performatively enter the "we," joining the story in the mode of the "and" that is also its central point of content.

If there is an irresistible beauty to the passage, of the smooth flow that immerses us into a new world, then that flow makes all the more striking the moment when, later in the same entry, Arendt subtly disrupts the perfect, smooth plane of her story when "we" are no longer newcomers but must ourselves welcome "newcomers to whom we prove what we no longer quite believe, that they are not strangers" (*D* XIX.39.470). A split opens up in relation to the simple welcome of the start of the passage. A new perspective appears, so that over the course of the narrative the reader sees the same event is seen from two vantage points. This does not need to be read as a dissolution of the opening lines. On the contrary, Arendt needs both. We must feel welcome *and* retain a sense of the strangeness of the newcomer. The strangeness will be productive: It does not merely mean that the newcomer does not fit, but it is what allows that they can change the whole world while also having the sense that they have a place in it.[26]

The section ends: "We die in absolute singularity, strangers after all, who say farewell to a foreign place after a short stay. What goes on is the world of plurality" (*D* XIX.39.470). As the "we" dies, Arendt withdraws the narrative welcome she so elegantly extended. We, the readers, are returned to the key term "plurality." The final passage to consider before returning to an explicit consideration of Entry 21 in Notebook XIX (October 1953) helps clarify the end of this story. The repetition of the "and" at the end of the passage offers a clear connection to the narrative just considered:

> It is as if men since Plato have not been able to take the fact of having-been-born seriously, but rather only that of dying. In having-been-born the human establishes itself as an earthly kingdom, toward which one connects, in that it searches for and finds its place, without any thought that he will one day go away again.[27]

Arendt speaks of a way of thinking foreign to Plato in which the "eternity of the human species" was seen primordial, rather than the "mortality of humanity." She argues that we need to take the fact of being born seriously even though the period of history in which this was taken for granted is over. If, in that time one could count on linking "search and find" (*sucht und findet*) in a quick conjunction, Arendt looks deeper into the moment of the "and" in the modern period. She describes a strangely unreflective "kingdom" where one never thinks of death. In this respect she launches a pure attack on the higher world of metaphysical afterlife. At another level though, her own thought demands that we think the imminence of the political and its nonidentity, its ability to change from within.

Poetry and Body Politic

In the *Human Condition*, Arendt productively reformulates the double perspective that appears in the narrative death of the "we" in terms of a "second birth" that leads an individual beyond the welcome of the world. One takes one's stance in relation to the world by reflecting on the distinction between actual birth and an idea of freedom that emerges from thinking about birth. In Chapter 5, she writes: "With word and deed we insert ourselves into the human world, and this insertion is like a second birth, in which we confirm and take upon ourselves the naked fact of our physical appearance."[28] In the second birth, one realizes that the plurality of the world does not simply preexist but that our own arrival necessarily cosigns it ("confirms"), and thus implicitly contains the power of refiguring it.

Since the opening of the inquiry, it has become clear that although the logic of Entry 21 appears to hang up on the phrase "poetry or body politic," Arendt does not actually reject the body as way of envisioning the world. Instead, she highlights an aspect of birth that displaces a higher conceptual body like the leviathan in the direction of a horizontal, narrative accretion of support. In addition to this new "body politic" that demands constant maintenance, however, the phrase gestures to what I would call a "poetry politic" that shows how action can radically change the common world. So, while Arendt does fight the abstractions of Heidegger's thrownness and Hobbes's leviathan, a mere shift to the horizontal is not sufficient to understand her thinking. The "or" can break in at any moment when a new generation whose bodies get ahead of the institutions demand new beginnings.

More than simply naming poetry, the lines "Futility of action = need / for permanence— / Poetry or body politic" read like poetry, and this suggests another approach to the entry's layout. If Kant's antinomies provided a model for approaching the entry from the German philosophical tradition, thinking of the entry in the tradition of avant-garde poetry around 1900 offers another way to take its spacing seriously.[29] Stéphane Mallarmé's 1897 poem "A Throw of the Dice" provides the blueprint for twentieth-century spatial poetics and helps us read two columns of text in their exposure of language across facing pages.[30] Critics have been fascinated by the multiple connections suggested by the poem's font sizes, use of italics and capitalization, and the way it opens semantic links across facing pages. Mallarmé's spacing operates on at least two levels: between the words on a page *and* across the spine, the hinge of a manuscript that physically holds it together. Reading the body politic poetically shows that plurality never really gives way to the unity of the body in the sense of a totality, because each person remains distinct, just as each word in the poem remains distinct.[31] Further, the space between the two pages, like the space between the two columns, reveals a basic distance between the singular and plural that constitutes the world for Arendt, even if, for the purposes of her political thought plurality holds the foreground. At the same time, Mallarmé's dice throw conserves the materiality of language in its specific fonts and careful layout, just as Arendt's thrownness keeps the animal body. For Arendt, the body both keeps one "in the throw" (Heidegger) *and* enables the capacity of the new throw in action.

If Rousseau grants the body a temporal force for liberation, Arendt not only brings time into the body politic but also keeps it open to the space of poetry. The "or" should not be seen as an alternative, as proposing two equally good choices. Instead, the phrase "poetry or body politic" splits up and becomes both "body politic" and "poetry politic."[32] Or, to put it another way, in the *Thought Diary*, Arendt offers a poetry of the body politic.

NOTES

1. Jean-Jacques Rousseau, *On the Social Contract* (New York: St. Martin's Press, 1978), 46. "*L'homme est né libre, et partout il est dans les fers.*" Rousseau, *Du Contract Social*. In *Oeuvres Completes*, ed. B. Gagnebin and M. Raymond (Paris: Plon, 1959–95), 3:351.

2. Seeking to carry the insights of the Enlightenment directly into the political world, *The Declaration of the Rights of Man and of the Citizen* (1789) keeps the "and" but profoundly stabilizes Rousseau's temporality in its first article: "Men are born and remain free [*naissent et demeurent*] and equal in rights." *The Declaration of the Rights of Man and of the Citizen* (1789) can be accessed at www.conseil-constitutionnel.fr/conseil-constitutionnel/root/bank_mm/anglais/cst2.pdf.

3. Hannah Arendt, *The Human Condition* (Chicago: University of Chicago Press, 1958), 9.

4. Ibid., 247.

5. Portions of my readings of Arendt that follow have appeared in an earlier form on the blog of the Hannah Arendt Center website: www.hanna harendtcenter.org.

6. Hannah Arendt, *D* XIX.21.461.

7. Arendt's drafts of the 1954 lectures at Notre Dame are held by the Library of Congress. A revised version of the third lecture was published as "Philosophy and Politics" *Social Research* 57, no. 1 (spring, 1990). This essay is included (under the new heading "Socrates), along with other related drafts of papers from the same time in *The Promise of Politics*, ed. Jerome Kohn (New York: Schocken Books, 2005). These posthumously published writings from the 1950s offer important insights into her reading of Marx.

8. The Gauss lectures are available online at the Library of Congress website: http://memory.loc.gov/ammem/arendthtml/mharendtFolderP05 .html.

9. Arendt, *The Human Condition*, 7.

10. Throughout *The Origins of Totalitarianism*, Arendt refers to racial purity as the condition of the "body politic" under the Nazis. Hannah Arendt, *The Origins of Totalitarianism* (New York: Harcourt, 1968). In *On Revolution*, she frequently employs "body politic" as a synonym for "form of government." See, for example, Hannah Arendt, *On Revolution* (New York: Penguin Books, 1963) 214. For a thorough treatment of the Nazi conception of the body politic see Andreas Musolff, *Metaphor, Nation and the Holocaust*. Chapter 9 of this study, "German Conceptual and Discursive Traditions of the Body Politic Metaphor," offers important background that places the Nazi use of the pure body in a historical context. For work on the changing images of bodies that burst forth during the French Revolution, see Antoine de Baecque, *The Body Politic: Corporeal Metaphor in Revolutionary France, 1770–1800*, trans. Charlotte Mandell (Stanford: Stanford University Press, 1997).

11. See Aristotle, *Politics* (Chicago: University of Chicago Press, 1984), 40–41.

12. Ernst Kantorowicz, *The King's Two Bodies: A Study in Mediaeval Political Theology* (Princeton: Princeton University Press, 1957).

13. Jonathan Hess, *Reconstituting the Body Politic: Enlightenment, Public Culture and the Invention of Aesthetic Autonomy* (Detroit: Wayne State University Press, 1999), 88–92.

14. While agreeing with the general direction of Hess's reading, I see Hobbes as both affirming *and* denying the artificial nature of the state. Strictly speaking, the order and direction of the ruler dominates, but the

very contradictions within his logic offer an opening for freedom and change. See my remarks on the role "terror" plays in Hobbes's account of the state's irreversibility: Jeffrey Champlin, "Introduction," *Terror and the Roots of Politics* (New York: Atropos Press, 2013), 10–12.

15. Louis Althusser, "Ideology and Ideological State Apparatuses," *Lenin and Philosophy and Other Essays* (New York: Monthly Review Press, 1972), 121–176.

16. Sigrid Weigel, "Poetics as a Presupposition of Philosophy: Hannah Arendt's *Denktagebuch,*" *Telos* 146 (2009): 97–110, at 105. Weigel describes the *Thought Diary* as an explicit decision on Arendt's part to turn from the personal and literary reflections of her earlier diaries to explicit reflection on questions of political philosophy following the publication of *The Origins of Totalitarianism* in 1951. However, in contrast to the earlier split in Arendt's writing between the private diary and public work of the academic dissertation on Augustine, in the *Thought Diary* "poetics no longer designates the other of philosophy . . . but, rather, it now describes *the path of or to thought*" (102).

17. Jürgen Habermas, "Hannah Arendt's Communications Concept of Power," *Social Research* 44, no. 1 (1977): 8.

18. Ibid.

19. Arendt, *The Human Condition*, 181, quoted in ibid., 9.

20. Habermas, "Hannah Arendt's Communications Concept of Power," 24.

21. Hannah Arendt, D XXI, 68:549–60: "*Heidegger hat unrecht: 'in die Welt' ist der Mensch nicht 'geworfen'; wenn wir geworfen sind, so—nicht anders als die Tiere—auf die Erde. In die Welt gerade wird der Mensch geleitet, nicht geworfen, da gerade stellt sich seine Kontinuität her und offenbart seine Zugehörigkeit. Wehe uns, wenn wir in die Welt geworfen werden!*" My translation.

22. Martin Heidegger, *Being and Time*, trans. John Macquarrie and Edward Robinson (London: Blackwell, 2000). See especially sections 35–38 at 211–224.

23. Hannah Arendt, "The Crisis in Education," in *Between Past and Future* (New York: Viking Press, 1961).

24. Peg Birmingham, *Hannah Arendt and Human Rights: The Predicament of Common Responsibility* (Bloomington: Indiana University Press, 2006), 149; Stephan Kampowski, *Arendt, Augustine, and the New Beginning: The Action Theory and Moral Thought of Hannah Arendt in the Light of Her Dissertation on St. Augustine* (Grand Rapids, Mich.: Eerdmans, 2009), 229.

25. I develop a reading of the figural dimension of natality in the *Human Condition* in "Born Again: Arendt's 'Natality' as Figure and Concept," *Germanic Review* 88, no. 2 (2013): 150–164.

26. The double perspective in this passage contributes to recent work on Arendt's engagement with the narrative conception of knowledge associated

with Hegel. Allen Speight points out that for Hegel the ultimate judge is institutionalized world history, while for Arendt the world is the space that reveals "the who" (which is already implicitly perceivable in the *daimon*). See Allen Speight, "Arendt on Narrative Theory and Practice," *College Literature* 38, no. 1 (Winter 2011): 115–130.

27. Arendt, D XIX.24.469–70: "*Es ist, als haben die Menschen seit Plato das Faktum des Geborenseins nicht ernst nehmen können, sondern nur das des Sterbens. Im Geborensein etabliert sich das Menschliche als ein irdisches Reich, auf das hin sich ein Jeder bezieht, in dem er seinen Platz sucht und findet, ohne jeden Gedanken daran, dass er selbst eines Tages wieder weggeht.*"

28. Arendt, *The Human Condition*, 176.

29. A spoken performance of the text reveals other connections: reading the right-hand column aloud reveals that alliteration plays a key role ("Fear," "Faith," "Labor," Loneliness"), while the left-hand column builds up a certain rhythm around single key terms before slowing down on the "Futility of action."

30. For an edition that presents the columns with a facing translation, see Stéphane Mallarmé, "Un coup de dés," in *Collected Poems*, trans. Henry Weinfield (Berkeley: University of California Press, 1994), 121–146. If Kant provides the great dual-column text of the eighteenth century and Mallarmé that of the nineteenth, Derrida's *Glas* takes the typographical challenge into the twentieth century with an intricate reading of Hegel and Genet in side-by-side columns. Jacques Derrida, *Glas*, trans. John P. Leavey Jr. and Richard Rand (Lincoln: University of Nebraska Press, 1987).

31. Robert Greer Cohn writes in language that resonates, albeit difficulty, with Arendt, of the near tautology of Mallarmé's "world in which . . . all terms are profoundly identical while yet being distinct." Robert Greer Cohn, *Mallarmé's "Un coup de dés": An Exegesis* (New Haven: Yale University Press, 1949), 16.

32. Roger Berkowitz identifies a connection between Jacques Rancière and Arendt that suggests a connection between what I here call Arendt's "poetry politic" and democracy; while "Rancière sees political action as manifesting 'dissensus' [Rancière's alternative to the cohesion of consensus], Arendt insists that political action be spontaneous and capable of beginning something new into the world. Which is why Arendt argues that 'the modern concept of revolution, inextricably bound up with the notion that the course of history suddenly begins anew, that an entirely new story, a story never known before, is about to unfold' is at the very center of modern democratic politics." www.hannaharendtcenter.org/?p=4705.

CHAPTER 9

Facing the End: The Work of Thinking in the Late *Denktagebuch*

Ian Storey

> Everything that is appears; everything that appears disappears;
> everything that is alive has an *urge* to appear; this urge is called
> vanity; since there is no *urge* to disappear and disappearance is the
> *law* of appearance, the urge, called vanity, is in vain. "Vanitas
> vanitatum vanitas"—all is vanity, all is in vain.
>
> —(*D* XXVII.84.796)

The twenty-seventh notebook is the last substantive section of Arendt's *Denktagebuch*, before the twenty-eighth trails off into a bare succession of dates and places.[1] It concludes abruptly with a brief note that her husband, Heinrich Blücher, has died—"so suddenly, so quickly" (*D* XXVII.86.797)—followed by a fragment of Berthold Brecht's "Ballade vom Mazeppa":

> One man road out with the things that were most his own:
> with earth and horse, with endurance and silence,
> then he was joined by vultures and sky.[2]

The notebook that follows begins with an equally brief and poignant entry: "1971 Without Heinrich. Free—like a leaf in the wind" (*D* XXVIII.1.801).

Even before its poignant conclusion, though, Notebook XXVII is preoccupied with thinking about ends, and Arendt weaves the multiple senses of the word in both English and German together into a series of meditations on the relationships between thinking, death, and purpose. These meditations, which interlace philosophy and poetry, show us a period when what would become the volume *Thinking*—which makes its first appearance in the form of an initial outline (*D* XXVII.64.784–85)—is crystallizing into an argument about the nature of appearance (and disappearance) and the "thinking-I." They also show us, in a way perhaps more intimate than nearly any other section of the thought-diary, how consummately absorbed in the world in which she lived Arendt's thoughts were, and the depth with which she thought and felt through her own embodied place in it.

The centrality of ends in these entries highlights one of the unique virtues of the *Denktagebuch* as a lens through which to look at Arendt's thought more broadly: its ability to bring to the fore dimensions of Arendt's published work otherwise easily lost and help trace threads of those dimensions across different periods and writings. Instrumentality and the orientation toward particular ends were a perennial concern for Arendt's work in the late 1950s and early 1960s, and the critiques she puts forward in that period have been a central part of the rise in popularity of her thought in political theory and philosophy. In a series of works, particularly *The Human Condition* and the several iterations of "Culture and Politics," Arendt highlighted the dangers of reducing the *vita activa*—particularly the sphere of action and politics—to the calculation and pursuit of predictable ends. "This instrumentalization," Arendt warned, could result only in the "limitless devaluation of everything existing," degrading "nature and the world into mere means, robbing both of their independent dignity."[3]

One might be tempted, then, to read the turn in Notebook XXVII (and subsequently in *Thinking*) toward a concern for the place of ends in human life as a shift in Arendt's thought, perhaps even a reversal on her previous decrial of those who would reduce the vibrancy of the public world to the service of means and ends. But reading Notebook XXVII in the context of Arendt's early work also brings out the ways in which the place Arendt accords to ends in the *vita contemplativa* already had significant echoes in her account of the *vita activa* that have gone underappreciated in the obvious salience of her discussions of ends-orientation for political thought. Perhaps ends were never such incorrigible villains for Arendt after all, but always had a role to play for what might be called her curious species of Platonism, in which each dimension in her account of the human condition was necessary but dangerous outside of its proper place. This is part of what makes the *Denktagebuch* compelling as an intellectual archive: It not only helps us better understand the nuances and interconnections of Arendt's thought, but can sometimes allow us to reread our own readings of her, and reconsider what we thought we understood of her texts.

In Notebook XXVII, philosophy stands astride the senses of end, and brings them together as an examination of the "final ends of human life," as she says quoting Kant, or with Leibniz's "first question," "why there should be something, rather than nothing" (*D* XXVII.68.786). For Arendt here, the end of life returns us to the question of the ends of life, and thinking is a necessary "anticipation of dying," a retreat from the world in which all things appear to each other, in order to give that world the meaning which its raw appearance alone cannot provide. In *Thinking*, thought's mode of engaging the appearing world through removal finds its closest companion in art, "which transforms sense-objects into thought-things, tears them first of all out of their context in order to de-realize and thus prepare them for their new and different function."[4] This intimacy between thinking, which makes meanings "for its own sake" (*T* 64), and art, the only ends/objects we make that are "strictly without any utility whatsoever" (*HC* 167), is not only a repeated theme in Arendt but also a theme that connects those works most known for their apparent hostility toward ends-orientation (*The Human Condition* and the culture writings) and this work that is preoccupied with ends, both purposes and deaths. The curious continuity makes it worth revisiting that well-documented anti-instrumentality of Arendt's to see if, at the very least, there might not be just a bit more to the story.

Arendt's Case against Ends

If nothing more than simply by dint of the object involved, it is not surprising that a large part of the attention in political thought has focused on Arendt's account of action as the defining activity of political and public life. This attention, both positive and negative, has in turn heavily structured the contemporary reception of *The Human Condition*. Arendt's analysis of action and speech as the "primordially and specifically human" (*HC* 178) capacity through which we "insert" ourselves "into the human world" (*HC* 184) contains much of what is most novel and arresting in Arendt's work, and it has become such a prolific wellspring of political thought in part because Arendt is able to contrast her understanding of action sharply with what she diagnoses as the primary misunderstandings of the political in our age. Chief among these, a misapprehension Arendt argues structured the turn in the social sciences toward econometrics and in turn the bureaucratic world of Washington toward the social sciences, is the attempt to understand and judge politics according to the standards of work, to reduce the meaning of political action to its means and ends, the usefulness of its outcomes.

For Arendt, one of the greatest dangers to action's fragile power of allowing humans to "reveal actively their unique personal identities and thus make their appearance" (*HC* 179) is, as Dana Villa succinctly puts it, the "instrumentalization of action and its degradation of the world of appearances."[5] *Homo faber*, one who works, in as much as what she is doing is working, approaches the world according to the value system germane to work and the creation of products: "everything is judged in terms of suitability and usefulness for the desired end" (*HC* 153). According to Arendt, famously and contentiously, this way of understanding and evaluating the world is antithetical to the possibility of political action. For action to succeed at providing a sphere of expression and freedom, it needs an audience able to view it as such: "every act, seen from the perspective not of the agent but of the process in whose framework it occurs and whose automatism it interrupts, is a 'miracle'—that is, something which could not be expected."[6] "The issue," as she puts it in *The Human Condition*, "is, of course, not instrumentality, the use of means to achieve an end, as such, but rather the generalization of the fabrication experience in which usefulness and utility are established as the ultimate standards for life and the world of men" (*HC* 157). In other words, the danger is not from instrumentality as such—without instrumentality and the world-building work of *Homo faber*, there can be no shared world in which actors can appear to each other through action—but from evaluating all life, particularly political life and the other nonfabricating dimensions of the *vita activa*, through the lens of means and ends.

Perhaps the most vivid account of what happens when politics is reduced to utility comes when that possibility intersects the human capacity for self-deception, as it did, in Arendt's analysis, during the decision-making processes of the Vietnam conflict. For Arendt, the problem of the Vietnam War's organizers was neither their nearly endless capacity to lie—for "the fact that the Pentagon Papers revealed hardly any spectacular news testifies to the liars' failure to create a convinced audience"[7]—nor even their equally endless capacity to deceive themselves. The only way to find an answer to the "How Could They?" of decision making concerning Vietnam was to realize how deadly had been the marriage of the capacity to deceive with an understanding of decision making itself that saw choices to act as reducible to quantified data out of which instrumental outcomes could be calculated. It was the conjunction of the power to lie to oneself and others and an overridingly instrumental view of the conduct of war that brought disaster:

> The problem-solvers who knew all the facts regularly presented to
> them in the reports of the intelligence community had only to rely on
> their shared techniques, that is, on the various ways of translating

qualities and contents into quantities and numbers with which to calcu-
late outcomes—which then unaccountably, never came true—in order
to eliminate, day in and day out, what they knew to be real. ("LP" 36)

As Arendt frames it in *The Human Condition*, the terminal trouble with
the universalization of *Homo faber*'s framework of instrumentality is that it
unravels work's own capacity to do what it must, to build a world for
enduring habitation. The criteria of work not only threaten the possibility
of beginning something unexpected in the world, they also, when applied
to that work's own output, ensure that the end-products of work themselves can never be valued as anything more than means to other, as yet
undetermined ends. There is, for Arendt, a fairly literal sense in which the
instrumentality of work makes value itself impossible, leaving our relationship to our world "in the unending chain of means and ends without ever
arriving at some principle which could justify the category of means and
end, that is, of utility itself" (*HC* 154). Outside the world of politics, this is
at its most dangerous for Arendt when applied to those products of work
which, in their "outstanding permanence," most "defy the equalization
through a common denominator such as money" (*HC* 167), works of art.

The work of art occupies a unique place in Arendt's account of politics
and action, a kind of unstable bridge from the instrumental world of the
worker to a public space that depends on it for survival. The artwork can
perform its task of building "a home for mortal men, whose stability will
endure and outlast the ever-changing movement of their lives and actions,
only insomuch as it transcends both the sheer functionalism of things
produced for consumption and the sheer utility of things produced for
use" (*HC* 173). Works of art, for Arendt, are what allow action to survive
the moment of its passing, the literal substance of which the stories of who
we have been are made. As such, the most immediate danger to these
"most intensely worldly of all tangible things" issues from the very mentality necessary to create them, the impulse to understand *materiel* as
means to an end.

At the birth of modern mass society, this threat took (and takes) on a
specific figure to which Arendt attaches the much older name of "philis-
tine," one who "seized upon [cultural objects] as a currency by which bought
a higher position in society . . . in this process, cultural values were treated
like any other values, they were what values always have been, exchange
values."[8] The rise of a form of society that "evaluated and devaluated cultural things into social commodities, used and abused them" in turn paved
the way for a translation of the social value of cultural objects into consum-

ables, little more than another product to "serve the life process of society, even though they may not be as necessary for life as bread and meat" ("CC" 205). This descent from the lonely status of invaluable preservers of the world-space of "mortal men" to merely another piece of "the biologically conditioned cycle of labor," to "a metabolism feeding on things by devouring them," presents the last real possibility that works of art might cease to be able to hold open the space of appearance. "Many great authors of the past," Arendt warns, "have survived centuries of oblivion and neglect, but it is still an open question whether they will be able to survive an entertaining version of what they have to say" ("CC" 208).

It would seem, then, that thinking and experiencing our world in terms of its ends, both past and projected, represented for Arendt a potentially mortal danger to the public and its space of appearance, and to action and its always unpredictable capacity to begin something new and reveal who we are to each other. Certainly, Wout Cornelissen makes a persuasive case in his essay here that in the early *Denktagebuch* this was still very much a driving concern for Arendt, and that she extends that set of concerns to thinking as well, when she writes that in reducing our experience of the world to making we have "everything has been split into contemplative thought, in which the 'Ideas,' the ends, etc. are given, and into violent action, which realizes these contemplated ends by violent means."

One response to this problem is to search for a way to understand thinking—in fact a way to think—which removes thinking from the realm of making, *Herstellen*, and transforms it into something else, something less violent, an approach Wout Cornelissen in this volume points out Arendt attributed to Jaspers, and to some extent undertook herself, with mixed results. Another approach, however, one that Arendt seems to take in the late *Denktagebuch*, is to ask whether the troubled family relation between thinking and means-and-ends might not be so wholly destructive as one strand of her thought might suggest. Notebook XXVII shows, in part, that the seeds of this reconciliation were already present in her narrative about making and action, thinking and art. But the *Denktagebuch* also provides the intervening figure between the critique of instrumentality in *The Human Condition* and the end-filled character of thought in *Thinking*, the analytic knot that ties the two together: Arendt's relationship to death, both the end of one part of the story of a who and, paradoxically, the beginning or origin of thought. While Elisabeth Young-Bruehl is right to say that the substance of Arendt's move from Heidegger lies in the fact that she adds an equal "concern with birth" to way that the latter's "work is weighted toward the future experience of death,"[9] Notebook XXVII seems in many ways to return to the emphatic interconnection of ends that Heidegger was only beginning to articulate when Arendt studied with him. The notebook begins to fill out Arendt's suggestion that thinking needs ends to do what it does, and that the ends of thought might be as integral part of what it means to take one's place in the world of appearances as the action which reveals our "who" to others. Perhaps this is a change of heart, a softening toward ends as the world seemed more full of them, but perhaps Arendt was also simply returning to the scene of ends' crime, so to speak, to do something like right by their place in her own story.

Thinking, Philosophy, and the End

It is a curious enough moment, given her historical hostility toward being called a philosopher, to find Arendt, as she mulls thinking and the ends of thought, invoking Hegel's understanding of philosophy as "thinking, insofar as it refers only to itself," that "special case of thought" which takes as its "end" "its own self-recognition" (*D* XXVII.67.785–6). After all, this thinking about the ends of thinking is precisely what Arendt has taken on, in what would be her last completed work, which brought her work closest to *Philosophy*, the magnum opus of her great friend and mentor Karl Jaspers.[10] To be sure, Arendt's late thoughts on this peculiar species of thinking are not an unambivalent endorsement of that of which she was once so vocally suspicious. She wryly observes, "All metaphysical fallacies are the fallacies of professional thinkers" (*D* XXVII.68.786), and it is often difficult to tell, without looking in *Thinking* for an endpoint that is not yet there in the *Denktagebuch*, whether her notes on Kant and Hegel are implying an agreement or setting the stage for a critique. But in taking on thinking about thought, Arendt brings philosophy into the dialogue begun by thought and art as evidence for the permanent interconnection of thought and our ends, both of means and of life.

Through philosophy's entry into Arendt's thoughts, the peculiar illuminating role that death plays in revealing the character of thought and philosophy appears here in a particularly beautiful form that survives only much diminished in *Thinking*. In Notebook XXVII, the primary characteristic of thought is that it is by its very nature deathly. The proximity of the two is not just an organizing metaphor for her understanding of the function of thought in the human life-world, but in the lives of men and women forms a fabric of what they are able to think, and when. Arendt finds in this tie between life-horizon and thought an explanation for the central paradox of what she calls the Greek (Platonic) view on philosophy, that it can be practiced only by "the youth" and "the elderly."[11] The paradox is only a paradox, according to Arendt, if one does not place thought in the context of the birth and death of a singular Who.

Remembering that thought can only occur in one who has been born and who will die, and never without those two conditions, reminds us not only of one limit to thought, but also begins to answer the question, "What makes us think?" (*D* XXVII.58.782). "When we are born," Arendt writes, "we are confronted with what appears only once, with the sensuously perceptible. Since we are born as a stranger in it . . . we are overwhelmed with astonishment, and our questions are aimed at becoming recognized in it" (*D* XXVII.55.780). Thus the condition of natality, of being and being capable of the radically new, meant for the Greeks that philosophy was "reserved for the new," "the youth" (*D* XXVII.55.781). This centrality of natality appears very early in Arendt's work, and Jeff Champlin's essay here examines its appearances earlier in the *Denktagebuch*. This last notebook provides the other end of that story, for although "our astonishment decreases proportionately as we become acquainted with the world," as we approach the end of life the confrontation with death "again calls everything into question." At the end, the question is no longer that posed by the irreducible particularity of the sensuous world "with which we had become familiar," but "the 'whole point,'" "and that is why philosophy is, then again, a matter for the elderly, or those who can imagine / have been introduced to the end" (*D* XXVII.55.781).

If Arendt's self-description in *Thinking* of her own philosophical project is one of reversing the historical prioritization of the internal world of the soul and mind in order to center the shared world, the world of appearances, then from the perspective of that shared world thinking itself is both a prelude and analog of death, of the end that will remove each who, but not their story, from the space of appearance. "What in thinking only occasionally and quasi-metaphorically happens, to retreat from the world of appearances, takes place in aging and dying as an appearance . . . in this sense thinking is an anticipation of dying (ceasing, 'to cease to be among men') just as action in the sense of 'to make a beginning' is a repetition of birth" (*D* XXVII.76.792). Disappearance is simply the law of the appearing world, the "the price we the living pay for having lived," and "to not want to pay this price," Arendt muses, "is miserable" (*D* XXVII.66.785).

Thinking doubly mimics this impending disappearance: We retreat from the shared world into our selves, and in making that shared world into the object of thought, we remove from it the sensuous quality that it had in order to prepare it for thinking. As Arendt later puts it in *Thinking*,

thinking requires a kind of repetition of the world, and "by repeating in [our] imagination, we *de-sense* whatever had been given to our senses" (*T* 87); or in the *Denktagebuch*, "in thinking everything is un-realized. I can think everything, but as something thought it is no longer actual" (*D* XXVII.67.786). Thinking, "when I enter most intimately into what I call myself" (*D* XXVII.53.780),[12] involves the end of both our selves as appearances, and the world we remake in thought.

This deathly character of thought raises the question of the ends of life, but it also raises the question of the ends of thought itself. Why, Arendt asks with Kant, think at all, if it can be practiced only as the metaphorical death of our selves and our world? "No one will doubt that in thinking I withdraw from the world," she writes, "even if my thought concerns world-objects. The first question is: What do I lose, what do I gain through this withdrawal?" (*D* XXVII.52.779). It is in exploring this question, via the operation of thinking itself, that Arendt introduces a term that might look paradoxical, looked at from the viewpoint of Arendt's own description of thought as without end: the thought-object.

Perish the Thought

The intimate connection between the end of life and ends of thought leaves thinking in an apparent paradox, one that will turn out to reflect on more than the thinking activity, alone. For all that Arendt is at pains to remind us that thought is itself endless in general and seemingly has no purpose but its own continuation, she notes that it nevertheless requires ends to go about its work, and though it has no purpose but its own, that is not the same thing as saying that it is endless. Thought is then endless only from the perspective of human being as the thinking-I, the secondary spectator of sorts to its own thought, an I that understands its existence as bounded by its own end; viewed from the perspective of its process, thinking is itself a kind of making of ends. Just as thought requires withdrawal from the world, so too must all things which are thought be withdrawn from appearance to join the thinking-I. It is through the deathly process of desensation that the world of appearances is made into something that can be thought, translated from the raw data of the sensory into a mental image. This power, for Arendt via Augustine, is called imagination, in a cleverly literal interpretation of the term: to generate the image by removing things from the world of appearances and, in their withdrawal, prepare them for the possibility of being thought.

Imagination is only the first step in the "process of preparation" by which world-objects become this new thing called "thought-objects," however. To think a thing also requires remembering it, its recollection "from the storehouse of memory" to return as the "deliberately remembered object" (*T* 77).[13] "Thought-objects come into being only when the mind actively . . . remembers, recollects, and selects." Only once we have these thought-objects can we begin the activity of thought around them, and for Arendt this is precisely the operative term: thought occurs *around* thought-objects, even when that thought-object is understood to be the thinking-I itself, which we must remember to contemplate. I can only think about myself insofar as I remember having been made present to myself in the past, by thinking, and my thought circles whatever object I hold in front of it even if that becomes the permanently reflexive process of holding my thought before itself. With that thought of ourselves before us, we can "go further" and begin to understand "things that are always absent, that cannot be remembered because they were never present to sense experience."

This crucial last function of the imagination's pairing with memory— to bring thought-objects before our own mental gaze that were never literally a part of our material world—is, as Arendt began to shadow in her lectures on Kant at the New School and University of Chicago,[14] profoundly necessary to our capacity to be political. The ability to "remember" through imagination what we have never directly experienced is what allows us to make judgments in a world the political scope of which vastly exceeds our immediate perceptive capacity. Without the ability to imagine the worlds and subject-positions of others, to "train our mind to go visiting" (*LKPP* 43) corners of the human world we share yet nevertheless do not know, we would be unable to make judgments that reflect more than our particular preoccupations and self-interests. This specifically political inflection of thought and imagination's general capacity to create the thought-objects around which our minds can whirl already shadows, though, that there is a double analogy to the sphere of art—of the artist-worker, artwork, and spectator—only one side of which can be glimpsed in the earlier Kant Lectures without the *Denktagebuch*, and as such has largely escaped notice in the literature on Arendtian judgment.

In these late iterations in the *Denktagebuch* and *Thinking*, "thinking as such . . . every reflection that does not serve knowledge and is not guided by practical needs and aims" (*T* 64) enables our political capacities to be like those of a discerning spectator of art, working the perspectives of others into our own in advance without prioritizing our own material interests. Simultaneously, however, the imagining-remembering of thought-objects also brings our process of thought closest to the creative making of an artist. It is here that Arendt's late redemption of at least certain kinds of ends-making finds its resonance with certain kinds of work in "The Crisis in Culture" and *The Human Condition.* Scandal though it may be to the strand of philosophy from Plato to the German Romantics which sees the *vita contemplativa* as possible only in quietude and freedom from earthly cares (a strand which it seems Arendt might be happy to bring into scandal), imaginative reflection and meaning-making may for Arendt have more in common with the toils of the worker—at least, one particular kind of worker—than any other side of the *vita activa.*[15]

The central characteristic of the artwork which distinguishes it from the other products of work in *The Human Condition* is that despite being ends in one sense—some thing, an object produced through fabrication that on completion brings its fabricating process to a close—they nevertheless "are strictly without any utility whatsoever and . . . therefore defy equalization through a common denominator such as money" (*HC* 167), and as objects "almost untouched by the corroding effect of natural processes" "can attain permanence." In other words, artworks are endful only from one perspective, that of production, and are endless from both the perspective of the human being as a spectator (paradigmatically here the exchange market) and as a mortal bound by natality and death. The echo of *Thinking*'s construction of thought should already be apparent. While one could quibble with either characterization, Arendt's point is that the apparent paradox of an endless end appears a paradox only because in every other product of the sphere of work the three senses of end appear inextricable from each other. Artworks are the form of work-object which pry apart the three senses of end, and in so doing form a kind of object with a different status altogether from other products of work.[16] They can do so because, unlike "use things" whose "source" is "man's 'propensity to truck and barter,'" the "immediate source" of artworks "is the human capacity for thought" itself.

In *Thinking*, Arendt extends her story about this unique form of endfulness created by the proximity of art and thought to the direct products of thinking itself—metaphors and meanings—and in so doing partially dissolves the one major distinction between the mental products of thought and artworks as "thought things": the process of reification that "fabricates things of thought" (*HC* 169). This new frame of metaphors as "thought objects," itself a metaphor, hinges on the idea of "actualizing" a set of products that like artworks are ends only in the first sense of term, from the perspective of their production. The most telling version Arendt provides for extending the essential analogy between the imagining of thought-objects and the making of artworks comes when she describes thinking as "the mental activity that actualizes those products of the mind that are inherent in speech and for which language, prior to any special effort, has already found an appropriate though provisional home in the audible world" (*T* 109). These thought-objects, "analogies, metaphors, and emblems are the threads by which the mind holds on to the world" and in their endlessness ensure the continuity of that world even when "[the mind] has lost direct contact with it." In so doing, "the mind's language by means of metaphor returns to illuminate and elaborate further what cannot be seen but can be said" (*T* 109). Unlike knowledge as a productive process, "which uses thinking as a means to an end" (*T* 64), the objects of thinking are the products of a continuous process of "*appropriating* and, as it were, disalienating the world" in order "to come to terms with whatever may be given . . . whatever there may be or may have occurred" (*T* 100) through metaphorical connections which are in principle infinite.

In the *Denktagebuch*, this same idea is reiterated in a brief confrontation Kant, who Arendt claims saw that the imagination's function was first and foremost to "*compose*" (and it is telling that Arendt focuses on Kant's use of *dichten*) "under the strict supervision of reason" (*D* XXVII.49.776). However, Kant failed to understand that the importance of this compositional process lies in the fact that its products are not limited to an explanatory or expositive power (*erklären*) for grounding knowledge, but themselves make meanings, a thought-object which unlike an object of knowledge is "done for its sake" and begets a potentially endless train of further meanings, the "relentless and repetitive" (*HC* 110) activity of thought. The point echoes one made in her earlier "Truth and Politics" in which she distinguishes facts, which can be known, and meanings, which must be continuously created by humans in their web of social (and political) relations with each other.[17] In "Truth and Politics," the *Denktagebuch*, and *Thinking*, she repeatedly calls this process of world-making through the making of metaphors "the quest for meaning." The "faculty of thought," she writes, exists to "search" for meaning: as distinct from knowledge, thought "does not ask what something is or whether it exists at all—its existence is always taken for granted—*but what it means for it to be*" (*T* 57).

In a way, one might read the discussion of the relationship between art and thought in *The Human Condition* and *Thinking* as an analytic hourglass, the bottleneck of which lies in Notebook XVII's consideration of the ends of life. In *The Human Condition*, where the central concern of the relationship between thinking and the work of art is the latter's reification of "words and deeds," Arendt momentarily notes that "thought transforms [feeling's] mute and inarticulate despondency . . . until [it is] fit to enter the world and to be transformed into things, to become reified" (*HC* 108).[18] At this earlier point, though, because she is concerned with how the process of work can provide some kind of permanence to fragile a public world that is constantly perishing, Arendt emphasizes the distinctive importance of the "materializing reification" with which work, in the work of art, must interrupt the endless play of thought. Art appears to create the lone sense in which it is an end, despite its uselessness and permanence, only by sacrificing the endlessness of thought. *Thinking*, however, transforms *HC*'s brief suggestion on thought into the idea that art and reflective thinking both do the work of "transforming sense-objects into thought-things, [tearing] them first of all out of their context in order to de-realize and thus prepare them for their new and different function" (*T* 49) in the quest for meaning. Though briefly recognizing *HC*'s distinction between the two (*T* 57), *Thinking* is more concerned with the essential continuity in the activities of the work of art and the work of thought—that they are ends in one sense and not ends in two others—than with the particular media by which the two promise a fleeting world some degree of perpetuity. Between the two lies Notebook XVII, which pries apart the three senses of ends and their relation to each other in the thinking-I, as death, process, and purpose all push their way into Arendt's thoughts and life.

Yet None so Terrible as Man

The Human Condition and *Thinking* each, in their separate ways, articulate decisively the proximate stakes of unraveling the meanings of "end" for their liminal objects, the artwork and thought-thing.[19] In Arendt's narrative about the world-preservative power of art, our collective who's (we) need an end of a work process whose purpose is to lend its immortality (endlessness) through materiality to action, which would otherwise die in the moment of its birth. In her last thoughts on thinking, "things of thought"—metaphors and meanings—are made in order to give us mental objects that, as concretizations in memory of the flux of our inner and outer worlds which is otherwise constantly passing away, allow us to connect each piece of that life to another as we strive to find (really, create) a purpose to the finite process of our lives together.[20] The last thing that the intervening Notebook XXVII gives us is a glimpse of what joins the nature of these two strange types of objects to another kind of bearer of ends altogether, perhaps the ultimate stake in their disentanglement of ends: the human being herself. The specter of our end, as what drives those facing "the development of our disappearance" (philosophers and the dying) back to the old metaphysical questions, is what brings answers to the question of "why exist" under the sphere of *Kritik der Urteilskraft*, judgment. It is, predictably, the beginning of philosophy (D XXVII.64.784; 74.791). It is also—and Arendt calls missing this "the essential error of Kant's moral philosophy" (D XXVII.80.794)—the beginning of conscience.

Entry 80 is one of those moments in the *Denktagebuch* that, if left in the isolation that they appear in the reproduced notebooks themselves, are just rich and tantalizing enough to be utterly maddening in their truncation. It presents, in just two paragraphs, a brief, fragmentary, but potentially revolutionary alternative account of the nature of morality as grounded not in Kantian practical reason, but in the relationship of judgment to conscience. In itself, it gestures only at the fact that there must be some connection between the fact that we "hide" "the bad from the world," the exercise of taste, and the "instinct" (which is "probably nothing more than judgments of taste") by which anything we do is "exposed to conscience." Set against the backdrop against the ground Arendt has provided for disentangling the ends of human life, however, there is enough here to at least call this vision of conscience a promise, if not yet a theory.

Arendt closed her critique of instrumentalization in *HC* by noting that Kant's moral philosophy presented a first systematic attempt to free modern humanity from the grip of "the anthropocentric utilitarianism of *homo faber*" by relegating "the means-end category to its proper place and prevent its use in the field of political action" through his formula that "no man must ever become a means to an end." Kant's moralist solution to the political problem of "the blindness of *homo faber* to the problem of meaning"—rendering each person as an end-in-herself—though, could succeed only in inventing utilitarianism's "greatest expression." As long as "the standards which governed its coming into being are permitted to rule it after its establishment," every individual thing in *Homo faber*'s "world becomes as worthless as the employed material" (*HC* 155–156).

Articulated within the narrow frame of work's instrumentality, under which the highest ends of the human world work builds are ultimately reduced to means, the circuit of means-ends itself remains closed and unitary. Means remain the only terms through which to describe worth, because it is only in forms of usefulness that ends become valuable to *Homo faber*, and the categorical imperative, in accepting the terms of means-ends in exchange for putting humanity as the ultimate ends, remains mute to defend the worth of human life beyond means. In other words, *Homo faber*'s world is worthless for Arendt in a literal sense, as long as the only framework for articulating worth is as further means. Work can guarantee a lasting world, but only activities that break apart the closed circuit of means-ends can bring the appearing world into that space of permanence still bearing other values.

Up to this point, Arendt's point from the *HC* remains a familiar critique of Kant, not far from Nietzsche's or Marx's, albeit using her singular idiom. The combination of Arendt's distinctive account of political action and heightened focus on appearances in *Thinking*, though, means that her critique of value enters into a quite different conceptual terrain and vision of politics when it intersects her late approach to ends. If, for Arendt, the political can only be set in the world of appearances, the dictates of conscience—that is, a faculty of deciding how to act—too must be germane to that faculty structure not to convert those appearances to knowledge, but to make meanings of it. To know how to "do good or bad," to act in a world, begins with the acknowledgment that our fellow humans must *appear* to us just as our actions must appear to them. When they appear, they do so not as strict ends in themselves but as makers of ends: as this line of thought from *HC* through Notebook XXVII to *Thinking* describes, beings capable of unraveling the tight means-ends braid by making meanings through the partial ends of thought and art. In such a world, our reverence for others cannot be saved by rendering them as an end to which no value can be given even if they are never a means. Conscience can only belong to the faculty capable of making their appearance to us mean something, this is, bear noninstrumental value through made meanings. And so Entry 80's declaration of Kant "essential error": he missed the defining reorientation that his own late architecture of reason should have given him, that this faculty through which "I can figure out the good" was not practical reason, the capacity to navigate means and ends, but "a kind of thinking," reflective thinking, or "the capacity to judge."

Would this attempt to radically refigure the place of the good in a world of appearances have worked to construct a new vision of political conscience? Absent the terrible interruption of Heinrich's death and her own decline, could Arendt's working out in Notebook XXVII of the polyphony of certain kinds of ends—art, thought-objects, and ultimately human beings—have become a fully fledged ethics, in the book *Judging* that was never to be? Or would this line of reason simply have become mired in all the basic moral dilemmas that "aesthetic" accounts of politics have been accused of creating since Walter Benjamin's "Das Kunstwerk im Zeitalter seiner technischen Reproduzierbarkeit" and Isaiah Berlin's studies on the German and Russian Romantics, and which Seyla Benhabib had would soon accuse Arendt of having confused from the outset?[21]

Kant was famously plagued by the problems created by his separation of practical reason and judgment for political action. He seems to have resorted to a strict separation of perspectives—the perspective of the actor, who could only determine the right through moral reason; and the perspective of history, that of the spectator and judge—as the only apparent way out, and this lead him into such strange alleys as a view of revolution as simultaneously admirable and absolutely forbidden.[22] Arendt herself, in the last entry before Heinrich's death, notes this separation of the stance of the spectator and, in a fluid description that forms an almost surreal, dissonant echo with the entry it faces, calls this position a kind of "impartial" and "inhuman" wonder (*D* XXVII.85.796). Many since (for which we might assign a bit of blame to both the neo-Kantians and Hegel) have simply jettisoned the place of the spectator and treated Kant's account of practical reason as his guide to action, full stop, consigning his views on the good and the right to an unsurprisingly politically unsatisfying deontological moralism. Arendt's suggestion seems to be the opposite: that Kant should have pushed his account of how we should act in the public all the way in to the sphere of judgment, and embraced the last critical faculty as the place of politics. It is an intriguing proposition, from an enticing fragment, in an absorbing volume, of an arresting thinker's intellectual life— perhaps one worth taking to the end.

NOTES

1. Though the *Denktagebuch* does not mention its source, the Latin quote from Ecclesiastes used in the epigraph to this essay appeared much earlier in Arendt's writing as well, in the form of a warning in the chapter "Action" of what becomes "unavoidable wherever and whenever trust in the world as a place fit for human appearance . . . is gone." Hannah Arendt, *The Human Condition* (Chicago: University of Chicago Press, 1972), 204 (hereafter *HC*). Now, here, it appears not as a situation to be avoided by the preservation of a vibrant sphere of appearance, but rather an inescapable condition of the existence of a space in which we can appear.

2. This is Arendt's own translation of these lines, which she also invokes, with the caveat that they are untranslatable, in her elegy to Brecht, "What Is Permitted to Jove . . ." Otherwise in this essay, where the original entry is in German, translations are my own.

3. *HC*, 156–157. Hereafter "*HC*."

4. *The Life of the Mind* (San Diego: Harcourt, 1971) (hereafter *T*).

5. Dana Villa, "Beyond Good and Evil," *Political Theory* 20, no. 2 (May 1992): 276. Villa has been one of the most consistent and thorough English-language interpreters of the anti-instrumental dimension of Arendt's thought; of earlier importance was James Knauer's defense of Arendt's anti-instrumentality in "Motive and Goal in Hannah Arendt's Concept of Political Action," *American Political Science Review* 74, no. 3 (September 1980): 721–733.

6. "What Is Freedom," *Between Past and Future* (New York: Penguin Books, 1978), 459.

7. "Lying in Politics," *Crises of the Republic* (New York: Harcourt Brace, 1969), 35 (hereafter "LP").

8. "The Crisis in Culture," *Between Past and Future* (New York: Penguin Books, 1968), 204 (hereafter "CC"). It is this form of philistinism, which arose from a society in which the instrumental mentality produced members who "even when they had acquired release from life's necessities, could not free themselves from . . . their status and position in society and the reflection of this on their individual selves" (210–211), which in turn gave rise to the social problems of mass society, Arendt's deeper concern in the first half of the essay.

9. Elisabeth Young-Bruehl, *Hannah Arendt* (New Haven: Yale University Press, 1982), 76.

10. Karl Jaspers, *Philosophie* (Berlin: J. Springer, 1932).

11. For reasons of space and competence, I am bracketing the question of the source and accuracy of this characterization of the "Greek" view and hope that it will suffice suggest that Arendt is neither obviously right nor alone in this characterization, in that it can be found in several places in the post-Kantian trajectory of Schiller, Nietzsche, and Heidegger. In *Thinking*, she splits this description as between the Roman (the old) and Greek (the young) interpretations.

12. Quoting David Hume, *Treatise on Human Nature*, I:6.

13. This emphasis on the deliberateness of reconstruction in memory is odd (insofar as it seems that perhaps the most powerful of memories are precisely those that return unbidden, or will not return whatever we will), but it also seems unnecessary for Arendt's larger description of the operation of memory and thought to hold together.

14. Compiled and edited by Robert Beiner as *Lectures on Kant's Political Philosophy* (Chicago: University of Chicago Press, 1989) (hereafter *LKPP*).

15. This is already indicated by the argument of *HC*, in the midst of the section on the work of art, that "like fabrication itself, [cognition] is a process with a beginning and an end, whose usefulness can be tested, and which, if it produces no results, has failed" (171). There, however, the concern is a con-

trast this character of cognition with thinking as "relentless and repetitive"; if there is a dimension of the argument of *Thinking* that represents a distinct *shift* in Arendt's thought, it is on this specific sense of endfulness, and whether or not thinking shares with cognition this characteristic, and to what extent.

16. One important stake of this move in *The Human Condition*, which reappears in Notebook XXVII of the *Denktagebuch*, is that humans, too, as the workers of art and the thinkers of thoughts, represent for Arendt this same kind of end.

17. "Truth in Politics" was originally published in the "Reflections" section of *The New Yorker*, February 26, 1967.

18. Interestingly, Notebook XVII.79.793 appears to radicalize this claim to the point where it undercuts the connection between thinking and feeling itself. Arendt argues that "thinking and Feeling are in fact opposed to one another" because "to think, I need separation, distance; feeling takes on the felt in such an intensive proximity, that it is virtually one with its object. The distance even of knowing, not to mention recognizing, is completely destroyed in feeling."

19. With respect to the subhead: In a move that would inspire responses from Kafka in the opening of *Metamorphosis* and Heidegger in a lecture reprinted in *An Introduction to Metaphysics* (New Haven: Yale University Press, 1959), Hölderlin translates the opening of the choral "Ode to Man" in Antigone as:

> *Ungeheuer ist viel. Doch nichts*
> *Ungeheuer als der Mensch.*

20. A neat summary of this point can also be found at XXVII.52.779, where Arendt finds in Kant's *Critique of Pure Reason* the point that only the process of translating our sensations of the world makes it even possible to become conscious of our selves in the world: "To say: *Ich existiere denkend*, I need something (*Beharrliches*) permanent which is not given in inner intuition" without which "I could not even measure this flux against permanence." In other words, in order to insert ourselves into the world, on Arendt's reading of Kant, we must also remove ourselves from it.

21. Seyla Benhabib, "Judgment and the Moral Foundations of Politics in Arendt's Thought," *Political Theory* 16, no. 1 (1988): 29–51.

22. This problem has a long and rich history in Kantian interpretation; in judicious review, see Christine Korsgaard, "Taking the Law into Our Own Hands: Kant on the Right to Revolution," reprinted in *The Constitution of Agency* (Oxford: Oxford University Press, 2008), 233–262. Arendt examines the actor/spectator distinction extensively in *LKPP*; see, e.g., 44, 55.

ACKNOWLEDGMENTS

The authors would like to acknowledge the financial support from Bard College and the Hannah Arendt Center for Politics and the Humanities at Bard College for their hosting of the original conference that gave rise to the volume, and for their hospitality. We have all benefited not only from the opportunity to come together to explore and examine the *Denktagebuch*, but also to do so in the presence of one of its editors, Ursula Ludz, who has also contributed to this volume. We would also like to especially thank Patchen Markell and Christina Tarnopolsky, who, although they were unable to contribute to the volume, were luminous lights in the conference and who have influenced all of our pieces. This volume is the product of a fortunate confluence of thinkers who were given the opportunity to reflect together for an extended period by Bard College, and we hope the results will be edifying for the legacy of the *Denktagebuch* and Hannah Arendt's thought. Regardless, that generous support must be acknowledged.

CONTRIBUTORS

ROGER BERKOWITZ is Associate Professor of Political Studies and Human Rights at Bard College and Academic Director of the Hannah Arendt Center for Politics and the Humanities. In addition to editing a number of volumes and journal special issues, Berkowitz is the author of *The Gift of Science: Leibniz and the Modern Legal Tradition*.

JEFFREY CHAMPLIN is Associate Fellow at the Center for Civic Engagement and Human Rights at Bard and the Hannah Arendt Center for Politics and the Humanities, visiting assistant professor and chair of the Department of Literature and Society at the Bard Honors College at Al-Quds University, and lecturer on literature at Bard College Berlin. He is the author of *The Making of a Terrorist: On Classic German Rogues* and editor of *Terror and the Roots of Poetics*.

WOUT CORNELISSEN holds a doctorate in philosophy from Leiden University. He currently works as a research assistant professor at Vanderbilt University. His first book, on the relations between philosophy and politics in the writing of Karl Popper, Leo Strauss, and Hannah Arendt, is forthcoming with Fordham University Press.

URSULA LUDZ is a sociologist and translator who has edited multiple volumes of Arendt's work, including Arendt, *Ich will verstehen*; Arendt and Heidegger, *Briefe 1924–1975*; Arendt and Fest, *Eichmann war von empörender Dummheit* (with Thomas Wild). Ursula Ludz and Ingeborg Nordmann are the editors of Arendt's *Denktagebuch*.

ANNE O'BYRNE is Associate Professor of Philosophy and Doctoral Program Director at Stony Brook University. Her work focuses on the political and ontological questions that arise from gendered embodiment and labor, including translations of Jean-Luc Nancy and writings ranging across the major Continental thinkers of the twentieth century and Julia Kristeva, as well as a sustained investment in Irish studies. She is currently working on a book on genocide and generation.

IAN STOREY is Lecturer on Social Studies at Harvard University and Associate Fellow of the Hannah Arendt Center for Politics and the Humanities. In addition to articles on political aesthetics and German philosophy, he is the author of two forthcoming books, *Hungers on Sugar Hill: Hannah Arendt, The New York Poets, and the Remaking of Metropolis* and *The Taste of Politics: Kantian Judgment and Belonging in the Modern World.*

TRACY STRONG is Professor of Political Theory and Philosophy at the University of Southampton and Distinguished Professor of Political Science at the University of California, San Diego. He is the author of numerous books and translations, including *The Idea of Political Theory, Jean Jacques Rousseau and the Politics of the Ordinary*, and most recently David Easton Prize–winning *Politics without Vision.*

TATJANA NOEMI TÖMMEL is a research associate at the Institut für Philosophie, Literatur-, Wissenschafts- und Technikgeschichte at the Technische Universität Berlin. Her work centers on aesthetics, literature and culture history, and has recently published *Will and Passion: The Concept of Love in Heidegger and Arendt.*

THOMAS WILD is Associate Professor of German at Bard College and Research Director of the Hannah Arendt Center for Politics and the Humanities. Wild is the author of *Hannah Arendt: Life, Work, Reception* (2006) and *Nach dem Geschichtsbruch* (2009), a book on postwar German writers around Arendt. He edited several of Arendt's correspondences (e.g., with Joachim Fest and Uwe Johnson), and is currently preparing a critical edition, digital and print, of Arendt's complete works.

Index